CONTENTS

ABOVE | 'The Field of Waterloo, from the Picton Tree', by J. M. W. Turner, circa 1833. The painting severely exaggerates the steepness of the valley's slopes, but does convey the small size of the battlefield.

WATERLOO

THE HISTORY OF FOUR DAYS, THREE ARMIES, AND THREE BATTLES

BERNARD CORNWELL

HARPER

An Imprint of HarperCollins*Publishers*

To Will and Anne Clevelend

HarperCollins books may be purchased for educational, business, or sales promotional use. For information, please e-mail the Special Markets Department at SPsales@harpercollins.com.

First published in Great Britain by William Collins in 2014.

FIRST U.S. EDITION

Maps created by Martin Brown

Layout and production by Tom Cabot / ketchup

Library of Congress Cataloging-in-Publication Data has been applied for.

ISBN: 978-0-06-231205-1

15 16 17 18 19   OV/RRD   10 9 8 7 6 5 4 3 2 1

PICTURE CREDITS

All reasonable efforts have been made by the author and publishers to trace the copyright owners of the material quoted in this book and of any images reproduced in this book. In the event that the author or publishers are notified of any mistakes or omissions by copyright owners after publication, the author and publishers will endeavour to rectify the position accordingly for any subsequent printing.

BRIDGEMAN IMAGES: p. 35: National Gallery, London, UK – p. 36: (top left) Louvre, Paris, France / Giraudon; (top right) Musee de l'Armee, Paris, France / Giraudon; (bottom right) Musee National du Chateau de Malmaison, Rueil-Malmaison, France / Giraudon; (bottom left) Royal Collection Trust © Her Majesty Queen Elizabeth II, 2014 – p. 37: (top) Musee de l'Armee, Brussels, Belgium; (bottom left) De Agostini Picture Library / G. Costa – p. 58: (top) The Trustees of the Goodwood Collection – p. 77: Private Collection / Giraudon – p. 78/9: (top) Private Collection / The Stapleton Collection; (bottom) Musee de l'Armee, Brussels, Belgium / Patrick Lorette / Giraudon – p. 101: (top) Private Collection / The Stapleton Collection; (bottom right) Private Collection / © Look and Learn – p. 102: (top left) Private Collection / The Stapleton Collection; (bottom) National Gallery of Victoria, Melbourne, Australia – p. 103: (top) Private Collection / The Stapleton Collection; (bottom) Brown University Library, Providence, Rhode Island, USA – p. 129: Private Collection / Photo © Mark Fiennes – p. 130: (top) Private Collection / The Stapleton Collection; (bottom right) Château de Versailles, France; (bottom left) Musee du Val-de-Grace, Paris, France / Archives Charmet – p. 131: (top left) Private Collection / Photo © Christie's Images; (top right) © The Bowes Museum, Barnard Castle, County Durham, UK; (bottom) Private Collection / The Stapleton Collection – p. 151: (top) Private Collection / The Stapleton Collection; (middle) R.S.A.F. Enfield Lock, Middlesex, UK – p. 152: (top) Musee des Beaux-Arts, Bordeaux, France / Giraudon – p. 153: (top) Château de Versailles, France; (bottom) Private Collection / The Stapleton Collection – p. 177: (middle) National Army Museum, London; (bottom right) Musee des Beaux-Arts, Reims, France / Roger-Viollet, Paris; (bottom left) © The Bowes Museum, Barnard Castle, County Durham, UK – p. 178/9: Private Collection – p. 202/3: Leeds Museums and Galleries (Leeds Art Gallery) U.K. – p. 204: (top) © Samuel Courtauld Trust, The Courtauld Gallery, London, UK; (bottom right) Royal Collection Trust © Her Majesty Queen Elizabeth II, 2014 – p. 225: (top left) Private Collection / Topham Picturepoint; (bottom) National Army Museum, London – p. 254: (top) Bibliotheque Marmottan, Boulogne-Billancourt, Paris, France / Giraudon; (bottom) National Army Museum, London – p. 255: (top) Apsley House, The Wellington Museum, London, UK; (bottom) Private Collection / Photo © Christie's Images – p. 279: Private Collection / Photo © Bonhams, London, UK – p. 280/1: Hamburger Kunsthalle, Hamburg, Germany – p. 282/3: (bottom) Apsley House, The Wellington Museum, London, UK / © English Heritage Photo Library – p. 308: Musee de l'Armee, Brussels, Belgium – p. 309: (top) Brown University Library, Providence, Rhode Island, USA – p. 309: (bottom) National Army Museum, London – p. 310/11: Palace of Westminster, London, UK – p. 312: Deutsches Historisches Museum, Berlin, Germany / © DHM – p. 337: (top) Musee de l'Armee, Brussels, Belgium; (bottom) © Royal Hospital Chelsea, London, UK – p. 338: (top) Pushkin Museum, Moscow, Russia; (bottom) De Agostini Picture Library / G. Dagli Orti.

OTHER SOURCES: p. 4: Turner Worldwide / Sotheby's– p. 34: © INTERFOTO / Alamy – p. 37: (bottom right) Getty Images / ©The British Library Board – p. 58: (bottom left) © Musée historique de Lausanne; (bottom right) English Heritage / Mary Evans – p. 59: akg-images – p. 101: (bottom left) akg-images – p. 102: (top right) Getty Images / Art Media / Heritage Images – p. 151: (middle) © INTERFOTO / Alamy; (bottom) © INTERFOTO / Alamy – p. 152: bpk – p. 177: © RMN-Grand Palais (Château de Fontainebleau) / Gérard Blot – p. 204: (bottom left) © Paris-Musée de l'Armée, Dist. RMN-Grand Palais / Pascal Segrette – p. 205: painting hangs in The Great Hall, Edinburgh Castle / Reproduced by kind permission of Royal Hospital Chelsea / Photograph courtesy Eric Gaba, Wikimedia Commons – p. 225: (top right) © National Portrait Gallery, London – p. 226/7: © National Museums Scotland – p. 282/3: (top) akg-images / Erich Lessing – p. 342: © Rijksmuseum, Amsterdam.

FOREWORD

WHY ANOTHER BOOK ON Waterloo? It is a good question. There is no shortage of accounts of the battle, indeed it is one of the most studied and written-about battles in history. From the close of that dreadful day in June 1815, everyone who took part in the slaughter knew that they had survived something significant, and the result was hundreds of memoirs and letters describing the experience. Yet the Duke of Wellington was surely right when he said that a man might as well tell the history of a ball, meaning a dance, as write the story of a battle. Everyone who attends a ball has a different memory of the event, some happy, some disappointing, and how, in the swirl of music and ball gowns and flirtations, could anyone hope to make a coherent account of exactly what happened and when and to whom? Yet Waterloo was the deciding event at the beginning of the nineteenth century, and ever since men and women have tried to provide that coherent account.

There is an agreed story. Napoleon attacks Wellington's right in an attempt to draw the Duke's reserves to that part of the battlefield, then launches a massive attack on the Duke's left. That attack fails. Act Two is the great cavalry assault on the Duke's centre-right, and Act Three, as the Prussians arrive stage left, is the desperate last assault by the undefeated Imperial Guard. To those can be added the subplots of the assaults on Hougoumont and the fall of La Haie Sainte. As a framework that has some merit, but the battle was far more complicated than that simple story suggests. To the men who were present it did not seem simple, or explicable, and one reason to write this book is to try and give an impression of what it was like to be on that field on that confusing day.

The survivors of that confusion would surely be bemused by the argument that Waterloo really was not that important, that if Napoleon had won then he would have still faced overwhelming enemies and ultimate defeat. That is probably, though not certainly, true. If the Emperor had forced the ridge of Mont St Jean and driven Wellington back into a precipitate retreat, he would still have had to cope with the mighty armies of Austria and Russia that were marching towards France. Yet that did not happen. Napoleon was stopped at Waterloo, and that gives the battle its significance. It is a turning point of history, and to say history would have turned anyway is not to reduce the importance of the moment it happened. Some battles change nothing. Waterloo changed almost everything.

Military history can be confusing. Roman numerals (IV Corps) march to meet Arabic numerals (3rd Div), and such labels tend to blur in the non-military mind. I have tried to avoid too much confusion, though perhaps I have added to it by using the words 'battalion' and 'regiment' to mean the same thing, when plainly they do not. The regiment was an administrative unit in the British army. Some regiments consisted of a single battalion, most had two battalions, and a few had three or even more. It was extremely rare for two British battalions of the same regiment to fight alongside each other in the same campaign, and at Waterloo only two regiments had that distinction. The 1st Regiment of Foot Guards had its 2nd and 3rd battalions at the battle, while the 95th Rifles had three battalions present. Every other battalion was the sole representative of its regiment, so if I refer to the 52nd Regiment I am meaning the 1st Battalion of that regiment. I sometimes use the term Guardsman for clarity, though in 1815 the privates of the British Guards were still referred to as 'Private'.

All three armies at Waterloo were divided into Corps, thus both the British–Dutch army and the Prussian army were divided into three Corps. The French had four, because the Imperial Guard, though not referred to as a Corps, was effectively the same thing. A Corps could be anything from 10,000 to 30,000 men or more, and was intended to be an independent force, capable of deploying cavalry, infantry and artillery. In turn a Corps was divided into divisions, thus the French 1st Army Corps was divided into four infantry divisions, each between 4,000 and 5,000 strong, and one cavalry division with just over 1,000 men. Each division contained its own supporting artillery. A division might then be further split into brigades, thus the 2nd Infantry Division of the 1st Army Corps contained two brigades, one of seven battalions, the other of six. Battalions were split into companies; a French battalion had eight companies, a British had ten. The most common term in this book will be battalion (sometimes called a regiment). The largest British infantry battalion at Waterloo had over 1,000 men, but the average battalion, in all three armies, was around 500 men. So, in brief, the hierarchy was Army, Corps, Division, Brigade, Battalion, Company.

Some readers may be offended by the usage 'English army' when plainly the reference is to the British army. I have used the term 'English army' only where it occurs in original sources, choosing not to translate *Anglais* as British. There was no such thing as the English army, but in the early nineteenth century it was a term in common usage.

The battles of 16 June and 18 June 1815 make for a magnificent story. History is rarely kind to historical novelists by providing a neat plot with great characters who act within a defined time-period, so we are forced to manipulate history to make our own plots work. Yet when I wrote *Sharpe's Waterloo* my plot almost entirely vanished to be taken over by the great story of the battle itself. Because it is a great story, not only in its combatants but in its shape. It is a cliffhanger. No matter how often I read accounts of that day, the ending is still full of suspense. The undefeated Imperial Guard climbs the ridge to where Wellington's battered forces are almost at breaking point. Off to the east the Prussians are clawing at Napoleon's right, but if the Guard can break Wellington's men then Napoleon still has time to turn against Blücher's arriving troops. It is almost the longest day of the year, there are two hours of daylight left and time enough for one or even two armies to be destroyed. We might know how it ends, but like all good stories it bears repetition.

So here it is again, the story of a battle.

PREFACE

IN THE SUMMER OF 1814 His Grace the Duke of Wellington was on his way from London to Paris to take up his appointment as British ambassador to the new regime of Louis XVIII. He might have been expected to take the short route from Dover to Calais, but instead a Royal Navy brig, HMS *Griffon*, carried him across the North Sea to Bergen-op-Zoom. He was visiting the newly created Kingdom of the Netherlands, an awkward invention, half French, half Dutch, half Catholic and half Protestant, which lay to the north of France. British troops had been posted in the new nation as guarantors of its existence, and the Duke had been asked to inspect the defences along the French border. He was accompanied by 'Slender Billy', also known as the 'Young Frog', the 23-year-old Prince William, who was Crown Prince of the new kingdom and who, because he had served on the Duke's staff in the Peninsular War, believed himself to possess military talent. The Duke spent a fortnight touring the borderlands and suggested restoring the fortifications of a handful of towns, but it is hard to believe he took the prospect of a renewed French war too seriously.

Napoleon, after all, was defeated and had been exiled to the Mediterranean island of Elba. France was a monarchy again. The wars were over, and in Vienna the diplomats were forging the treaty that would remake the boundaries of Europe to ensure that another war did not ravage the continent.

And Europe had been ravaged. Napoleon's abdication had ended twenty-one years of warfare that had begun in the wake of the French

Revolution. The old regimes of Europe, the monarchies, had been horrified by the events in France and shocked by the executions of Louis XVI and his queen, Marie Antoinette. Fearing that the ideas of the Revolution would spread to their own countries, they had gone to war.

They had expected a swift victory over the ragged armies of Revolutionary France, but instead they sparked a world war which saw both Washington and Moscow burned. There had been fighting in India, Palestine, the West Indies, Egypt and South America, but Europe had suffered the worst. France had survived the initial onslaught, and from the chaos of revolution there emerged a genius, a warlord, an Emperor. Napoleon's armies had shattered the Prussians, the Austrians and the Russians, they had marched from the Baltic to the southern shores of Spain, and the Emperor's feckless brothers had been placed on half the thrones of Europe. Millions had died, but after two decades it was all over. The warlord was caged.

Napoleon had dominated Europe, but there was one enemy he had never met and whom he had never defeated, and that was the Duke of Wellington, whose military reputation was second only to Napoleon's. He had been born Arthur Wesley, the fourth son of the Earl and Countess of Mornington. The Wesley family were part of the Anglo-Irish aristocracy and Arthur spent most of his youth in Ireland, the country of his birth, though most of his education was at Eton, where he was not happy. His mother, Anne, despaired of him. 'I don't know what I shall do with my awkward son Arthur,' she complained, but the answer, as for so many younger sons of the nobility, was to arrange a commission in the army. And so began an extraordinary career as the awkward Arthur discovered a talent for soldiering. The army recognized that talent and rewarded it. He first commanded an army in India, where he won a series of astonishing victories, then he was recalled to Britain and entrusted with the small expeditionary army that was trying to keep the French from occupying Portugal. That small army had grown into the mighty force that liberated Portugal and Spain and invaded southern France. It had won victory after victory. Arthur Wellesley (the family had changed the surname from Wesley) had become the Duke of Wellington and was recognized as one of the two greatest soldiers of the age. Alexander I, the Czar of Russia, was to call him '*Le vainqueur du vainqueur du monde*', the conqueror of the world's conqueror, and the world's conqueror was, of course, Napoleon. And in twenty-one years of war the Duke and the Emperor had never fought each other.

The Duke was constantly being compared to Napoleon, but when in 1814 he was asked whether he regretted that he had never fought the Emperor in battle, he replied, 'No, and I am very glad.' He despised Napoleon the man, but admired Napoleon the soldier, reckoning the Emperor's presence on a battlefield was worth 40,000 men. And the Duke of Wellington, unlike Napoleon, had never lost a battle, but facing the Emperor might well mean losing that extraordinary record.

Yet in the summer of 1814 the Duke could be forgiven for thinking that his fighting days were over. He knew he was good at warfare, but, unlike Napoleon, he had never taken delight in battle. War was a regrettable necessity. If it was to be fought then it should be fought efficiently and well, but the object of war was peace. He was a diplomat now, not a general, yet old habits die hard and as his entourage travelled across the Kingdom of the Netherlands the Duke found many places which, as he noted, were 'good positions for an army'. One of those good positions was a valley which, to most people's eyes, was merely an unremarkable stretch of farmland. He had always possessed a keen eye for ground, for judging how slopes and valleys, streams and woodland might help or hinder a man commanding troops, and something about that valley south of Brussels caught his attention.

It was a wide valley, its slopes not particularly pronounced. A small roadside tavern called La Belle Alliance, 'the beautiful friendship', stood on the ridge marking the valley's southern side, which was mostly higher than the crest of the northern ridge that rose about 30 metres above the valley floor, say 100 feet, though the slope was never steep. The two ridges were not quite parallel. In some places they were fairly close together, though where the road ran northwards from ridge to ridge the distance between the crests was 1,000 metres, or just over half a mile. It was a half-mile of good farmland, and when the Duke saw the

valley in the summer of 1814, he would have seen tall crops of rye growing either side of the road, which was heavily used by wagons carrying
coal from the mines around Charleroi to the fireplaces of Brussels.

The Duke saw a lot more than that. The road was one of the main
routes from France to Brussels, so if war was to break out again this was
a possible invasion route. A French army coming north on the road
would cross the southern crest by the tavern and see the wide valley
ahead. And they would see the northern ridge. Ridge is really too
strong a word; they would have seen the straight road dropping gently
into the valley and then rising, just as gently, to the long swell of farmland, the northern ridge. Think of that ridge as a wall, and now give the
wall three bastions. To the east was a village of stone houses huddled
about a church. If those buildings and the village's outlying farms were
occupied by troops it would be the devil's own job to get them out.
Beyond those stone houses the land became more rugged, the hills
steeper and valleys deeper, no place for troops to manoeuvre, so the
village stood like a fortress at the eastern end of the ridge. In the centre
of the ridge, and standing halfway down the far slope, was a farm called
La Haie Sainte. It was a substantial building, made of stone, and its
house, barns and yard were surrounded by a high stone wall. La Haie
Sainte blocked an attack straight up the road, while off to the west was
a great house with a walled garden, the Château Hougoumont. So the
northern ridge is an obstacle with three outlying bastions, the village,
the farm and the château. Suppose an army came out of France and
suppose that army wanted to capture Brussels, then that ridge and
those bastions were blocking their advance. The enemy would either
have to capture those bastions or else ignore them, but if he ignored
them his troops would be squeezed between them as they attacked the
northern ridge, vulnerable to crossfire.

The invaders would see the ridge and its bastions, yet just as important was what they could not see. They could not see what lay beyond
the crest of the northern ridge. They would have seen treetops in the
country beyond, but the ground to the north was hidden, and if that
French army decided to attack troops on that northern ridge they

would never know what happened on that far hidden slope. Were the defenders moving reinforcements from one flank to the other? Was an attack assembling there? Was cavalry waiting out of sight? The ridge, even though it was low and its slopes were gentle, was deceptive. It offered a defender enormous advantages. Of course an enemy might not be obliging and make a simple frontal assault. He might try to march around the western flank of the ridge where the countryside was flatter, but nevertheless the Duke made a mental note of the place. Why? So far as he knew, indeed so far as all Europe knew, the wars were over. Napoleon was exiled, the diplomats were codifying the peace in Vienna, yet still the Duke made a point of remembering this place where an invading army, marching from France towards Brussels, would find life horribly difficult. It was not the only route an invading army might follow, and not the only defensive position the Duke noted in his two weeks of reconnaissance, but the ridge and its bastions stood athwart one of the possible invasion routes a French army might follow.

The Duke rode on, passing La Haie Sainte, to find a crossroads at the top of the ridge and, just beyond, a small village. If the Duke had asked what the place was called they would have said Mont St Jean, which was mildly amusing because the mountain of Saint John was nothing but that gentle swell in the wide fields of rye, wheat and barley. North of the village the road was swallowed into the great forest of Soignes and a couple of miles up that road there was a small town, another unremarkable place, though it possessed a handsomely domed church and a large number of inns for thirsty and tired travellers. In 1814 fewer than two thousand people lived in the town, though they had lost at least twenty young men to the long wars, all of them fighting for France, because this was the French-speaking area of the province of Belgium.

We do not know whether the Duke stopped in the small town in the summer of 1814. We do know he had taken notice of Mont St Jean, but the nearby country town with its fine church and lavish inns? Did he remember that place?

In time he would never forget it.

It was called Waterloo.

WATERLOO

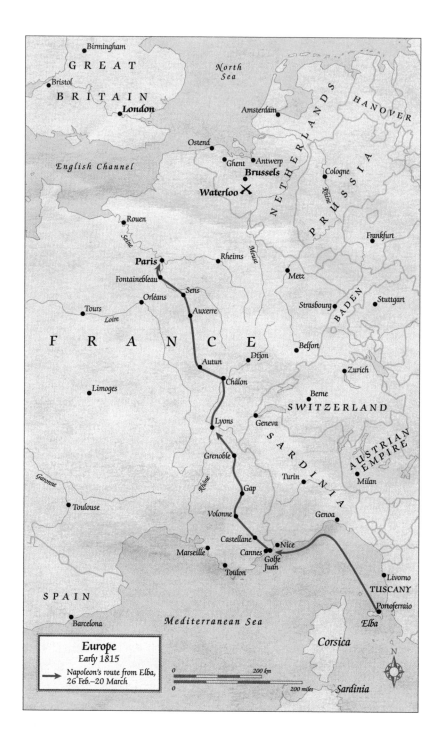

Birmingham

GREAT
Bristol
BRITAIN
London

North
Sea

Amsterdam

NETHERLANDS

HANOVER

Ostend
English Channel
Ghent ●Antwerp
Cologne
Brussels
Waterloo ✕

PRUSSIA

Rhine

Rouen

Frankfurt

Seine

Paris
Fontainebleau
Rheims

Meuse

Metz

Orléans
Sens
Auxerre

Tours
Loire

F   R   A   N   C   E

Strasbourg
Stuttgart
BADEN

Autun
Dijon
Belfort

Limoges
Châlon

Zurich

Berne
Lyons
Geneva
SWITZERLAND

Grenoble
SARDINIA
AUSTRIAN
EMPIRE

Garonne
Rhône
Gap
Turin
Milan

Toulouse
Volonne
Genoa

Castellane ●Nice
Marseille
Cannes
Golfe
Juan
Toulon

SPAIN

Livorno
TUSCANY

Portoferraio
Elba

Barcelona
Mediterranean Sea

Corsica

N

Europe
Early 1815
➤ Napoleon's route from Elba,
26 Feb.–20 March

0   200 km
0   200 miles

Sardinia

14

CHAPTER ONE

Glorious news! Nap's landed again in France, Hurrah!

'MY ISLAND IS NONE too BIG!' Napoleon declared when he found himself ruler of Elba, the tiny island that lies between Corsica and Italy. He had been Emperor of France and ruler of 44 million people, yet now, in 1814, he governed just 86 square miles and 11,000 subjects. Yet he was determined to be a good ruler, and no sooner had he arrived than he began issuing a string of decrees that would reform the island's mining industry and its agriculture. Little escaped his attention; 'Inform the intendant', he wrote, 'of my dissatisfaction at the dirty state of the streets.'

His plans extended far beyond street-cleaning. He wanted to build a new hospital, new schools and new roads, but there was never enough money. The restored monarchy in France had agreed to pay Napoleon a subsidy of 2 million francs a year, but it soon became apparent that the money would never be paid, and without money there could be no new hospitals, schools or roads. Frustrated by this failure, the Emperor retired into a sulk, passing the days by playing cards with his attendants, and all the while aware of the British and French warships that guarded Elba's coast to make certain he did not leave his Lilliputian kingdom.

The Emperor was bored. He missed his wife and son. He missed Josephine too and he was inconsolable when the news of her death reached Elba. Poor Josephine, with her black teeth, languid manner and lissom body, a woman who was adored by every man who met her, who was unfaithful to Napoleon, yet was always forgiven. He loved her even though, for dynastic reasons, he had divorced her. 'I have not passed a day without loving you,' he wrote to her after her death as though she still lived, 'I have not spent a night without clasping you in my arms ... no woman was ever loved with such devotion!'

He was bored and he was angry. He was angry at Louis XVIII, who was not paying the agreed subsidy, and furious at Talleyrand, once his own Foreign Minister, who now negotiated for the French monarchy at the Congress of Vienna. Talleyrand, sly, clever and duplicitous, was warning the other European envoys that Napoleon could never be kept safe on a small Mediterranean island so close to France. He wanted the Emperor sent far away to some remote place like the Azores, or better still to a West Indian island where the yellow fever raged, or perhaps to some speck in a distant ocean like Saint Helena.

Talleyrand was right while the British Commissioner, sent to Elba to keep a watchful eye on the Emperor, was wrong. Sir Neil Campbell believed that Napoleon had accepted his fate and wrote as much to Lord Castlereagh, Britain's Foreign Minister. 'I begin to think', he reported, 'that he is quite resigned to his retreat.'

The Emperor was anything but resigned. He followed the news from France and noted the dissatisfaction with the restored monarchy. There was widespread unemployment, the price of bread was high, and people who had greeted the Emperor's abdication with relief now looked back on his regime with regret. And so he began to make plans. He had been allowed a puny navy, nothing large enough to threaten the French and British ships that guarded him, and in mid-February 1815, he ordered the *Inconstant*, the largest of his brigs, brought into port; 'have its copper bottom overhauled,' he commanded, 'its leaks stopped and ... have it painted like the English brigs. I want it in the bay and ready by the 24th or 25th of this month.'

He ordered two other large ships to be chartered. He had been allowed to take 1,000 soldiers to Elba, including 400 veterans of his old Imperial Guard and a battalion of Polish lancers, and with those troops he would attempt to invade France.

And Sir Neil Campbell suspected nothing. Sir Neil was a decent man, thirty-nine years old in 1815, with a successful military career which almost ended in 1814 when he was appointed Military Attaché to the Russian army invading France. He had survived battles in Spain, but at Fère-Champenoise he was mistaken by an over-enthusiastic Cossack for a French officer and savagely wounded.

He survived his wounds and was appointed British Commissioner to His Highness the Emperor Napoleon, ruler of Elba. Lord Castlereagh stressed that Sir Neil was not the Emperor's jailer, but of course part of his job was to keep a close eye on Napoleon. Yet Sir Neil had been lulled, and in February 1815, while the *Inconstant* was being disguised as a British ship, he told the Emperor that he needed to sail to Italy to consult with his doctor. That may well have been true, but it is also true that Signora Bartoli, Sir Neil's mistress, lived in Leghorn, and that is where he sailed.

The Emperor wished Sir Neil well and hoped he would return by the end of the month because the Princess Borghese was giving a ball, and Sir Neil promised he would do his best to attend. The Princess Borghese was Napoleon's beguiling sister, the lovely Pauline, who had joined her brother in exile. Penury had forced the sale of her lavish house in Paris, which had been purchased by the British government for use as their embassy. That meant that for five months it had been home to the Duke of Wellington, who had been appointed Britain's ambassador to the court of Louis XVIII. The house, on the rue du Faubourg St-Honoré, is a jewel, and is still Britain's embassy.

Sir Neil sailed to Leghorn in the Royal Navy brig *Partridge*, which usually blockaded Elba's main harbour. With the *Partridge* flown the Emperor could put his plans into effect and on 26 February his small fleet sailed for France with just 1,026 troops, 40 horses and 2 cannon. The voyage lasted two days and on 28 February the Emperor landed in France again. He led a puny army, but Napoleon was nothing if not confident. 'I will arrive in Paris', he told his troops, 'without firing a shot!'

The peace was over, struck by a thunderbolt.

* * *

During the winter of 1814 to 1815 many women in Paris wore violet-coloured dresses. It was not just fashion, but rather a code which suggested that the violet would return in the spring. The violet was Napoleon. His beloved Josephine had carried violets at their wedding, and he sent her a bouquet of the flowers on every anniversary. Before his exile to Elba he had said he would be modest, like the violet. Everyone in Paris knew what the colour violet represented, and if at first the French had been relieved that the Emperor was dethroned and that the long destructive wars were over, they soon found much to dislike in the Emperor's replacement. The restored monarchy, under the grossly obese Louis XVIII, proved rapacious and unpopular.

Then the violet returned. Most people expected that the Royalist army would swiftly defeat Napoleon's risible little force, but instead the King's troops deserted in droves to the returned Emperor and within days French newspapers were printing a witty description of his triumphant journey. There are various versions, but this one is typical:

The Tiger has left his den.
The Ogre has been three days at sea.
The Wretch has landed at Fréjus.
The Buzzard has reached Antibes.
The Invader has arrived at Grenoble.
The Tyrant has entered Lyon.
The Usurper has been glimpsed fifty miles from Paris.
Tomorrow Napoleon will be at our gates!
The Emperor will proceed to the Tuileries today.
His Imperial Majesty will address his loyal subjects tomorrow.

His Imperial Majesty, Napoleon Bonaparte, was forty-six years old as he entered the Tuileries Palace in Paris, where an excited crowd awaited his arrival. They had been gathered for hours. The King, fat Louis XVIII, had fled Paris, going to Ghent in the Kingdom of the Netherlands, and the carpet of his abandoned throne room was tufted with embroidered crowns. Someone in the waiting crowd gave one of the crowns a dismissive kick and so loosened it to reveal that the royal tuft hid a woven bee. The honey-bee was another of Napoleon's symbols, and the excited crowd went to its knees to tear off the crowns, thus restoring the carpet to its old imperial splendour.

It was evening before Napoleon arrived at the palace. The waiting crowd could hear the cheering getting closer, then came the clatter of hoofs on the forecourt and finally the Emperor was there, being carried shoulder-high up the stairs to the audience chamber. An eyewitness said 'his eyes were closed, his hands reaching forward like a blind man's, his happiness betrayed only by his smile'.

What a journey it had been! Not just from Elba, but from Napoleon's unpromising birth in 1769 (the same year as the Duke of Wellington's birth). He was christened Nabulion Buonaparte, a name that betrays his Corsican origin. His family, which claimed noble lineage, was impoverished and the young Nabulion flirted with those Corsicans who plotted for independence from France and even thought of joining Britain's Royal Navy, France's most formidable foe. Instead he emigrated to France, frenchified his name and joined the army. In 1792 he was a Lieutenant, a year later, aged twenty-four, a Brigadier-General.

There is a famous painting of the young Napoleon crossing the St Bernard Pass on his way to the Italian campaign which rocketed him to fame. Louis David's canvas shows him on a rearing horse, and every-thing about the painting is motion; the horse rears, its mouth open and eyes wide, its mane is wind-whipped, the sky is stormy and the General's cloak is a lavish swirl of gale-driven colour. Yet in the centre of that frenzied paint is Napoleon's calm face. He looks sullen and unsmiling, but above all, calm. That was what he demanded of the painter, and David delivered a picture of a man at home amidst chaos.

The man who was carried up the Tuileries staircase was much changed from the young hero who had possessed rock-star good looks.

By 1814 the handsome, slim young man was gone, replaced by a pot-bellied, short-haired figure with sallow skin and very small hands and feet. He was not tall, a little over five foot seven inches, but he was still hypnotic. This was the man who had risen to dominate all Europe, a man who had conquered and lost an empire, who had redrawn the maps, remade the constitution and rewritten the laws of France. He was supremely intelligent, quick-witted, easily bored, but rarely vengeful. The world would not see his like again until the twentieth century, but unlike Mao or Hitler or Stalin, Napoleon was not a murderous tyrant, although like them he was a man who changed history.

He was a superb administrator, but that was not how he wanted to be remembered. Above all, he was a warlord. His idol was Alexander the Great. In the middle of the nineteenth century, in the American Civil War, Robert E. Lee, the great Confederate General, watched his troops executing a brilliant and battle-winning manoeuvre and said, memorably, 'It is well that war is so terrible, or we should grow too fond of it.' Napoleon had grown too fond of it, he loved war. Perhaps it was his first love, because it combined the excitement of supreme risk with the joy of victory. He had the incisive mind of a great strategist, yet when the marching was done and the enemy was outflanked he still demanded enormous sacrifices of his men. After Austerlitz, when one of his generals lamented the French lying dead on that frozen battlefield, the Emperor retorted that 'the women of Paris can replace those men in one night'. When Metternich, the clever Austrian Foreign Minister, offered Napoleon honourable peace terms in 1813 and reminded the Emperor of the human cost of refusal, he received the scornful answer that Napoleon would happily sacrifice a million men to gain his ambitions. Napoleon was careless with the lives of his troops, yet his soldiers adored him because he had the common touch. He knew how to speak to them, how to jest with them and how to inspire them. His soldiers might adore him, but his generals feared him. Marshal Augereau, a foul-mouthed disciplinarian, said, 'This little bastard of a general actually scares me!', and General Vandamme, a hard man, said he 'trembled like a child' when he approached Napoleon. Yet Napoleon led them all to glory. That was his drug, *la Gloire*! And in search of it he broke peace treaty after peace treaty, and his armies marched beneath their Eagle standards from Madrid to Moscow, from the Baltic to the Red Sea. He astonished Europe with victories like Austerlitz and Friedland, but he also led his *Grande Armée* to disaster in the Russian snow. Even his defeats were on a gargantuan scale.

Now he must march again, and he knew it. He sent peace feelers to the other European powers, saying that he had returned to France in response to the public will, that he meant no aggression, and that if they accepted his return then he would live in peace, but he must have known those overtures would be rejected.

So the Eagles would fly again.

* * *

The Duke of Wellington's life was in danger. Appointing him as Ambassador to France was not, perhaps, the most tactful move the British government made, and Paris was filled with rumours about impending assassination attempts. The government in London wanted the Duke to leave Paris, but he refused because such a move would look like cowardice. Then came the perfect excuse. Lord Castlereagh, the Foreign Secretary and the chief British negotiator at the Congress in Vienna, was urgently needed in London and the Duke was appointed as his replacement. No one could depict that move as a fearful flight from danger because it was plainly a promotion, and so the Duke joined the diplomats who laboriously attempted to redraw the maps of Europe.

And while they talked Napoleon escaped.

Count Metternich, the cold, clever, handsome Foreign Minister of Austria, was perhaps the most influential diplomat in Vienna. He had gone to bed very late on the night of 6 March 1815 because a meeting of the most important plenipotentiaries had lasted until 3 a.m. He was tired, and so he instructed his valet that he was not to be disturbed, but the man woke the Count anyway at 6 a.m. because a courier had arrived with an express despatch marked 'URGENT'. The envelope bore the inscription 'From the Imperial and Royal Consulate at Genoa', and the Count, perhaps thinking that nothing vital would be communicated from such a minor consulate, put it on his bedside table and tried to go to sleep again. Finally, at around 7.30 in the morning, he broke the seal and read the despatch. It was very short:

> *The English commissioner Campbell has just entered the harbour asking whether anyone has seen Napoleon at Genoa, in view of the fact that he had disappeared from the island of Elba. The answer being in the negative, the English frigate put to sea without further delay.*

It might seem strange that Sir Neil Campbell had sailed to Italy in search of the missing Napoleon rather than looking for the errant Emperor in France, but there was a widely held assumption that Napoleon, if he landed in France, would be swiftly captured by Royalist forces. 'None would hear of France,' the Duke of Wellington recalled, 'all were sure that in France he would be massacred by the people when he appeared there. I remember Talleyrand's words so well, *"Pour la France? Non!"'* A landing in Italy seemed far more likely, especially as his brother-in-law, Joachim Murat, was King of Naples. Murat, who owed his throne to Napoleon's generosity, had made his peace with the Austrians, but realized the Congress in Vienna would almost certainly strip him of his petty kingdom. As soon as he heard of Napoleon's escape he changed sides again, attacking the Austrians, an adventure that failed utterly and led eventually to a firing squad.

Napoleon, of course, did go to France, but for days the diplomats in Vienna had no idea where he was, only that he was on the loose. The Congress, which had dithered and dallied and danced and debated, suddenly became decisive. 'War', Metternich recalled, 'was decided in less than an hour.' That swiftness was made possible because almost everyone that mattered, the decision-makers, were present at Vienna. The King of Prussia, the Emperor of Austria, the Czar of Russia, all were there, and Napoleon's reappearance galvanized them. They did not declare war on France, because so far as the powers at Vienna were concerned France was still a monarchy ruled by Louis XVIII; instead they declared war on one man, Napoleon.

Four countries, Russia, Prussia, Austria and Great Britain, each agreed to raise an army of 150,000 men. Those armies would converge on France. Great Britain was unable to raise such a large army, so she agreed to pay subsidies to the other three instead. By now couriers were criss-crossing Europe, and one of them brought a letter to the Duke of Wellington from Lord Castlereagh: 'Your Grace can judge where your personal presence is likely to be of the most use to the public service … either to remain at Vienna or to put yourself at the head of the army in Flanders.'

The Czar of Russia, Alexander I, had no doubt what the Duke's choice would be. 'It is up to you', he told the Duke, 'to save the world again.'

The Duke was doubtless flattered, but probably rather suspicious of such high-flown sentiments. Nor did he have any difficulty in deciding where he was likely to be of the most use to the public service. He replied to the government in London, 'I am going into the Low Countries to take command of the army.' He left Vienna at the end of March and was in Brussels by 6 April.

History rarely provides such a striking confrontation. The two greatest soldiers of the era, two men who had never fought against each other, were now gathering armies just 160 miles apart. The world's conqueror was in Paris while the conqueror of the world's conqueror was in Brussels.

Did Napoleon know that Wellington had been described as his conqueror? Diplomats are rarely discreet about such things, and it is more than possible, even likely, that the Emperor was told of that derisory remark. It would have angered him. He had something to prove.

And so the armies gathered.

* * *

There was confusion in France when Napoleon returned. Who ruled? Who should rule? For a few days no one could be sure what was happening. Colonel Girod de l'Ain was typical of many of the officers who had fought under Napoleon. With the return of the monarchy he had been forced to retire on half-pay and, though he was newly married, he wanted to rejoin the Emperor as soon as he could. He was living in the French Alps, but decided he should go to Paris:

*The whole country was in turmoil. I travelled in uniform, but I
took the precaution of providing myself with two cockades, one
white and the other a tricolour, and depending on which colour
flag I saw flying from the bell-towers of any town or village we
passed through, I quickly decorated my hat with the appropriate
cockade.*

Colonel de l'Ain reached Paris and discovered his old regimental
commander had already declared for Napoleon, as did almost the
whole of the royal army, despite the oaths of loyalty they had sworn to
Louis XVIII. Their officers might stay loyal to their royal oath, but the
men had different ideas. Count Alfred-Armand de Saint-Chamans
commanded the 7th Chasseurs, and as soon as he heard of Napoleon's
return he told his regiment to be ready to campaign, 'because I believed
we were going to fight the ex-Emperor'. His battalion, though, had a
quite different objective:

*Someone told me that several officers had gathered in the café
and were determined to take their troops to join the Light
Infantry of the Guard to support the Emperor, that others were
having tricolour flags made which they planned to give to the
men and so provoke a mutiny ... I began to see the true state of
affairs and to feel the misery of my position. What could I do?
Any hopes I had of giving the King a fine loyal regiment to
support the throne at this fateful hour were dashed to the ground.*

The loyalty of the French army to Louis XVIII melted in a moment,
giving Napoleon 200,000 troops. Thousands of veterans, like Colonel
de l'Ain, were also volunteering, but Napoleon knew he needed an even
larger army to defend against the attack that would surely come. One
of Louis XVIII's few popular measures had been the abolition of
conscription, and Napoleon hesitated to reintroduce it, knowing how
much people hated it, but he had no option, and that would raise
another 100,000 men, though all would need training and equipping

before they were ready to march, so the Emperor decreed that the National Guard, a local-based militia, would give him 150,000 troops. It was still not enough. The allies, he knew, would bring over half a million men to attack him.

France, in those first weeks, was frantic with preparations. Horses were requisitioned, uniforms made and weapons repaired. It was a compelling display of Napoleon's administrative genius because, by early summer, he had one army ready to march and others placed to defend France's frontiers. He still had too few men to resist the onslaught he knew was coming, and he needed yet more troops to suppress Royalist unrest in the Vendée, a region in the west of France which had always been Catholic and Monarchist, but by early summer Napoleon had a total force of 360,000 trained men, the best of whom were destined to assemble in northern France, where 125,000 experienced soldiers would form *l'Armée du Nord*, the army of the north.

Napoleon could have remained on the defensive that summer, stationing most of his men behind massive fortifications and hoping that the allied armies would batter themselves to destruction. That was not appealing. Such a war would be fought on French soil and Napoleon had never been a passive general. His skill was manoeuvre. In 1814 he had faced overwhelming odds as the Prussians, Austrians and Russians approached Paris from the north and east, and he had dazzled them with the speed of his marches and the suddenness of his attacks. To military professionals that campaign was Napoleon's finest, even though it did end in defeat, and the Duke of Wellington took care to study it. Napoleon himself claimed:

The art of war does not need complicated manoeuvre; the simplest are the best, and common sense is fundamental. From which one might wonder why generals make blunders; it is because they try to be clever. The most difficult thing is to guess the enemy's plan, to find the truth from all the reports. The rest merely requires common sense; it is like a boxing match, the more you punch the better it is.

The Emperor was being disingenuous. War was never quite that simple, but in essence his strategy was simple. It was to divide his enemies, then pin one down while the other was attacked hard and, like a boxing match, the harder he punched the quicker the result. Then, once one enemy was destroyed, he would turn on the next. The best defence for Napoleon in 1815 was attack, and the obvious enemy to attack was the closest.

It would take time for the massive Russian army to cross Europe and reach the French frontier, and the Austrians were still not ready in May. But just to the north of France, in the old province of Belgium that was now part of the Kingdom of the Netherlands, two armies were gathering: the British and the Prussian. Napoleon calculated that if he could beat those two armies then the other allies would lose heart. If he defeated Wellington and drove the British back to the sea, there could even be a change of government in London which might bring a Whig administration inclined to let him stay as ruler of France. The enemy alliance would then fall apart. It was a gamble, of course, but all war is a gamble. He could have waited to raise and train more men until the French army almost matched the allies in number, but those two armies north of the border were too tempting. If they could be divided then they could be beaten, and if they could be beaten then the enemy coalition might collapse. It had happened before, so why not now?

The army he would take north was a good one, filled with experienced troops. If it had a weakness it was in the high command. Napoleon had always depended on his Marshals, but of the twenty Marshals still living four remained loyal to Louis XVIII, four more defected to the allies and two simply lay low. One of those two was Marshal Berthier, who had been Napoleon's Chief of Staff and had a genius for organization. He fled to Bavaria, where on 1 June he fell to his death from a third-floor window of Bamberg Castle. Some suspect murder, but the most likely explanation is that he simply leaned too far out to watch some Russian cavalry pass through the square beneath. He was replaced by Nicolas Jean de Dieu Soult, a hugely experienced soldier who had risen from the ranks. Napoleon once called him 'the greatest manoeuvrer in Europe', but when Soult commanded armies in Spain he found himself constantly outfought by Wellington. He was a difficult man, prickly and proud, and it remained to be seen whether he possessed Berthier's administrative talents.

Two of the Emperor's most brilliant Marshals, Davout and Suchet, did not accompany *l'Armée du Nord*. Davout, a grim and relentless fighter, was made Minister for War and stayed in Paris, while Suchet was appointed commander of the Army of the Alps, a grand name for a small and ill-equipped force. Napoleon, asked which were his greatest generals, named André Masséna and Louis-Gabriel Suchet, but the first was in ill health and Suchet was left behind to defend France's eastern frontier against an Austrian attack.

Napoleon created one new Marshal for the coming campaign: Emmanuel, Marquis de Grouchy. Davout advised against the appointment, but Napoleon insisted. Grouchy was an aristocrat from the *ancien régime* and had been fortunate to survive the slaughters of the French Revolution. He had made his reputation as a cavalryman; now he would be given command of one third of *l'Armée du Nord*.

Then there was the Marshal who was called the 'bravest of the brave', the mercurial and fearsome Michel Ney, who, like Soult, had risen from the ranks. He was fiery, red-haired and passionate, the son of a barrel-maker. He was forty-six years old in 1815, the same age as Napoleon and Wellington, and he had made his reputation on some of the bloodiest battlefields of the long war. No one doubted his courage. He was a soldier's soldier, a warrior who, when Napoleon landed from Elba, had famously promised Louis XVIII to bring the Emperor back to Paris in an iron cage. Instead he had defected with his troops. He was renowned for his extraordinary courage and inspiring leadership, but no one would ever call Ney cool-headed. And, ominously, Soult detested Ney, and Ney detested Soult, yet the two were expected to work together in that fateful summer.

The Marshals were important, and none more so than the Chief of Staff, because it was his job to translate the Emperor's wishes into mundane orders of march. Berthier had been a brilliant administrator, foreseeing problems and sorting them efficiently, and it remained to be seen whether Marshal Soult had the same ability to organize over a hundred thousand men, to feed them, move them and bring them to battle according to his Emperor's wishes. The other Marshals would have the heavy responsibility of independent command. If the Emperor's tactic was to pin one enemy army and keep it in place while he defeated the other, then a Marshal would be the man doing the pinning. At the opening of hostilities it was Marshal Ney's job to keep Wellington busy while Napoleon fought the Prussians, and two days later Marshal Grouchy had to divert the Prussians while Napoleon destroyed Wellington's men. Those tasks were not done by just following orders, but by imaginative soldiering. A Marshal was expected to take the difficult decisions, and Napoleon was entrusting them to Grouchy, new to his high rank and nervous of failure, and to Ney, whose only mode of battle was to fight like the devil.

L'Armée du Nord would face two armies in Belgium, of which the largest was the Prussian. It was led by the 74-year-old Prince Gebhard Leberecht von Blücher, who had first fought for Sweden against the Prussians, but after being captured was commissioned into the Prussian army by Frederick the Great. He was vastly experienced, a cavalryman with the nickname of *Marschall Vorwärts*, Marshal Forwards, because of his habit of shouting his men forward. He was popular, much loved by his troops and, famously, prone to bouts of mental illness during which he believed himself pregnant with an elephant fathered by a French infantryman. There was no trace of this madness during the summer of 1815; instead Blücher marched with a fanatical determination to defeat Napoleon. He was bluff, courageous, and if he was not the smartest general he had the sense to employ brilliant staff officers. In 1815 his Chief of Staff was August von Gneisenau, a man of vast ability and long experience, some of which had been gained fighting alongside the British during the American Revolution. That had soured his views of the British army, and Gneisenau was extremely suspicious of British abilities and intentions. When Baron von Müffling was appointed as the liaison officer to Wellington he was summoned by Gneisenau, who warned him:

> *To be much on my guard with the Duke of Wellington, because*
> *by his relations with India and his transactions with the deceitful*
> *Nabobs, this distinguished general had so accustomed himself to*
> *duplicity that he had at last become such a master in the art as to*
> *outwit the Nabobs themselves.*

It defies imagination to know how Gneisenau got hold of this strange opinion, but given Gneisenau's responsibilities and Blücher's high regard for his advice, it hardly boded well for future relations between the British and Prussians. There was mistrust anyway between the two countries over Prussia's ambition to annex Saxony, a disagreement that had soured the Congress of Vienna. The British, French and Austrians were so opposed to this expansion of Prussian power that they had agreed to go to war rather than permit it. Russia had similar ambitions for the whole of Poland, and at one time it looked as if a new war would break out in Europe with Prussia and Russia fighting against the rest. That had been averted, but the bad blood remained.

Now the Prussian army was in the province of Belgium. It was an untested army. The Prussians had experienced defeat, occupation, reorganization and, after Napoleon's abdication in 1814, demobilization. There were good, experienced troops in Blücher's ranks, but not enough, and so the numbers were made up by volunteers and by the *Landwehr*, the militia. The call to arms was answered enthusiastically in 1815. Franz Lieber was just seventeen years old when he heard that call, so he and his brother went to Berlin, where they discovered:

> *a table was placed in the centre of a square … at which several*
> *officers were enlisting those who offered themselves. The crowd*
> *was so great that we had to wait from ten until one o'clock before*
> *we could get a chance to have our names taken.*

He reported to his regiment at the beginning of May, had one month's training and then was marched into the Low Country to join Blücher's forces. Lieber was intrigued to discover that one sergeant in his regiment was a woman who had so distinguished herself in combat that she had been awarded three gallantry medals. So by the summer of 1815 Blücher led at least one woman and 121,000 men, a formidable army on paper, but as Peter Hofschröer, an historian very sympathetic to the Prussians, writes, 'a substantial part of Blücher's forces consisted of raw levies capable of two basic manoeuvres: going forwards in a state of disorder, or going backwards in a state of chaos.' That is witty and, as things turned out, those raw levies proved capable of fighting too, but it remained to be seen whether Gneisenau would overcome his Anglophobia and cooperate with the army gathering on the Prussian right.

That was the British–Dutch army led by the Duke of Wellington, who, famously, described it as 'an infamous army'. And so it was when he first arrived in Brussels. It was under-strength, many of the Dutch regiments were from the French-speaking province of Belgium, and the Duke was wary of those troops because so many of them were veterans of Napoleon's armies. The French-speaking Belgians were unhappy that their land had been given to the Kingdom of the Netherlands, and the Emperor knew of that dissatisfaction. Pamphlets were being smuggled across the French border and distributed among the Belgian troops in the Duke's army. 'To the brave soldiers', the pamphlets read, 'who have conquered under the French Eagles, the Eagles which have led us so often to victory have reappeared! Their cry is always the same, glory and liberty!' The Duke doubted the reliability of those regiments and took the precaution of separating them, brigading them with battalions whose loyalties were unquestioned.

Those loyal battalions were either British troops or the 6,000 men of the King's German Legion (KGL), a unit which had fought brilliantly for the Duke during the long Peninsular War. The Legion had been raised in Hanover, which of course shared a King with Great Britain, and in 1815 Hanover sent another 16,000 men to join Wellington's army.

Those 16,000 were untested and so, like the Dutch army, they were split up and brigaded with either British or KGL battalions. It was not a popular decision. 'It was a severe blow to our morale,' Captain Carl Jacobi of the 1st Hanoverian Brigade complained:

> *The English generals were totally unfamiliar with the traditions of the Hanoverians ... In their eyes, everything was imperfect, even open to criticism if it did not conform to English concerns and institutions. There was no camaraderie among the allied troops, not even among the officers. The ignorance of the other's language, on both sides, the major difference in pay and the resulting great difference in life styles prevented any closer companionship. Even our compatriots in the King's German Legion did not associate with us; the fifteen year old ensign with the red sash looked down on the older Hanoverian officer.*

By summer, when the war began, Wellington had some 16,000 Hanoverians and just under 6,000 men from the King's German Legion. The Dutch army, which was part of his 'infamous' army, numbered almost 40,000, of whom half were in regiments that were French-speaking and so of doubtful reliability. The rest of his army, some 30,000 men, were British, and the Duke wished he had more of them.

But Britain had just fought a war with the United States, and many of the best regiments, veterans of Wellington's victories, were still across the Atlantic. They were returning, and some battalions found themselves travelling straight from America to the Netherlands. The Duke would have been far more confident if he had possessed his Peninsular army, which had been one of the best that ever fought under British colours. A few weeks before Waterloo he was walking in a Brussels park with Thomas Creevey, a British parliamentarian, who rather anxiously asked the Duke about the expected campaign. A red-coated British infantryman was staring at the park's statues and the Duke pointed at the man. 'There,' he said, 'there. It all depends upon that article whether we do the business or not. Give me enough of it, and I am sure.'

In the end there was just enough of it. A little over 20,000 British infantry were to fight at Waterloo, and they were to bear the brunt of the Emperor's attacks. Napoleon's generals warned him of those red-coated soldiers, saying how staunch they were. General Reille annoyed Napoleon by saying that British infantry were *inexpugnable*, impregnable, while Soult told the Emperor that 'In a straight fight the English infantry are the very devil.' And so they were. The Emperor had never fought against them and he dismissed the warnings, but Wellington knew their worth, and the similar worth of the King's German Legion. Four years after the battle, walking the field of Waterloo, the Duke remarked, 'I had only about 35,000 men on whom I could thoroughly rely; the remainder were but too likely to run away.'

The Duke had twenty-two British battalions, of whom fifteen had fought with him in Spain or Portugal. It was just enough. Yet even those experienced battalions were, like the Prussian regiments, filled with new recruits. The largest and one of the best battalions at Waterloo was the 52nd, the Oxfordshire Light Infantry, which had been in more or less continuous combat from 1806 until Napoleon's first abdication. At Waterloo the battalion numbered 1,079 men, but of those 558 had joined since its last battle. The Guards Division was the same. Ensign Robert Batty of the 1st Foot Guards said the division was filled with 'young soldiers and volunteers from the militia who had never been exposed to the fire of an enemy'.

Yet the old hands, the veterans, were full of confidence. Frederick Mainwaring was a Lieutenant in the 51st, a Yorkshire battalion that had fought at Corunna, Fuentes d'Onoro, Salamanca, Vitoria and in the battles of the Pyrenees and southern France. It was stationed at Portsmouth when the news of Napoleon's return reached Britain. Mainwaring recalled:

I was seated with two or three others at breakfast in the mess-room, the Bugle-Major came in with the letters and as usual laid the newspaper on the mess-table. Someone opened it and glanced his eyes carelessly over its contents when suddenly his countenance brightened up, and flinging the newspaper into the air like a madman, he shouted out 'Glorious news! Nap's landed again in France, Hurrah!' In an instant we were all wild … 'Nap's in France again' spread like wildfire through the barracks … the men turned out and cheered … our joy was unbounded!

Captain Cavalié Mercer commanded a troop of Royal Horse Artillery at Colchester when the news arrived and tells the same story as Lieutenant Mainwaring. The order to march was 'received with unfeigned joy by officers and men, all eager to plunge into danger and bloodshed, all hoping to obtain glory and distinction'.

The French and Prussians were no different. Eager volunteers had flocked to the Prussian colours, and in France most soldiers were over-joyed at the Emperor's return. Many had been prisoners-of-war in the dreadful British prisons, either on Dartmoor or in the pestilential hulks that were great dismasted ships that lay at permanent anchor, and those men wanted revenge. They wanted glory. Captain Pierre Cardron, an infantry officer, recorded a scene that happened again and again across France. His regiment had sworn loyalty to the King, but after Napoleon's return the Colonel summoned all the officers. They stood in two ranks 'asking one another what was going on? What was there? In the end we were filled with worry', Cardron remembered, but then their Colonel appeared:

holding in his hands, what? You would not guess in a hundred years … Our eagle, under which we had marched so many times to victory and which the brave Colonel had hidden inside the mattress of his bed … At the sight of the cherished standard cries of 'Vive l'Empereur!' could be heard; soldiers and officers, all overwhelmed, wanted not only to see, but to embrace and touch it; this incident made every eye flow with tears of emotion … we have promised to die beneath our eagle for the country and Napoleon.

No wonder that one French general wrote home that his men were in a 'frenzy' for the Emperor. And in that frenetic atmosphere Napoleon decided on a pre-emptive blow against the British and the Prussians. He would attack them before the Austrian and Russian armies could reach the French frontier, and for his attack he had 125,000 men and 350 cannon. Facing him was Blücher with 120,000 men and 312 cannon and Wellington's army of 92,000 men and 120 guns. The Emperor was outnumbered, but that was nothing new and he was a master of manoeuvre. His task now was to divide the allies then destroy them one by one. War, he had declared, was simple. 'It's like a boxing match, the more you punch the better it is.'

And in June of 1815 he set out to punch Blücher and Wellington into oblivion.

Franz Lieber was just seventeen years old when he heard the Prussian army's call to arms, and he and his brother volunteered in Berlin. He reported to his regiment at the beginning of May, had one month's training and then was marched into the Low Country to join Marshal Blücher's forces. He would go on to have a distinguished career in America, emigrating in 1827, where he became Professor of Political Economics at South Carolina College. He moved to the north before the Civil War and taught at Columbia University, where he compiled the Lieber Code, credited as the first attempt to codify the rules of war. He lived till 1870.

'The Duke of Wellington', by Francisco Goya. When in 1814 the Duke was asked whether he regretted that he had never fought the Emperor in battle, he replied: 'No, and I am very glad.' He despised Napoleon the man, but admired Napoleon the soldier.

CLOCKWISE FROM TOP LEFT | *Portrait of the Empress Josephine, by Pierre-Paul Prud'hon.* | *'Napoleon, Fontainebleau, 31 March 1814', by Paul Delaroche – the handsome, slim young man was gone, replaced by a pot-bellied, short-haired figure with sallow skin.* | *Czar Alexander I of Russia, 1814, by Baron François Gérard: 'It is up to you,' he told the Duke of Wellington, 'to save the world again.'* | *'Clemens Lothar Wenzel, Prince Metternich, 1815', by Sir Thomas Lawrence: 'War', Metternich recalled, 'was decided in less than an hour.'*

CLOCKWISE FROM TOP | *'The Arrival of Napoleon at the Tuileries': It was evening before Napoleon arrived at the palace. The waiting crowd could hear the cheering getting closer, then came the clatter of hoofs on the forecourt and finally the Emperor was there.* | *A souvenir made to mark Napoleon's return to Paris in March 1815. The violet was Napoleon. His beloved Josephine had carried violets at their wedding, and he sent her a bouquet of the flowers on every anniversary.* | *Portrait of Louis XVIII of France with the coronation robe, by Pierre-Narcisse Guérin.*

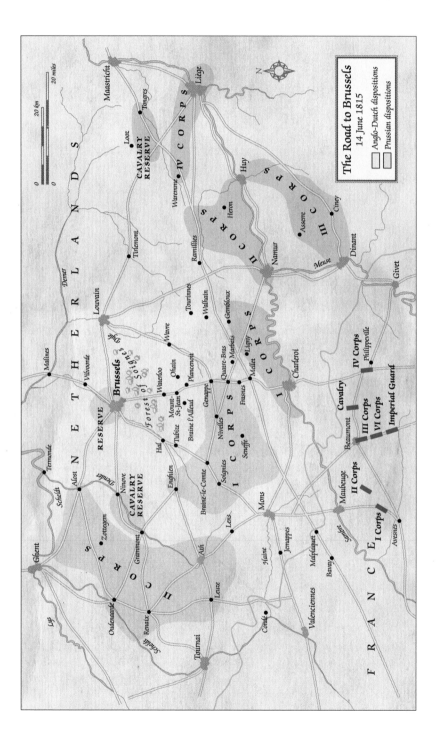

The Road to Brussels
14 June 1815

☐ Anglo-Dutch dispositions
☐ Prussian dispositions

CHAPTER TWO

Napoleon has humbugged me, by God!

NAPOLEON WAS SURELY RIGHT when he claimed that the most difficult thing in war was 'to guess the enemy's plan'. And that was precisely the difficulty that Marshal Blücher and the Duke of Wellington faced. What was the Emperor planning?

The first question was whether the Emperor would attack at all, and if the answer was yes, then they needed to know where and when that attack would occur. Yet only three days before the storm burst the Duke of Wellington was persuaded that no onslaught was coming. He planned to give a ball in Brussels on 21 June, the anniversary of his great victory at Vitoria, and when the Duchess of Richmond asked whether it would be sensible for her to give a ball on 15 June he reassured her, 'You may give your ball with the greatest safety without fear of interruption.' On Tuesday, 13 June, he wrote to a friend in England:

> *There is nothing new here. We have reports of Buonaparte's joining the army and attacking us, but I have accounts from Paris of the 10th, on which day he was still there; and I judge from his speech to the Legislature that his departure was not likely to be imminent. I think we are now too strong for him here.*

That letter was written on Tuesday, and on the day before, Monday, 12 June, Napoleon had left Paris to join *l'Armée du Nord* in Flanders. On 14 June that army closed up to the frontier and the allies still suspected nothing. Blücher shared Wellington's opinion. He had written to his wife, 'Bonaparte will not attack us,' but Bonaparte was poised to do just that. He had closed France's borders – 'Not a stage or carriage must pass,' he ordered – while north of the frontier, in the province of Belgium, the British and Prussian armies were spread across a swathe of country over a hundred miles wide.

That dispersal was necessary for two reasons. The allies are in a defensive posture. They will not be ready to attack until they have overwhelming force, when the Austrians and Russians have reached the French frontier, so for the moment Wellington and Blücher are waiting and, of course, they know that the Emperor may attack them before they move against him. Wellington may have thought such an attack unlikely, but he still must guard against the possibility, and that means watching every route that the French might take. With hindsight it seems obvious that Napoleon would strike at the junction of the Prussian and British armies, to separate them, but that was not so obvious to either Blücher or to Wellington. Wellington's fear was that Napoleon would choose a route further west, through Mons and so on to Brussels or even towards Ghent, where Louis XVIII had taken refuge. Such an attack would cut Wellington off from the coast, and so sever his supply lines. Whatever happened Wellington wanted to be certain that his army had a way to retreat to safety if it was outfought, and that safe retreat led west to Ostend, where ships could evacuate the army to Britain. Blücher had the same concern, only his retreat would be eastwards, towards Prussia.

So the two armies are spread wide because they need to guard against every possible French attack. The most westerly Prussian forces, General von Bülow's Corps, are a hundred miles to the east of Wellington's western flank. That dispersal was also necessary to feed the armies. The troops depended on buying local supplies and too many men and too many horses in a single place soon exhausted the available food.

So the allies were spread across a hundred miles of country, while Napoleon was concentrating his army south of the River Sambre on the main road which led through Charleroi to Brussels. So why did the allies not detect this? In Spain the Duke of Wellington had a superb intelligence service; indeed his problem had been that he received too much intelligence, but in Flanders, in 1815, he was virtually blinded. Before the frontier was closed he had received plenty of reports from travellers coming north out of France, but most of those reports were fanciful and all were contradictory. He was also denied his favourite intelligence instrument, his Exploring Officers.

The Exploring Officers were reliable men who scouted enemy country and depended on their superb horses to escape French pursuit. They rode in full uniform, so they could not be accused of spying, and they were extremely effective. Chief among them was a Scotsman, Colquhoun Grant, and Wellington demanded Grant's presence in Belgium as the head of his Intelligence Department. Grant arrived in Brussels on 12 May and immediately set about establishing a network of agents on the French frontier, in which activity he was severely disappointed because the local population, all French-speaking, was either sympathetic to Napoleon or sullenly apathetic. Nor could Grant send Exploring Officers south of the border because, officially, the allies were not at war with France, only with Bonaparte.

But Grant did have superb contacts in Paris. This was by accident, because in 1812 Grant had the misfortune to be captured by the French in Spain. The French, knowing his value to Wellington, refused to exchange or parole him, but sent him to France under close guard, though not close enough, because, once over the frontier in Bayonne, the Scotsman escaped and learned that General Joseph Souham, a French officer who had risen from the ranks, was staying in the town and planning to travel to Paris. In an act of superb bravado Grant introduced himself to Souham as an American officer and asked to travel in the General's carriage. He was still wearing the red coat of the British 11th Regiment of Foot and no one thought to question it. What did Frenchmen know of American uniforms? Once in Paris the intrepid Grant found a source in the Ministry of War and contrived to send reports to the Duke in Spain. Grant eventually made his way back to England, but his source still existed in Paris and, once established as head of Wellington's Intelligence Service, Grant managed to make contact again. The source gave him much valuable information about *l'Armée du Nord*, but not what he really wanted to know: was Napoleon going to attack? And if so, where? The French were not making it easy to guess; the earliest contacts between the armies were on the road to Mons where French cavalry patrols exchanged shots with allied picquets, suggesting that Napoleon was reconnoitring the direct route to Brussels.

The map on page 38 shows the allied positions. The Prussians occupy a spread of land to the east of the main road leading north from Charleroi, the British are widely spread to the west of that road. The British headquarters is in Brussels, while Marshal Blücher's is almost 50 miles away in Namur, guarding the best routes the Prussians might need if they are forced to retreat. This is important. If Napoleon punches really hard and defeats both his enemies, then he shatters any chance they have of cooperating, because the Prussians will retreat eastwards and the British will withdraw westwards, both seeking the safety of their homelands. This, in essence, is Napoleon's plan, to divide the allies and, once divided, to deal with them separately. And to achieve this, on 14 June, he concentrates his army just south of Charleroi. Now he is ready to launch his men like a spear into the heart of the widespread allied dispositions.

Napoleon attacked on Thursday, 15 June. He crosses the frontier and his troops march on Charleroi. The Prussian cavalry screen skirmishes with French horsemen and messengers gallop north with the news of the French advance, but when those messages reach Wellington he mistrusts them. The Duke fears that any French advance on that road is really a feint intended to distract him while the real attack is launched on his right wing. Hindsight condemns the Duke for his caution, claiming that Napoleon would never have attacked in the west because such an assault would have driven Wellington back onto

Blücher's army, but the Duke knows he must expect the unexpected from Napoleon. So the Duke remains cautious. In Brussels there is a rumour that the army will march on 25 June, but it is only one rumour among many. Edward Healey, an undergroom in the service of a British staff officer, noted the rumour in his diary, and added that officers were taking their swords to ironmongers' shops to be ground and purchasing cloth from linen-drapers to make bandages, 'but in a general way,' he adds, 'things were going on as if nothing was the matter.'

The Emperor marched close to the frontier on 14 June. Next night, the Duchess of Richmond gives a ball in Brussels. The Duke attends.

While everything to the south is going wrong for the allies.

*　*　*

Charlotte, Duchess of Richmond, was married to the fourth Duke, a not too successful soldier whose real passion was cricket. He was given command of a small reserve force that was posted in Brussels and his Scottish wife, herself the daughter of another duke, is one of society's hostesses. She was forty-seven in 1815, the mother of seven sons and seven daughters. Wellington had assured the Duchess that her ball would not be interrupted by unwelcome news, though he had also advised her against throwing a lavish picnic in the countryside south of Brussels. There had been too many reports of French cavalry patrols, so it was better for the Duchess to entertain in Brussels itself.

The Duke and Duchess had rented a large mansion with a capacious coach-house which was transformed into a dazzling ballroom. The humble coach-house was decorated with great swathes of scarlet, gold and black fabric, while chandeliers hung between the pillars that were wreathed with foliage, flowers and still more fabric. The guest list glittered too, headed by the Prince of Orange, also known as Slender Billy or the Young Frog. He was twenty-three, Crown Prince of the newly created Kingdom of the Netherlands, and something of a thorn in the Duke's side, though the Duke liked him personally. The problem was the Young Frog's father, King William I, who insisted that his eldest son hold high command in the Anglo-Dutch army. Wellington was forced to cede this demand or else manage without the Dutch troops, which meant that a large part of the Duke's army was under the command of a young man whose only qualification for such responsibility was the fortune of royal birth. He commanded the 1st Corps and, because of Wellington's insistence that unreliable or inexperienced battalions were brigaded with loyal and veteran units, the Prince commanded some of the Duke's best British and Hanoverian troops.

The Prince had been an aide-de-camp to the Duke for almost three years in Spain, an experience that had given him a highly exaggerated opinion of his own military talents. He was called Slender Billy because of his strangely long and thin neck, and the Young Frog because he had a high, receding hairline, a wide mouth and prominent eyes. He was supposedly engaged to Princess Charlotte, only daughter of Britain's Prince Regent, but after she saw Slender Billy get drunk at the Ascot races she broke off the engagement. Slender Billy airily dismissed her rejection, believing, falsely, that she would change her mind. He had similarly dismissed his father's French-speaking subjects, the Belgians, as 'idiots', and because he had been educated at Eton was much more at home among the British than among his compatriots. In the next few days he would be in command of almost a third of Wellington's army, but fortunately the Young Frog was well served by capable staff officers who, the Duke must have prayed, would rein in his inexperience, self-regard and enthusiasm.

The guests at the ball were the cream of Brussels society, a beribboned throng of diplomats, soldiers and aristocrats, one of whom was General Don Miguel Ricardo de Álava y Esquivel, a soldier who had been appointed Spain's ambassador to the Netherlands. He had begun his military career in the Spanish navy and had been present at the battle of Trafalgar as a combatant fighting against Nelson's ships, but the exigencies of war had meant Spain becoming an ally of the British, and Álava, who had joined the Spanish army after Trafalgar, had been appointed as liaison officer to Wellington. Relations between the British and Spanish had been fraught with jealousies, difficulties and mutual misunderstandings, and would have been much worse had it not been for Álava's cool-headed and sensible advice. A lifelong friendship sprang up between him and the Duke, and the Spaniard would be at the Duke's side throughout the next few days. He had no business being at Waterloo, but friendship alone made him share the dangers, and Wellington was grateful. Álava has the rare distinction of being one of the very few men who were present at both Trafalgar and Waterloo, though a good number of French also had that distinction, because at least one battalion who fought at Waterloo had served as marines aboard Villeneuve's doomed fleet.

Sir Thomas Picton was at the ball. He was newly arrived in Brussels, come to command the Duke's Second Corps, and welcome he was, because Picton was a fighting general who had seen long and successful service in Portugal and Spain. 'Come on, ye rascals,' he had shouted as he led an attack at Vitoria, 'come on, ye fighting villains!' He was an irascible Welshman, burly and unkempt, but indubitably brave. 'A rough, foul-mouthed devil,' the Duke of Wellington described him, but by 1814 the rough, foul-mouthed devil was suffering from what we would know as combat stress reaction. He had written to the Duke begging to be sent home, 'I must give up. I am grown so nervous, that when there is any service to be done it works upon my mind so that it is impossible for me to sleep at nights. I cannot possibly stand it.'

When Wellington took command of his 'infamous army' he sent for Picton. He needed every Peninsular veteran he could find, and the Welshman was a man he could trust to lead and inspire troops. Picton was still suffering. Before leaving Britain he lay down in a newly dug grave and remarked morbidly, 'I think this would do for me.' Despite that gloomy premonition he had come to Brussels, though somehow he had managed to mislay his luggage with his uniform, so that he went to battle in a shabby greatcoat and a mouldy brown hat. He must have cut a strange figure among the dazzling uniforms at the ball, amidst all the lace and gold thread, epaulettes and aiguillettes, not to mention the low-cut dresses of the ladies, many of them young English women like the 22-year-old Lady Frances Wedderburn-Webster, who, though married and pregnant, had been seen meeting the Duke of Wellington in a Brussels park just a few days before. A

British staff officer had seen the Duke strolling alone in the park, then an open carriage had stopped and Lady Frances stepped out and the couple, the officer wrote, 'descended into a hollow, where the trees completely screened them'. In time a London newspaper, the *St James's Chronicle*, would spread rumours of their affair, claiming that Lady Frances's husband was threatening a divorce, a report that led to a libel case and severe damages against the *Chronicle*, but it is interesting, if not significant, that the Duke found time both on the eve of Waterloo and on the day immediately following the battle, to write to Lady Frances.

Wellington liked the company of women, except for his wife, whom he detested. In that taste he was quite unlike Napoleon, who once remarked, 'We have ruined everything by treating women too well, we have committed the great mistake of putting them almost on a level with ourselves. Nature created them to be our slaves.' Wellington was more at ease with women, especially clever women, than with men, and he liked it even more if the women were young, pretty and aristocratic. There was gossip in Brussels: the Duke 'makes a point of asking all the Ladies of Loose character' complained Lady Caroline Capel, sister to Wellington's second in command, Lord Uxbridge, who had himself run off with Wellington's sister-in-law. The Duke was pointedly warned against one such 'loose' woman, Lady John Campbell; her character, he was told, was 'more than Suspicious'. 'Is it, by God!' he responded. 'Then I will go and ask her myself!', whereupon 'he immediately took his hat and went out for the purpose'. There were no suspicious rumours about the seventeen-year-old Lady Georgiana Lennox, daughter of the Duchess of Richmond, who dined next to Wellington at her mother's ball. She asked if the rumours were true and that the French were marching and he nodded. 'Yes,' he said, 'they are true, we are off tomorrow.'

It was that imminence of battle which gives the Duchess of Richmond's ball such piquancy. On the night of 15 June there was a throng of beautifully uniformed officers dancing by candlelight, and within twenty-four hours some would be dead, still wearing their silk stockings and dancing shoes. Wellington's critics, naturally, carp that he had no business attending a ball when he knew that the French were marching, but the Duke, as ever, had his reasons.

In the first place he did not want to display panic. He had been taken by surprise, and by the time he arrived at the ball, at 10 p.m., he knew he had been wrong-footed by Napoleon, but this was no time to show alarm. He knew he was being observed, so it was necessary to display confidence. The second reason was eminently practical. The Duke needed to issue urgent orders, and virtually every senior officer in his army was at the ball, making it easy for him to find and direct them. The ball, in truth, served as an orders group, and it would have been foolish of the Duke to pass up such an opportunity. Lady Hamilton-Dalrymple, who shared a sofa with him for part of the evening, recollected that 'frequently in the middle of a sentence he stopped abruptly and called to some officer, giving him instructions'.

So what had happened to invest the ball with such threat?

Hell had broken loose on the road from Charleroi.

*　*　*

One of Napoleon's difficulties was self-inflicted. He had ordered the main roads north out of France to be destroyed. The roads were made from a layer of compacted gravel over a bed of larger stones, and for some miles south of the frontier the roads had been hacked and trenched to make it difficult for an enemy army to advance into France. It made it equally difficult for the French to travel the other way. The broken roads were no obstacle for infantry or cavalry, they were used to marching in the fields either side of any road, but it was a nuisance for all the wheeled vehicles: the supply wagons and the guns.

Once Napoleon decided to attack he moved fast, concentrating his army just south of the River Sambre. Crews repaired the roads, letting the guns and wagons travel north, but the infantry and cavalry had to use the fields which, for the most part, were planted with rye. The rye grew taller in the early nineteenth century, so the advancing army was faced with thick, close-set, fibrous stalks as tall as a man. The crop was trampled flat, but one cavalryman recalled how the horses stumbled on the tangled mess underfoot, and that inconvenient rye will play a small part in the unfolding events.

Yet despite the stumbling horses and the road-repairs, Napoleon's army closed on the frontier, so that, by nightfall on 14 June, the day before the Duchess of Richmond's ball, *l'Armée du Nord* was bivouacked a few miles south of Charleroi. The Emperor ordered them to attempt concealment by camping behind hills, yet still their cooking fires lit up the night. That glow in the sky should have been the first signal to the allies that something ominous was brewing south of the frontier, but though it was noticed it did not provoke any particular alarm.

The 15th of June dawned fine, and French soldiers were on the march by daybreak. Their first task was to cross the River Sambre, which lay just to the north of the frontier, and three columns approached the river from the south. The central column marched to Charleroi, where the bridge was barricaded, and there was a delay until sufficient infantry had arrived to storm the barrier. The Prussian defenders were few in number, really nothing more than an advanced picquet, and they withdrew northwards as the French occupied the town. By now it was afternoon and Napoleon's army was crossing into Belgium, where strong cavalry patrols fanned out to discover where the allied armies lay.

This was not the only French activity. Much further west other cavalry patrols were probing north towards Mons. That morning the 2nd Battalion of the 95th Rifles encountered a patrol of French lancers on the frontier close to Mons. Richard Cocks Eyre, a Second Lieutenant (a rank in the Rifles equivalent to an Ensign in the rest of the army), described the encounter as 'play', but for the Duke of Wellington such reports were deadly serious. They could be evidence of an enemy advance that would cut him off from the North Sea ports. He also heard reports of French activity around Charleroi, but his first instinct was to protect his right flank, and so he ordered the army's reserve, which he commanded himself, to remain in Brussels, and the rest of the army to stay in their cantonments to the west. This could have been disastrous. Napoleon was thrusting men across the river and slowly pushing the

Prussians back, but Wellington, instead of sending his men towards the danger point, was watching the roads leading to Ostend where most of his troops, guns and supplies were shipped from Britain. Napoleon could not have wished for anything better.

The story of 15 June, the day of the famous ball, is one of mystery. The fog of war is a cliché, yet it applies to that day. Napoleon commits his army to an attack across the Sambre, beginning at dawn, the Prussians retreat slowly and stubbornly, and Wellington, despite messages from his allies, does nothing decisive; indeed he does something frivolous, he goes to a dance. He has been accused of deliberately ignoring the Prussian messages, though why he should do that is also a mystery. He first hears of the French advance at about 3 p.m. The messages have taken a long time to reach him and the Duke's critics contend that as soon as he heard he should have issued orders that would have taken his troops east towards the fighting, but instead he waits. Baron von Müffling was his Prussian liaison officer and it was Müffling who brought Wellington the news:

> When General von Zieten was attacked before Charleroi on the 15th of June, an event which opened the war, he despatched an officer to me, who arrived at Brussels at three o'clock. The Duke of Wellington, to whom I immediately communicated the news, had received no intelligence from the advanced post at Mons.

Two things are interesting about Müffling's account. We know that the first clash between Napoleon's army and the Prussians occurred around 5 a.m., yet Müffling, who has no reason to lie about the matter, is certain that the news does not reach Brussels until 3 p.m., ten hours later. Charleroi lies 32 miles south of Brussels and a despatch rider could easily make the journey in under four hours. Yet it took ten. We do not know why, though Wellington once suggested that 'the fattest officer in the Prussian army' was chosen as the courier.

The Prussians insist that General von Zieten, whose troops were being pushed back by the French, sent a message to Wellington early on that morning, but proof that the message was sent is not proof that it was received. A huge amount of ink, temper and recrimination has been spilled over this dispute. Gneisenau later said that the Duke was slow in assembling his army and added snidely, 'I still do not know why.' Of course he knew, but his dislike of the Duke would not let him admit that there was a reasonable explanation. The sad thing about this animosity is that Gneisenau and Wellington shared much in common: they were both highly intelligent, hard-working, painstaking, disciplined, intolerant of either foolishness or carelessness, and both were committed to the same goal, the utter destruction of Napoleon's power, yet Gneisenau insisted Wellington was untrustworthy. And trust is important to the story of Waterloo. The allied campaign was predicated on trust, that Blücher would come to Wellington's aid and Wellington to Blücher's, because both commanders knew that their individual armies could not defeat Napoleon's veterans single-handed. They had to combine their forces to win, and if they could not combine they would not fight.

So why, on that fateful Thursday, did Wellington not concentrate his army? Because he still was not sure where he would have to fight. He received news that French forces were seen close to Thuin, their presence near that town, though close to Charleroi, could have indicated a general advance towards Mons, and there had been that clash between British riflemen and French lancers on the Mons road itself. Wellington's fear was that Napoleon would attack in the west, and that was why he waited to hear more from his troops at Mons. He is specific about this. When Müffling presses him, urging the Duke to concentrate his forces closer to the Prussians, Wellington explains his reluctance.

> *If all is as General von Zieten supposes, I will concentrate on my left wing … Should, however, a portion of the enemy's army come by Mons, I must concentrate more to my centre. For this reason I must positively wait for news from Mons before I fix the rendezvous.*

That seems clear enough. Far from betraying his allies or treating their warnings with disdain, the Duke was being cautious because, so far, he had no conclusive evidence that the French attack through Charleroi was the main effort. It could have been a ruse designed to draw his men eastwards while the real attack was launched to his right. So he waited. He had said before the campaign that 'one false movement' could open him to a devastating attack from Napoleon, and it seemed preferable to make no movement at all. More messages arrived from Blücher in the early evening, and still the Duke waited because he still feared that attack up the road to Mons. It was not till late at night, while the Duke was in the gaudy ballroom, that he heard from Mons that all was quiet there, and he became convinced that Blücher had been right all along and that the French were making their attack on the Charleroi road. News was arriving thick and fast that evening, and one of the crucial messages came from the Baron Jean-Victor Constant-Rebecque, who was Slender Billy's Chief of Staff and a good man. He reported that the French had advanced north from Charleroi as far as a crossroads called Quatre-Bras and that he had sent troops to oppose them.

What followed is one of the most famous incidents in the Duke's life. It was after midnight and the Duke was leaving the ball, and as he was escorted through the hall he turned to the Duke of Richmond and whispered, 'Have you a good map in the house?'

Richmond took Wellington into his study, where a map was spread on the table. The Duke studied it by candlelight, then exclaimed, 'Napoleon has humbugged me, by God! He has gained twenty-four hours march on me!'

Napoleon's troops were poised to separate the allies. The Emperor's plans were working.

* * *

The wonderfully named Hyacinthe-Hippolyte de Mauduit was a Sergeant in Napoleon's Imperial Guard. That made him *crème de la crème*. He was in the Old Guard, part of the second battalion of the first regiment of Grenadiers. The Imperial Guard was Napoleon's favourite unit, the shock troops of the French empire. Every man was a veteran, they received privileges, wore a distinctive uniform and were fiercely loyal to the Emperor they guarded. Benjamin Haydon, a spendthrift British painter, caught a glimpse of the Guard just after Napoleon's first abdication and wrote:

> More dreadful-looking fellows than Napoleon's Guard I had never seen. They had the look of thoroughbred, veteran, disciplined banditti. Depravity, indifference and bloodthirstiness were burnt in their faces; black moustachios, gigantic caps, a slouching carriage and a ferocious expression were their characteristics. If such fellows had governed the world, what would have become of it?

Sergeant Hippolyte de Mauduit was one of these *banditti* and, while the Duke of Wellington was at the ball, the Sergeant was settling into the courtyard of an ironmaster's house in Charleroi which was Napoleon's temporary headquarters.

> We busied ourselves cooking food for a morning meal as well as for an evening meal because we had been on the march for nearly eighteen hours without being able to even unhook our cooking pots and everything indicated it would be the same next day ... Aides-de-camp and staff officers came and went constantly and in the course of rushing around they often knocked over our piles of muskets.

The soldiers of the Guard had no real idea what was happening. They had marched all day, heard the sound of firing, marched again, and now, like the veterans they were, they were making certain they had food in their knapsacks. But one of the guardsmen had an old map of Flanders and Hippolyte recalls how they crowded round and worked out from the map what the Emperor's plan might be.

Did Napoleon even have a plan? He had said, often enough, that the best plan was to make contact with the enemy and only then make the crucial decisions. That day, 15 June, the French had made contact with the Prussians. The first fighting had been south of Charleroi, but resistance stiffened once the French crossed the Sambre and pushed north, and what Hippolyte de Mauduit and his companions would have seen on their map was the main road to Brussels running north out of Charleroi. Just a couple of miles out of town that main road crossed a second road, an old Roman highway, and the Prussians, it seemed, were using that second road for their fighting retreat. They were going eastwards, towards distant Prussia, and no one, it appeared, was defending the main road north to Brussels.

The Waterloo campaign is all about roads. Roads and crossroads. The armies needed the roads. Cavalry and infantry could advance across country without roads, though their progress would be painfully slow, but guns and supply wagons had to have roads. To understand the road map north of Charleroi is to comprehend the problems that the three commanding generals faced, and on the night of the Duchess of Richmond's ball the problems were almost all on the allied side. Napoleon had grasped the situation, and his strategy of dividing the allies was working. Indeed, Wellington's caution was making it even easier for the Emperor.

The Prussians are not retreating far. On the night of 15 to 16 June, while the Emperor is in Charleroi and the Duke of Wellington is dancing, the Prussians halt at a small village called Sombreffe. There they will make a stand. Why Sombreffe? Because here another road is important, a road which crosses the Roman road and leads westwards, and the British–Dutch army is off to the west. That minor road, usually known as the Nivelles road, crosses the Charleroi-to-Brussels highway at an insignificant hamlet called Quatre-Bras. So if the Prussians retreat any farther east then they risk losing contact with Wellington's forces. The Nivelles road is the last connecting road which will let the British come to the aid of the Prussians, so Blücher orders a stand there.

There is a problem, though. The Duke of Wellington waited too long and the British–Dutch army is assembling late. The Emperor has stolen a march, and the vital crossroads of Quatre-Bras, the place where the British–Dutch must assemble if they are to help Blücher, is virtually undefended. Seize that crossroads and the Duke of Wellington's army cannot march to help the Prussians.

And at dawn on 16 June the Emperor sends Marshal Ney to capture Quatre-Bras.

It is a hot day, a sweltering summer's day in Belgium. The Imperial Guard leave Charleroi late, at around 9 a.m., and follow the Emperor's main forces towards Sombreffe. The Emperor has found the enemy and he knows exactly what he must do. Marshal Ney will capture the vital crossroads at Quatre-Bras, thus keeping Wellington away from the battle the Emperor will fight at the village of Ligny, which is close to Sombreffe. That battle will be between France and Prussia. If Napoleon wins that battle then the Prussians can be driven away east towards their homeland, and the Emperor can turn on the British.

Hippolyte and his fellow guardsmen march behind their regimental band. They pass the unburied corpses of the men killed in the previous day's skirmishes between the Prussian rearguard and the advancing French. Hippolyte recalls that he more or less understood the Emperor's plan, the map helped him understand it, but in truth that plan is not his business. All he needs to know is that his beloved Emperor has chosen to fight, that the enemy is in disarray, and that if the battle becomes desperate then the Imperial Guard will be thrown into the fight. That is their purpose, to win battles, and their boast is that they are undefeated. They are the Emperor's picked men, the bravest soldiers of France, the indomitable Guard.

The Imperial Guard would doubtless have liked to call themselves 'the bravest of the brave', except that soubriquet belonged to Marshal Michel Ney, who only joined the army that hot morning of June 16th. 'Ney,' the Emperor greeted him, 'I am glad to see you,' and while Hippolyte and the rest of the army marched east to deal with the Prussians, Ney was given 9,600 infantry, 4,600 cavalry and 34 cannon and ordered to seize the crossroads at Quatre-Bras. It was, truly, the simplest of tasks, and Ney possessed an overwhelming force with which to achieve it.

Capture Quatre-Bras and the Prussians are almost certainly doomed.

Capture Quatre-Bras and the British will be Napoleon's next victims.

It has all started so well for the Emperor. Then a Dutchman decided to be disobedient.

* * *

Major-General Baron Jean-Victor Constant-Rebecque was born in Switzerland and was to die in what is now Poland. His first military service was with the French, but after the Revolution he joined the Dutch army. He was forty-three in 1815 and knew the British well because when Slender Billy, the Crown Prince, had been made an aide-de-camp to Wellington in the Peninsula, Rebecque had accompanied the young man. Now he was Chief of Staff to Slender Billy.

Rebecque was a level-headed, intelligent man. On 15 June he had received orders to assemble the 1st Corps, which was commanded by the Crown Prince, at Nivelles, a town which lies to the west of the Charleroi-to-Brussels highroad. The orders had come late because the Duke of Wellington had hesitated all day, still fearing that French attack through Mons, but at last the Anglo-Dutch army was moving.

And Rebecque decided it was moving to the wrong place.

Nivelles was not a bad place for part of Wellington's army to assemble. A road went eastwards from the town, the Nivelles road, and led to where Blücher had decided to make his stand. Except between Nivelles and Sombreffe was that insignificant crossroads called Quatre-Bras. Napoleon had grasped the importance of that crossroads and ordered Marshal Ney to capture it. If the French held Quatre-Bras then they had come between Nivelles and Sombreffe, between Wellington and Blücher. Capture Quatre-Bras and Napoleon's aim of dividing the allies was achieved.

And Rebecque understood that.

So despite the orders to assemble at Nivelles, Rebecque sent troops to Quatre-Bras. They were not many, just over 4,000 men of the Dutch army, but they were at the crossroads and, even while Wellington was dressing for the ball, they fought off the advancing French. Those Frenchmen were patrolling and, just south of Quatre-Bras, came under fire from Dutch artillery and infantry. The French did not press their attack. They probed, discovered the Dutch forces, and then retreated. It was late, the sun was almost down, and the attack on the crossroads could wait till morning. The Dutch troops who repelled the French probes were actually Germans from Nassau. They were in Dutch service because, in the same manner that the ruler of Hanover had become the King of England in Europe's game of musical thrones, so the Prince of Nassau had become King William I of the Netherlands. The men who fought off the first French attacks were under the command of a 23-year-old Colonel, Prince Bernhard of Saxe-Weimar, and that night, as the chandeliers were being lit for the Duchess of Richmond's ball, the young Colonel sent a report of the day's action to his immediate superior. He reported that he had repelled French cavalry and infantry, but was worried because he had no contact with any other allied troops. He was quite alone, in the dark, without any supporting allies. There was worse:

> *I need to confess to Your Excellency that I am too weak to hold here long. The Second Battalion of Orange Nassau still have French muskets and are down to 10 cartridges per man … every man is likewise down to 10 cartridges. I will defend the post entrusted to me as long as possible. I expect to be attacked at daybreak.*

So as night fell on Belgium the Emperor's plan seemed to be working. His army had crossed the Sambre and pushed northwards. The Prussians had retreated north and east, but had stopped close to the village of Ligny, where they planned to make a fight of it. Blücher was depending on Wellington coming to his aid, but the British had been slow in concentrating their forces, and were still a long way from their Prussian allies. They could still reach Ligny, but only if the Nivelles road was open, and that meant holding the crossroads at Quatre-Bras where a small force of Germans in Dutch service was now isolated and almost out of ammunition. Those 4,000 Germans expected to be attacked in the morning, and that attack would come from Marshal Ney, 'bravest of the brave'.

Thus as the sun rose early on 16 June the allies could expect two battles, one at Ligny and the other at the vital crossroads of Quatre-Bras. And Napoleon understood the importance of that crossroads. Capture Quatre-Bras and he would have divided his enemies. Yet the fog of war was thickening. While Wellington danced the Emperor was under the illusion that Ney had already captured Quatre-Bras. On the morning of the 16th he sent even more troops to reinforce Ney, who would now command over 40,000 men. Those extra troops were not sent to help Ney capture the crossroads, so far as Napoleon was aware Ney had already done that; instead their task was to hold the crossroads and so stop Wellington's troops from joining Blücher's. There was more: 'You will march for Brussels this evening, arriving there at seven o'clock tomorrow morning. I shall support you with the Imperial Guard.'

So Napoleon believed he could shove the Prussians further away, then switch his attack to the British. It was all going to plan and the Emperor would take breakfast in Brussels's Laeken Palace on Saturday morning.

Except Ney had still not captured Quatre-Bras.

THIS PAGE, CLOCKWISE FROM TOP | *'The Duchess of Richmond's Ball, 15 June 1815', by Robert Alexander Hillingford. Virtually every senior officer in his army was at the ball, making it easy for Wellington to find and direct them – the ball, in truth, served as an orders group.* | *Field-Marshal August Neidhart, Count of Gneisenau, by George Dawe. Gneisenau complained that Wellington was slow in assembling his army and added snidely: 'I still do not know why'.* | *Major-General Baron Jean-Victor Constant-Rebecque, by J. B. Van Der Hulst: 'Then a Dutchman decided to be disobedient.'*

FACING PAGE | *The formidable 71-year-old Prince Gebhard Leberecht von Blücher – nicknamed 'Marschall Vorwärts' … Marshal Forwards. Wood engraving after a drawing by Adolph Menzel.*

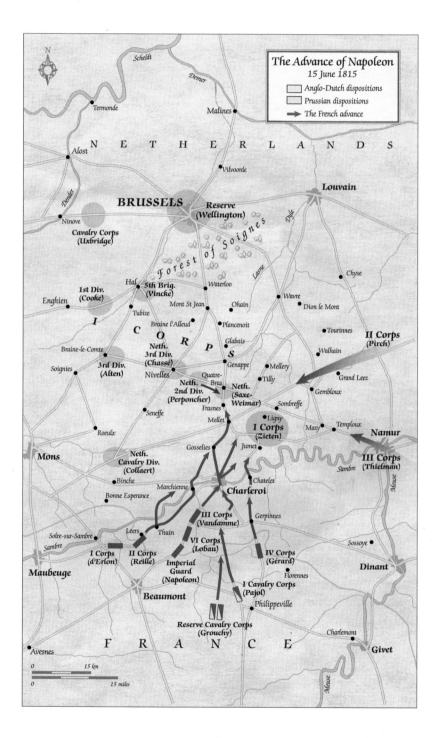

The Advance of Napoleon
15 June 1815

Anglo-Dutch dispositions
Prussian dispositions
The French advance

CHAPTER THREE

The fate of France is in
your hands!

THE 16TH OF JUNE was a Friday. It dawned hot and sweltering. The Prussians were assembling their army close to the small town of Sombreffe, the French were advancing towards them, while the British–Dutch army was desperately trying to regain that lost day's march. Wellington, realizing the importance of that insignificant crossroads at Quatre-Bras, had ordered his army to march there, but he had left the order late. Too late? Some troops marched from Brussels by moonlight, leaving the city at two in the morning, but most waited until dawn. The city was close to panic. Captain Johnny Kincaid, an officer of the 95th Rifles, slept on a pavement, or rather he tried to sleep:

> *But we were every instant disturbed by ladies as well as gentlemen; some stumbling over us in the dark, some shaking us out of our sleep, to be told the news … All those who applied for the benefit of my advice I recommended to go home to bed, to keep themselves perfectly cool and to rest assured that, if their departure from the city became necessary (which I very much doubted) they would have at least one whole day to prepare for it as we were leaving some beef and potatoes behind us, for which, I was sure, we would fight rather than abandon!*

Few did sleep that night, though the Duke snatched a couple of hours before leaving for Quatre-Bras. English visitors to Brussels, and there were many, said their goodbyes to the soldiers. One of those visitors, Miss Charlotte Waldie, recalled 'the tumult and confusion of martial preparation':

Officers looking in vain for their servants, servants running in pursuit of their masters, baggage waggons were loading, trains of artillery harnessing ... As the dawn broke the soldiers were seen assembling from all parts of the town, in marching order, with their knapsacks on their backs, loaded with three days' provisions ... Numbers were taking leave of their wives and children, perhaps for the last time, and many a veteran's rough cheek was wet with the tears of sorrow. One poor fellow, immediately under our windows, turned back again and again to bid his wife farewell, and take his baby once more in his arms; and I saw him hastily brush away a tear with the sleeve of his coat as he gave her back the child for the last time, wrung her hand, and ran off to join his company which was drawn up on the other side of the Place Royale.

Miss Waldie does not say what nationality that poor soldier was, though it is very possible he was British. A small number of wives and children were allowed to accompany a battalion on foreign service. They were chosen by lottery on the eve of departure and the women were expected to be launderers and cooks, but the families had been instructed to stay in Brussels as the troops marched south. Lieutenant Basil Jackson of the Royal Staff Corps watched the exodus:

First came a battalion of the 95th Rifles, dressed in dark green, and with black accoutrements. The 28th Regiment followed, then the 42nd Highlanders, marching so steadily that the sable plumes of their bonnets scarcely quivered.

Lieutenant Jackson had been awake most of the night, delivering a message eastwards, and now he had a moment to rest before mounting his tired horse and following those steady Highlanders towards the crisis.

And it was a crisis. Quatre-Bras marked the last place where the allies had easy access to each other. Lose Quatre-Bras and the only connecting roads would be country lanes which twisted through hilly country and were obstructed by narrow bridges, so if Napoleon could thrust the British away from the crossroads then communication between the British–Dutch and the Prussians would become far more difficult. All the French needed to do was push, and the Emperor had massively reinforced Ney's force. Indeed, by the morning of the 16th, the French had over 40,000 troops with which to overwhelm the small Dutch contingent under Saxe-Weimar. Those Nassauers had little ammunition left, just ten rounds a man. 'I will defend the post entrusted to me as long as possible,' Prince Bernhard of Saxe-Weimar had promised, but how long could 4,000 men who were short of ammunition hold out against Ney's overwhelming force?

But Marshal Ney, astonishingly, did nothing. He could have captured the crossroads any time that morning with little effort. He had an overwhelming advantage in numbers, yet still 'the bravest of the brave' hesitated. He claimed later to be waiting for further orders from Napoleon, yet he had not even obeyed the Emperor's previous orders, which were clear enough, capture Quatre-Bras, and while he waited the British–Dutch reinforcements were marching from Nivelles and from Brussels. Many explanations have been offered for Ney's inactivity: that he really was confused and waiting for orders, or that he misunderstood the Emperor's intentions, or, perhaps, that he was being extremely cautious.

Ney knew he was facing the British–Dutch army that was commanded by the Duke of Wellington, and Ney had faced Wellington before. He had been at Busaco in 1810 when 65,000 French troops had attacked Wellington's 50,000 and been bloodily repulsed. Ney had commanded an army Corps that had attacked the centre of the British line, and all seemed to be going well as the French troops advanced uphill against a fairly scattered skirmish line of British and Portuguese troops, but just as the Corps reached the heights of Busaco the British sprang their trap and two concealed battalions of redcoats stood and fired a tremendous volley at close range and followed it with a bayonet charge that sent Ney's men reeling in panic down the hill.

Wellington was a master of the 'reverse slope'. Very simply, that means he liked to conceal his troops behind a hill. At Busaco the British objective was to hold the high hill, but if Wellington had positioned his men on the crest, or on the forward slope, then they would have become targets for the deadly efficient French artillery. By placing them just behind the crest, on the reverse slope, he kept them safe from most artillery fire and concealed his dispositions from the enemy. One biographer of Napoleon called this a 'tired old dodge', which is a remarkably stupid comment. It was, perhaps, an obvious tactic, but concealing and protecting troops is neither a 'dodge' nor 'tired', and the surprising thing is how rarely other commanders used the tactic.

Ney, south of the crossroads, could not see what awaited him at Quatre-Bras. His view northwards was obstructed by thick woods, by some gentle undulations in the ground and, especially, by those tall crops of rye and other cereals. His experience in Spain, and his knowledge that he faced Wellington, could well have convinced him that the innocent-looking landscape actually concealed the whole of the British–Dutch army. This was a moment when Wellington's reputation served him well. In truth the British–Dutch army was still marching on dusty roads under a sweltering sun and the crossroads was there for the taking, but Ney hesitated.

'In three hours the campaign will be decided,' Napoleon claimed that day, but Ney was wasting those hours. Napoleon had decided on his tactics for the day. He divided his army. One of the rules of war is never to divide an army, but Napoleon only meant the division to be temporary. He would attack the Prussians around the village of Ligny and fully expected that Ney would throw back any British attack at Quatre-Bras and then march eastwards from the crossroads to assault the flank of the Prussians. Napoleon, by attacking the Prussians from their front, would hold them in place until Ney's strong force fell on their right flank to destroy them. Then, with the Prussians defeated and his army reunited, Napoleon would turn on the British–Dutch.

Blücher's hopes for the day were almost a mirror-image of Napoleon's. The Prussians would hold their position about the village of Ligny and wait for the British to arrive from Quatre-Bras, then the British–Dutch forces would fall on the left flank of the French army and so give the allies a famous victory.

Wellington, meanwhile, just hoped to hold Quatre-Bras. He was fully aware of Blücher's hopes and doubtless wished he could join the battle that was to develop at Ligny, but his first priority was to keep the French from capturing the vital crossroads. He arrived at Quatre-Bras at about ten in the morning to discover that the enemy was inexplicably supine. The French were in force to the south of the crossroads, but showed no signs of attacking, and so Wellington rode three miles west to meet Blücher at a windmill in the village of Brye, which is close to Ligny.

Blücher explained that he meant to fight, and requested that Wellington send him troops. Wellington, meanwhile, was inspecting the Prussian deployment and, perhaps tactlessly, criticized it. Many of Blücher's men were arrayed on open ground, dangerously exposed to artillery fire. 'I said that if I were in Blücher's place,' the Duke of Wellington recalled, 'I should withdraw all the columns I saw scattered about the front, and get more of the troops under shelter of the rising ground.' In other words to use the reverse slopes of the gently undulating fields that lay between the villages. The advice was not welcome, 'they seemed to think they knew best, so I came away very shortly.'

The Prussians asked that he bring his army to their aid, but to do that Wellington needed to hold Quatre-Bras and he knew that, despite Ney's somnolence, the crossroads must soon be under severe attack. 'Well,' he told them, 'I will come, provided I am not attacked myself.'

Much has been made of this meeting. The Duke of Wellington's critics claim that he made a solemn promise to come to the aid of the Prussians, and that he broke the promise. It has even been suggested that the Duke deliberately lied about his intentions because he wanted the Prussians to fight and so give him time to concentrate his army, though there is not the slightest evidence to back up that contention. Wellington certainly did not want the Prussians to be routed, because then his smaller army would have to face Napoleon's larger army alone, so why would he risk a Prussian disaster? The evidence suggests that he was being realistic. He could not march to Ligny until he had fought off the expected French attack at Quatre-Bras. If there was no attack, then he would send men, but if he was defending the crossroads against Ney's considerable force then he would probably have no men to spare.

Which meant the Prussians would almost certainly have to face Napoleon on their own, but by early afternoon Blücher had assembled 76,000 infantry, 8,000 cavalry and 224 guns to oppose the Emperor's 58,000 infantry, 12,500 cavalry and 210 cannon.

Napoleon had not reckoned on facing such a large force. He had thought the Prussians were still retreating and would leave around 40,000 men as a rearguard, but he was not dismayed at the disparity of numbers. In the first place the Prussians had decided against using the 'tired old dodge' of sheltering their troops, and that refusal left many of Blücher's regiments vulnerable to Napoleon's efficient artillery. More importantly, the Emperor had troops in reserve, primarily a very strong Corps of 22,000 men under the command of Count d'Erlon, who, in expectation that the Prussians would assemble a much smaller force, had been sent to reinforce Ney. Napoleon also fully expected that Ney's massive force would fall like a hammer blow on the Prussian right. So although the Emperor would begin the battle with inferior numbers, he was confident that by nightfall his army would be reunited and the Prussians defeated. At 2 p.m. that afternoon the Emperor sent Ney more instructions:

> *It is His Majesty's intention that you attack whatever force is presently in front of you and after driving it vigorously back you will turn in our direction in order to bring about the encirclement of these enemy troops, though if the latter are defeated first then His Majesty will manoeuvre in your direction to assist you.*

In brief, Ney is to hurl the defenders away from Quatre-Bras and march to attack the Prussian right, though if Napoleon has already defeated the Prussians then the Emperor would march to join in the fight against the British–Dutch.

The hostilities at Ligny began in the early afternoon, and the Emperor found he had a much stiffer fight on his hands than he had anticipated. His artillery, as the Duke of Wellington had forecast, did grim work with the exposed Prussian infantry. A French officer recalled that the Emperor's guns 'played havoc with the Prussian columns which presented themselves without cover and received all the shot fired by the numerous batteries along our line'. The slaughter those guns made was horrific. Hippolyte de Mauduit, the Sergeant in the Imperial Guard, had seen many battlefields, but after the fight at Ligny he was appalled by what he saw on the long, exposed slopes where the Prussian infantry had waited for the French attack:

A vast number of corpses, both men and horses, were scattered about, horribly mutilated by shells and cannon balls. The scene was different from the valley where almost all the dead preserved a human appearance because canister, musket balls and bayonets were practically the only instruments of destruction used there. Here, as a contrast, it was limbs and scattered body parts, detached heads, ripped out entrails and disembowelled horses.

That was why Wellington used the 'tired old dodge' of sheltering his troops on the reverse slope. A brook ran along the valley that Sergeant de Mauduit mentioned, and it was a considerable obstacle to the French, because in that shallow valley was a chain of small villages that served as fortresses for the Prussians. Most of the fighting was in Saint-Amand and in Ligny, the village that was to gi e the battle its name. An anonymous Prussian officer described Ligny in bucolic terms: 'a village built of stone and thatched with straw, on a small stream which flows through flat meadows'.

The day's bright sunshine disappeared as heavy clouds rolled across the sky. Artillery smoke billowed and lingered, and out of that smoke emerged the first French columns marching to attack the battered Prussians. Those columns were greeted with a storm of cannon fire from the Prussian artillery. Their cannon were firing roundshot and shells, their targets the densely packed attack columns of blue-coated French infantry that needed to capture the villages if they were to drive Blücher back. The Prussians defended the villages staunchly and Napoleon, realizing that he needed more troops, sent another message to Ney, commanding him to come at once and fall on the Prussian rear. 'Do not lose a moment,' the Emperor wrote to Ney, because Blücher's army 'is lost if you act quickly! The fate of France is in your hands!'

The fate of France might be in Ney's hands, but Quatre-Bras was not. The Emperor still believed that the crossroads had been captured, but Ney could not march to Napoleon's aid because he was still dithering.

Yet there was other help available. Count d'Erlon commanded those 22,000 men who were still marching to assist Ney. D'Erlon could not, of course, march on the straight road which led from Quatre-Bras to Ligny because both ends were in enemy hands, so instead of that simple five-mile march he was forced to go twice as far on lesser roads, first southwards, then north-westwards. D'Erlon was summoned back to Napoleon's army, and his men, who had almost reached Ney's forces, turned round and retraced their steps.

Meanwhile the Prussians and French were in desperate battle. Napoleon's plan was to hold the Prussian left with assaults from Grouchy's Corps while his main effort was hurled against the centre of Blücher's line where the villages were so stoutly defended. Grouchy's attacks would stop the Prussians from reinforcing their centre with men from their left flank, but the right flank would be left unengaged, thus tempting Blücher to weaken it by drawing reinforcements from that part of his defensive line. Then, when the Prussian right wing was weakened Ney or, more likely, d'Erlon would attack from the west.

But while d'Erlon marched back the rest of Napoleon's army was thrown against the Prussian defences. Charles François was a Captain in the 30th Regiment of the Line, which was ordered to assault the village of Ligny. 'Within two hundred yards of the hedges which hid thousands of Prussian sharpshooters,' he wrote, 'the regiment took up battle order while still on the march.' What François means by that is that his battalion went from column into line, and they did it without halting. That showed a fine discipline. The terms 'line' and 'column' will make frequent appearances in the story of the Waterloo campaign, and deserve some explanation. The basic fighting deployment of infantry was in line, which is simple enough to understand. A battalion made a straight line of, in the French and Prussian armies, three ranks, which faced towards the enemy. The British preferred a line of two ranks.

The line is an efficient way of utilizing a battalion's firepower, but it is an extremely fragile formation. Attempting to march a line forward across anything except the smoothest parade ground led to disorder. Men straggled, stumbled, wavered, and the line would soon lose all cohesion. Worse, a line was very vulnerable to cavalry attack, especially if the enemy horsemen could attack from either end.

So the preferred method of advancing men across open country was to form a column. That is a slightly misleading term, suggesting a long thin block of men advancing like a spear shaft towards the enemy line. In fact the column was short and squat. A French battalion of around 500 men arrayed in column, such as that in which Captain François approached Ligny, might have a frontage of one or two companies. If the 30th of the Line closed on Ligny in a column just one company wide, then the Prussian defenders would have seen thirty men in the French front rank, and seventeen other ranks behind them. So the column is roughly twice as wide as it is deep. A two-company front (which was probably how François's battalion attacked) had a front rank of about sixty men and only nine ranks in all.

The column had three advantages over the line. It was much easier to manoeuvre over rough ground, it was much less vulnerable to cavalry because there is no weak point that can be overwhelmed, and the very density of the formation was good for morale. In their haste to raise large armies at the beginning of the Revolution the beleaguered French discovered that large columns were doubly useful. Half-trained men could be marched into battle easily, and enemies were often over-awed by the sheer size of the attacking columns. François's 30th was not alone; his battalion was just one of several closing on the Prussians. In a couple of days the French would deploy a whole Army Corps in column, a massive block of men. A line, especially a British line just two ranks deep, would look very fragile against the advance of a dense column.

Yet if the column was psychologically powerful it also had two weaknesses. A column was desperately vulnerable to cannon fire, and only the men in the outer two ranks and files could use their muskets. If a column has seventeen ranks of thirty men each, totalling 510 men, then only the sixty in the first two ranks, and the two men on the outside of each rank, can actually fire at the enemy. So of the 510 men, fewer than a quarter can shoot their muskets. If they are approaching a line then they will be massively outgunned, because every man in the line can fire.

By 1815 the French are well aware of this weakness. In Spain French columns were mauled again and again by British, Portuguese and Spanish lines. At Busaco, where Ney received his drubbing from Wellington, it was British lines that blasted his columns off the hill. The answer to the problem was to utilize the ease of the column as a means to advance troops over rough ground, and then deploy into line as the columns closed on the enemy. That was what Charles François's battalion did as they approached the hedges surrounding Ligny. But Captain François's troubles were far from over:

> *The charge was sounded and our soldiers went through the hedges. [We] went down a sunken road obstructed by felled trees, vehicles, harrows and ploughs and we got past these obstacles only after much difficulty and under fire from the Prussians*

concealed by the hedges. At last we overcame these obstacles and,
firing as we went, entered the village. When we reached the
church our advance was halted by a stream and the enemy, in
houses, behind walls and on rooftops inflicted considerable
casualties by musketry, grapeshot and cannon balls which
assailed us from in front and from the flanks.

François tells how three battalion commanders, five captains, two
adjutants and nine lieutenants were killed in this savage fighting. Out
of the two battalions that made the attack close to 700 men were killed
or wounded, and it was no surprise that a Prussian counter-attack
drove the French back out of the village. Franz Lieber, the seventeen-
year-old who had volunteered in Berlin, was part of the
counter-attacks:

Our ardour now led us entirely beyond the proper limits; the
section to which I belonged ran madly, without firing, towards
the enemy, who retreated. My hindman fell; I rushed on … the
village was intersected with thick hedges, from behind which the
grenadiers fired upon us, but we drove them from one to the
other. I, forgetting altogether to fire and what I ought to have
done, tore the red plume from one of the grenadiers' bearskin-
caps, and swung it over my head.

Franz Lieber reaches the centre of the village, steps round a house
and is faced by a French infantryman just a dozen paces away.

He aimed at me, I levelled my rifle at him. 'Aim well, my boy,'
said the sergeant-major, who saw me. My antagonist's ball grazed
my hair on the right side; I shot and he fell; I found I had shot
through his face; he was dying. This was my first shot ever fired
in battle.

The battle is a desperate struggle, reduced to hand-to-hand fighting in the villages. A French officer said the dead in the main street 'were piled two or three deep. The blood flowed from them in streams ... the mud was formed from crushed bones and flesh.' The clouded sky is thickened with great gouts of powder smoke belched by massive cannon that fill the air with man-made thunder. Prussian advantage of numbers is holding the French at bay, but the superior quality of the French troops is slowly eroding the Prussian defence. After one French counter-attack a Prussian gunner, Captain von Reuter, seeing a skirmish line approach, assumed it was from his own infantry and ordered his gunners to keep firing at the distant enemy cannon. It was his battalion surgeon who noticed that the skirmishers were French. 'I at once bellowed the order, "grape on the skirmishers!"' von Reuter recalled:

> At the same moment they gave us a volley . . and by that volley, and the bursting of a shell or two, every horse except one belonging to my left flank gun was killed or wounded ... in another moment I saw my left flank taken in the rear, from the Ligny brook, by a French staff officer and about fifty horsemen. As these charged us the officer shouted in German 'Surrender, gunners, for you are all prisoners!' With these words he charged down with his men and dealt a vicious cut at my wheel driver, who dodged it by flinging himself over his dead horse. The blow was delivered with such force that the sabre cut deep into the saddle and was stuck fast there. Gunner Sieberg snatched up the handspike of one of the twelve-pounders and with the words, 'I'll show him how to take prisoners,' dealt the officer such a blow on his bearskin that he rolled with a broken skull from the back of his grey charger.

As the afternoon shades into a grey evening the battle is still undecided. The Prussians are holding, but of course General d'Erlon's Corps is coming to fall like a thunderbolt on their exposed right flank.

Or rather it is supposed to fall like a thunderbolt, but instead the hapless General d'Erlon becomes the leading actor in a French farce. Jean-Baptiste Drouet, Count d'Erlon, was the son of a carpenter and as a youth had been apprenticed to a locksmith, but in 1780, aged seventeen, he joined the pre-Revolutionary army and rose to the rank of Corporal. It took the Revolution to reveal his talent, and after that his rise was swift until, by 1815, he is a Count and in command of the 1st Corps of *l'Armée du Nord*. He leads almost 17,000 infantry, 1,700 cavalry, a corps of engineers and 46 guns, and his first orders on that fateful Friday had been to march to Ney's support. His powerful Corps would help Ney clear Quatre-Bras, then swing right on the Nivelles road to fall on the Prussians, but Napoleon realizes he needs help sooner and so sends a messenger to recall d'Erlon, who had almost, at last, reached Ney's troops.

D'Erlon obediently reverses his march, a cumbersome process which takes time as the guns and their limbers are turned around on the narrow roads. He marches back towards the Emperor, but the orders have been confusing and, instead of taking his men north onto the Prussian flank he arrives on the flank of General Vandamme's Corps, which is engaged in the brutal fight for the village of Saint-Amand.

It is early evening, the sky is clouded, the terrain obscured by drifting gun smoke, and Vandamme at first believes that the approaching troops are Prussians, or maybe British. He sends an urgent message to Napoleon, who has just massed his Imperial Guard to make a last massive assault on the Prussian centre, and the Emperor, alarmed, delays that attack until he can discover the identity of these newly arrived troops. They are his own men, but in the wrong place, so a messenger rides to d'Erlon ordering him to turn northwards and assault the Prussian flank, but just then yet another courier arrives, this one from Marshal Ney, demanding that d'Erlon return to Quatre-Bras immediately.

D'Erlon assumes that Ney is in desperate trouble and so he turns his Corps around and sets off a second time for Quatre-Bras. The

Emperor has launched his great attack, but by the time he realizes d'Erlon is not engaged, the 1st Corps has vanished. Thus did those 22,000 men spend that Friday, marching between two battlefields and helping at neither. D'Erlon arrived at Quatre-Bras too late, the fighting had ended at sundown and his powerful Corps, which could have swung either the battle at Ligny or the fighting at Quatre-Bras, had achieved nothing. It is the French equivalent of the Grand Old Duke of York, except d'Erlon spent his day halfway between two fights, neither up nor down, and his prevarication denied Napoleon the crushing victory he expected.

Because Ligny was a victory. The final assault of the Imperial Guard captures the villages at the centre of the Prussian line and sends Blücher's army reeling back. The pretty village of Ligny, with its thatched houses, is a charnel house, especially the church and graveyard which saw the severest fighting. Marshal Blücher, despite his age, tried to restore the position by attacking with his own cavalry. He was unhorsed and ridden over by French heavy cavalry, but Blücher's aide-de-camp, with great presence of mind, draped a cloak over the Marshal's medals and braid, so obscuring his eminent status, and in the failing light the French cavalry did not recognize him, so that at last he could be rescued by his own men. He was bruised and dazed, and his army was beaten, but it was not destroyed. The 'ifs' of history are generally pointless, but there can be little doubt that d'Erlon's men, if they had done what the Emperor wanted, would have made the difference. The final successful attack would have been made earlier in the evening, giving the French more time to complete the enemy's destruction, and d'Erlon's Corps could have rolled up the Prussian right flank and, in all probability, caused such panic and chaos that Blücher's army might have ceased to exist.

But it did exist. It had been wounded, but the two flanks were still coherent, and Blücher was alive and, though they had been beaten, they managed to withdraw from the battlefield in reasonable order and the French made no effort to pursue in the gathering dark. One Prussian officer recalled:

The men looked dreadfully tired after the fighting. In the great heat gunpowder smoke, sweat and mud had congealed into a thick crust of dirt so that their faces looked like mulattos ... and many who had been unwilling to leave the ranks because of a slight wound wore bandages they had made themselves and in a number of men the blood was soaking through. As a result of fighting in the villages for hours and frequently crawling through hedges the men's tunics and trousers were torn so that they hung in rags and their bare skin showed.

Blücher was still recovering, and Gneisenau, the clever Chief of Staff, was temporarily in charge of the Prussians. Sixteen thousand Prussians had been killed, wounded or taken prisoner, and another 8,000 had simply disappeared in the darkness and were heading for home as fast as they could, but General von Bülow's Corps had never reached the battlefield, and was intact, and the remainder of the army was doing its best to regroup in the wet night. The diary of a senior Prussian officer – sadly his name is not known – records meeting Gneisenau that night:

I found him in a farmhouse. The village had been abandoned by its inhabitants and every building was crammed with wounded. No lights, no drinking water, no rations. We were in a small room where an oil-lamp burned dimly. Wounded men lay moaning on the floor. The General himself was seated on a barrel of pickled cabbage with only four or five people gathered about him. Scattered troops passed through the village all night long, no-one knew whence they came or where they were going ... but morale had not sunk. Every man was looking for his comrades so as to restore order.

So Ligny was a victory for Napoleon, but it had not achieved his first objective, which was to destroy one of the allied armies. It remained to be seen whether he had achieved his second objective, which was to drive the Prussians away from their British–Dutch allies. If that happened, if Blücher led his army eastwards towards Prussia, then Ligny would be a stunning victory.

But though the Prussian army had been defeated, it was still capable of fighting, as was its commander, Blücher. In the morning after the battle he sent for Colonel Hardinge, the British liaison officer who had lost his left hand in the battle, and called him *lieber Freund*, dear friend, and Hardinge remembered how the old Marshal stank of schnapps and rhubarb, the first a medicine taken internally, the second a liniment on his bruises. And Marshal Forwards was still belligerent. He had been defeated, not beaten. 'We lost the day,' Blücher remarked, 'but not our honour,' and he would live up to his nickname and fight again.

His army had survived because d'Erlon's Corps had failed to arrive.

But the British had also failed to arrive. That is another 'if' of history, what might have happened if Wellington had brought troops to Blücher's aid. He had promised to do so, 'provided I am not attacked myself', but while Blücher was engaged in his desperate struggle at Ligny another battle was being fought just five miles away.

The battle of Quatre-Bras.

FACING PAGE | *Marshal Michel Ney, c. 1804 (French school). 'Bravest of the brave', mercurial and fearsome, Ney, was fiery, red-haired and passionate – renowned for his extraordinary courage and inspiring leadership, no one would ever call Ney cool-headed.*

ABOVE | *'Battle of Ligny – Marshal Blücher stunned by the violent fall lay entangled under his horse'. Marshal Blücher, despite his age, tried to restore the position by attacking with his own cavalry. He was unhorsed and ridden over by French heavy cavalry, but Blücher's aide-de-camp, with great presence of mind, draped a cloak over the Marshal's medals and braid, so obscuring his eminent status, and in the failing light the French cavalry did not recognize him, so that at last he could be rescued by his own men.*

BELOW | 'Battle of Ligny, 16 June 1815'. The battle was a desperate struggle, reduced to hand-to-hand fighting in the villages. A French officer said the dead in the main street 'were piled two or three deep. The blood flowed from them in streams … the mud was formed from crushed bones and flesh.' The sky thickened with great gouts of powder smoke belched by massive cannon that fill the air with man-made thunder.

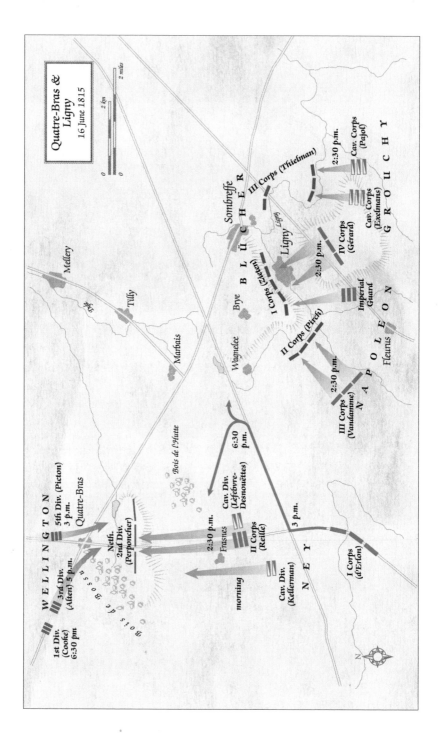

Quatre-Bras &
Ligny
16 June 1815

WELLINGTON

1st Div.
(Cooke)
6:30 pm

3rd Div.
(After) 5 pm

5th Div. (Picton)
3 p.m.
Quatre-Bras

Neth.
2nd Div.
(Perponcher)

Bois de Bossu

Bois de l'Hutte

Frasnes

Cav. Div.
(Lefebvre-
Desnoüettes)

6:30
p.m.

2:30 p.m.

II Corps (Reille)

morning

Cav. Div.
(Kellerman)

NEY

I Corps (d'Erlon)

3 p.m.

Mellery

Tilly

Marbais

Sombreffe

Brye

BLÜCHER

Wagnelee

I Corps (Zieten)

Ligny

II Corps (Pirch)

III Corps
(Vandamme)

Fleurus

Imperial
Guard

NAPOLEON

2:30 p.m.

2:30 p.m.

Ligny

IV Corps
(Gérard)

2:30 p.m.

III Corps (Thielman)

Cav. Corps
(Exelmans)

Cav. Corps
(Pajol)

2:30 p.m.

GROUCHY

2 km

2 miles

0

0

N

80

CHAPTER FOUR

Avancez, mes enfants, courage, encore une fois, Français!

ERNHARD OF SAXE-WEIMAR'S 4,000 troops at Quatre-Bras were reinforced early on that Friday morning with another 4,000 men from the Dutch army, but luckily for them Marshal Ney hesitated. He feared the landscape, thinking it might conceal Wellington's whole army, while in truth that army was still desperately trying to reach the crossroads.

The battle that was to develop at Quatre-Bras was a scrambling affair and one that stands out from all Wellington's others. He is usually depicted, somewhat disparagingly, as a great defensive general. He was indeed a great defensive general, choosing the ground on which he would fight and using that ground to his men's advantage as he had at Busaco, but to dismiss him as merely a defensive fighter is to wilfully ignore some of his greatest victories. When he was asked, much later in life, of what he was most proud he replied in one word, 'Assaye'. Assaye was a battle fought in India, against a much larger army, and he turned the enemy's flank, attacked and crushed them. Then there was Salamanca, in Spain, sometimes termed his masterpiece, where 40,000 Frenchmen were destroyed in 40 minutes. Salamanca was a brilliant offensive battle that took the French by surprise and routed them. Or

Vitoria, the battle that cleared the French from Spain, another offensive masterpiece that left the enemy in ruins. He was, in truth, a great attacking general, but attacks are, broadly speaking, more expensive in men than defensive tactics, and Britain's army was small and there were never enough replacements for battle casualties, and so the Duke preferred defensive battles where he could use the terrain to shelter his men from enemy artillery.

Quatre-Bras was, essentially, a defensive battle, but one fought on terrain that Wellington had not chosen. He had no time to prepare and little time to react to the enemy's assaults, and for almost all of the day he was outnumbered. The story of Quatre-Bras is essentially that of allied troops arriving in the nick of time to stave off another crisis, yet it all began quietly enough. Wellington reached the crossroads at about ten in the morning and, finding that the French were still hesitating, he rode east to meet Blücher. That was the conference at the Brye windmill where Wellington promised to send troops to help the Prussians 'provided I am not attacked myself'.

Yet by mid-afternoon he was being attacked and there would be small chance of sending any troops to assist the Prussians. Wellington needed every man who arrived. He had to defend the crossroads because that was his link to the allies, and the French had at last made up their minds to capture the vital junction. They were advancing in force and most of Wellington's men were still marching in the sweltering heat to reach Quatre-Bras.

Most of the British troops arrived from Brussels, a march of 22 miles. Once at Quatre-Bras they faced a tight battlefield. In front of them was a stretch of gently rolling countryside in which sturdy stone-built farmsteads stood like small forts. Not that any man could see much. The landscape was obscured by thick stands of trees and by the fields of high, obstinate rye which grew between the pastureland. It was also hidden by gun smoke which gradually thickened.

The fighting was to take place south of the Nivelles road, the highway which led east to the Prussians. The western side of the battlefield was defined by a thick, almost impenetrable wood, the Bossu Wood, where Saxe-Weimar's tired troops had taken refuge. A small stream rose inside the wood and trickled across the Brussels highway, though it was no obstacle to cavalry, infantry or guns. Where the highway met the stream, in the very centre of the battlefield, was a big stone-built farm called Gemioncourt. It would have helped Wellington enormously to hold that farm, but the French had driven out the Dutch defenders and had now garrisoned its thick walls. Once past the farm the streamlet trickled on to feed an artificial lake, the Materne Lake, beyond which was a hamlet called Piraumont which, to Wellington's consternation, was also held by French infantry. Those enemy infantrymen were perilously close to the Nivelles road and, being to the east of the battlefield, threatened to cut the vital link between Wellington and Blücher.

The Frenchmen in Piraumont never did cut the road because Wellington contained them with the first reinforcements to arrive, the 95th Rifles, who were helped by a battalion of Brunswick infantry. That meant his left flank was safe for the moment, while his right was protected by the thick undergrowth of the Bossu Wood. The major fighting would take place in the mile-wide stretch of undulating country between the lake and the wood, and when he returned from his meeting with Blücher, around 3 p.m., that stretch of farmland was swarming with Frenchmen.

Rebecque, the clever Dutchman, had managed to assemble 8,000 troops at Quatre-Bras, but the newcomers had retreated in panic from the French while Saxe-Weimar's men, still short of ammunition, had taken cover in the Bossu Wood. It must have seemed that there was nothing to stop the French advance, but fortuitously Sir Thomas Picton's fine division was just arriving from Brussels. The 95th led them and they were sent left to stop the French breaching the road to Ligny, while the rest were deployed to face the attack coming straight up the Brussels highway. Some newly arrived British artillery unlimbered south of the crossroads, but almost immediately came under fire from French skirmishers concealed in the tall fields of rye. There were still some Dutch skirmishers in the rye, but they were being pressed relentlessly back and the French could spare men to fire at the British gunners and at the newly arrived infantry. Lieutenant Edward Stephens of the 32nd, a Cornish regiment, described the fire of the French skirmishers as 'very galling … our men were falling in every direction'.

Skirmishers play a large part in the story of Waterloo. Essentially they are specialist infantrymen who fight neither in line nor in column (though they could and often did do both), but fought ahead of a line or column. They formed a skirmish line, a scatter of troops spread wide, whose job was to snipe at the enemy's formation. Every battalion possessed a Light Company, and some whole battalions were light troops like the battalions of the 95th Rifles. The French had expanded the numbers of their skirmishers because, like the artillery, they were useful for weakening an enemy line before the column attacked. The best defence against skirmishers was other skirmishers, so in battle both sides had their light troops in extended order way ahead of their formations. Their scattered formation made them difficult targets for inaccurate muskets and not worth the price of a cannonball, though they were vulnerable to canister, an artillery round which turned the cannon into a giant shotgun. They fought in pairs, one man firing while his companion loaded. In an ideal world the French skirmishers, who were called *voltigeurs* or *tirailleurs*, would go ahead until they were in musket range of the enemy line and then they would open fire, hoping to bring down officers. *Tirailleur*, the official name, simply means a shooter, from the verb *tirer*, to shoot, while a *voltigeur* is a vaulter, or gymnast, because the ideal skirmisher was an agile, quick-moving man. They knelt or lay down to fire, making themselves small targets, and enough skirmishers could seriously hurt a line of troops, but only if they could get close. French skirmishers usually outnumbered the British, though the British had the advantage that many of their skirmishers were armed with rifles, a weapon that Napoleon refused to employ. The rifle's drawback was that it was slow to load because the bullet, usually wrapped in a leather patch, had to be forced down the rifled barrel, and that took far longer than ramming a musket ball down a smoothbore barrel, but the advantage of the rifle was its accuracy. The British used the Baker rifle, a superb and dependable weapon, that was accurate far beyond the range of any musket.

Skirmishers dared not get too far ahead of their parent battalions because, in the deadly game of scissors, stone and paper which characterizes artillery, infantry and cavalry in the Napoleonic era, they were totally vulnerable to horsemen. Their scattered formation meant they could not form square or offer volley fire, so a few cavalrymen could decimate a skirmish line in a matter of seconds. But when Picton's Division arrives at Quatre-Bras there is no cavalry to scour the French skirmishers away. The Black Legion of Brunswick reached the battlefield at the same time as Picton's men, but the rest of the Duke's cavalry regiments are still hurrying to reach the battlefield and so Wellington decides to attack the French skirmishers with his line of infantry. There were columns of French infantry beyond the enemy skirmishers, but British lines had never had trouble defeating French columns, and so the six battalions were ordered forward.

They were severely outnumbered. The French were coming in three columns. The largest with over 8,000 men was attacking northwards close to the Bossu Wood, the central column, advancing along the highway, had 5,400 men, while to their right were another 4,200 infantry, all of them supported by over fifty cannon and by troops of cavalry. The six battalions of British infantry had around 3,500 men between them who had to face at least 17,000 infantry, as well as the artillery and cavalry, but these battalions were among the best and most experienced in Wellington's army.

What followed was typical of the day's confused fighting. One of those battalions was the kilted Highlanders, just over 500 men of the 42nd, the Black Watch. James Anton was a Sergeant in the battalion that first had to advance through the field of rye where the Dutch skirmishers were being overwhelmed by the heavy French attack:

The stalks of the rye, like some reeds that grow on the margins of some swamp, opposed our advance; the tops were up to our bonnets, and we strode and groped our way through as fast as we could. By the time we reached the field of clover on the other side we were very much straggled; however, we united in line as fast as time and our speedy advance would permit. The Belgic skirmishers retired through our ranks, and in an instant we were on their victorious pursuers. Our sudden appearance seemed to paralyse their advance. The singular appearance of our dress, combined no doubt with our sudden début, tended to stagger their resolution: we were on them, our pieces were loaded, and our bayonets glittered, eager to drink their blood. Those who had so proudly driven the Belgians before them turned now to fly ... we drove on so fast that we almost appeared like a mob [and] Marshal Ney, who commanded the enemy, observed our wild unguarded zeal and ordered a regiment of lancers to bear down upon us ... [We] took them for Brunswickers.

The Black Watch was now in an open field and still in line. There was cavalry on their flank, but they assumed they were the Brunswick horsemen who had arrived at Quatre-Bras about the same time as the 42nd. Brunswick was a German state which had fallen to the French, and in revenge the Duke of Brunswick had raised a regiment which had joined Wellington in Spain. They wore black uniforms and were known as the Black Legion, and were led at Quatre-Bras by their young Duke, Friedrich Wilhelm. The Brunswickers, though they had been allies of the British in Spain, were not popular, mainly because of their taste for dog meat. The Irish Rifleman, Private Edward Costello of the green-jacketed 95th Rifles, remembered a dog called Rifle who had accompanied his battalion in Spain:

A dog which had attached itself to our regiment and which could never be induced to leave us. We lost him on one or two occasions, but he always managed to rejoin us. We used to joke among ourselves at Rifle's antipathy to a red coat, for he had a decided preference for green. The poor fellow survived many of our skirmishes, in which he used to run about barking and expressing his delight as much as a dog could.

Then one day Rifle vanished altogether, and it was discovered that he had been eaten by the Black Legion. Legend insists that the Rifles got their revenge by slicing the buttocks from some dead Frenchmen, smoking them and then selling them as hams to the Brunswickers.

Sergeant James Anton and the 42nd Highlanders were still advancing in line across the open field of clover, ignorant that the cavalry to their right were not dog-eating Germans, but Frenchmen. Then a German staff officer galloped past the battalion shouting that the approaching cavalry were 'Franchee! Franchee!' The horsemen were lancers.

We instantly formed a rallying square; no time for particularity; every man's piece was loaded, and our enemies approached at full charge; the feet of their horses seemed to tear up the ground.

This was desperate work. A battalion in line was fearfully vulnerable to a cavalry charge, but an infantry square could defeat almost any attack by horsemen. Yet it took time to make a square and the Highlanders had no time and so the order was shouted to rally. This was almost a panic. Instead of the careful ordering of the companies into a rectangle bristling with bayonets, the 42nd simply ran towards the colours and formed a huddle with the men facing outwards. Some lancers were even trapped inside the hastily forming rally-square and were dragged from their horses and killed. The skirmishers, who were deployed ahead of the battalion, stood no chance and were ridden down by the lancers, as was the battalion commander, Sir Robert Macara. Sir Robert's death was witnessed by the 42nd and it enraged them. He had been wounded earlier and, just before the lancers appeared, was being stretchered to the rear in search of a surgeon. The stretcher was either two jackets with their sleeves threaded over a pair of muskets or, more likely, a blanket held by the four men carrying him. The French saw the wounded man's medals and braid and, presumably in search of plunder, callously slaughtered all five men. That was murder, not warfare, and it enraged the Scots. They drove off the lancers with musketry, but later in the day the officers of the 42nd had to restrain their men who were slaughtering surrendering Frenchmen with shouts of 'Where's Macara?'

Captain Archibald Menzies, who commanded the Grenadier Company of the 42nd, was also trapped outside the rally-square. He was a man of legendary strength who, preferring to fight on foot, had handed off his horse to a drummer boy. Menzies (pronounced Mingis) was wounded and fell next to Private Donald Mackintosh. The drummer boy abandoned the horse and ran to help, upon which a lancer tried to seize the valuable animal. Mackintosh, with his last effort, managed to shoot the lancer. 'You mauna tak that beast,' he is reported to have said, 'it belongs to our captain here!' A French officer, seeing Menzies trying to stand, attacked with his sabre:

> As he stooped from his saddle [Menzies] seized his leg, and managed to pull him off his horse upon him. Another lancer, observing this struggle, galloped up and tried to spear [Menzies, who], by a sudden jerk and desperate exertion, placed the French officer uppermost, who received the mortal thrust below his cuirass and continued lying on Menzies's body for near ten minutes, sword in hand. A pause in the battle permitted some men of the 42nd to carry their officer into the square of the 92nd, where he was found to have received sixteen wounds.

Menzies survived and lived until 1854. While he was tended in the 92nd's square his own battalion tried to form line again, this time to oppose an approaching column of French infantry, but almost immediately they were threatened by still more cavalry, this time cuirassiers. Cuirassiers were France's heavy cavalry and the riders wore metal breastplates. The 42nd formed square just in time to receive the charge. 'The Cuirassiers', Anton remembered, 'dashed full on two of [the square's] faces; their heavy horses and steel armour seemed sufficient to bury us under them,' but the horses sheered away from the Scottish bayonets:

A most destructive fire was opened; riders cased in heavy armour
fell tumbling from their horses; the horses reared, plunged, and
fell on the dismounted riders; steel helmets and cuirasses rang
against unsheathed sabres as they fell to the ground.

The murder of the wounded Macara had inflamed the Scots and is
a reminder of how good relations were between officers and men in
Britain's army. Again and again, in letters, diaries and memoirs, that
mutual affection shines through. Too often the British army of the early
nineteenth century is depicted as a mass of whipped soldiers led by
aristocratic fops, a picture which is utterly misleading. Most officers
came from the middle classes, clergymen's sons being especially prominent, and the long wars had honed their skills. The 42nd killed defenceless Frenchmen late in the day because they had been maddened by
Macara's murder, they wanted revenge, and that reaction sprang from
their affection for their commanding officer. There was more than
affection, there was admiration. An officer might be wealthy, certainly
wealthier than the average private, he was privileged and even, sometimes, aristocratic, yet he still shared the dangers of the battlefield.
Officers were expected to lead by example. Rifleman Costello, of the
95th, said the troops divided officers into two classes, the 'come on' and
the 'go on', 'and with us,' he said, 'the latter were exceedingly few in
numbers'. Rifleman Plunket once told an officer, 'The words "go on"
don't befit a leader, Sir.'

Not all officers were respected. Private Thomas Patton was an
Irishman in the 28th Foot, a Gloucestershire regiment, and at Quatre-
Bras they were in square and had been ordered to hold their fire. Enemy
horsemen had surrounded the square, but were making no effort to
break the red-coated ranks; it was a stand-off, but then Patton recalled
how a French officer, he thinks he was a general, 'came over our bayonets with his horse's head and encouraged his men to break into our
square'. Patton, who was in the third rank, lifted his musket and shot
the enemy officer dead, whereupon Lieutenant Irwin struck Patton
over the face with the flat of his sword. Patton protested and was told

he was being punished 'for firing without orders'. General Sir James Kempt was in the square and he quashed the Lieutenant: 'Silence … let the men alone; they know their duty better than you!'

The duty of the British infantry was now to stave off increasingly heavy attacks from cavalry, infantry and artillery. Lancers had led the French cavalry attacks, but they were reinforced by Kellerman's cuirassiers. General François Étienne de Kellerman, a long name for a diminutive man, was one of the most celebrated of Napoleon's cavalry commanders. When he arrived at Quatre-Bras he was immediately ordered by Ney to charge the enemy, an order Kellerman questioned, as he only had 700 cuirassiers under command, but Ney insisted. '*Partez!*' he shouted. '*Mais partez donc!*' Go! Go now! Kellerman did not want his men to see just how many enemy they were being ordered to charge and so, unusually, he took them straight into the gallop: '*pour charger au galop! En avant!*'

The cuirassiers first charged the Highlanders and were driven off. One French trumpeter, a lad just fifteen years old, was so astonished by the kilted regiments that he thought the British *cantinières* were fighting. *Cantinières* were women who followed the French army and sold food, drink and, often, other comforts to the troops. Kellerman led his men past the squares, storming on towards the crossroads that the French had been ordered to capture.

Reinforcements were arriving for both sides and had to be fed almost immediately into the chaos at the field's centre. The 44th, a regiment from East Essex, came to support the Highlanders and, like them, was surprised by cavalry. They had no time to form square so their commanding officer turned his rear rank about and saw the lancers off with a volley, though not before some of the horsemen reached the centre of the line where they tried to capture the colours. One of the battalion's officers recalled how:

> *A French lancer severely wounded Ensign Christie, who carried one of [the colours], by a thrust of the lance which, entering his left eye, penetrated to the lower jaw. The Frenchman then*

*endeavoured to seize the standard, but the brave Christie,
notwithstanding the agony of his wound, with a presence of
mind almost unequalled, flung himself upon it, not to save
himself, but to preserve the honour of the regiment. As the
Colour fluttered in its fall, the Frenchman tore off a portion
of the silk with the point of his lance; but he was not permitted
to bear even the fragment beyond the ranks. Both shot and
bayoneted by the nearest of the soldiers of the 44th, he was borne
to the earth, paying with his life for his display of unavailing
bravery.*

The 30th, a battalion from a Cambridgeshire regiment, came up behind the 44th. Ensign Edward Macready, just seventeen years old, had noted the smoke hanging thick over the battlefield as he approached and he also remarked on the birds flying in panic above the Bossu Wood. He described:

*The roaring of great guns and musketry, the bursting of shells,
and shouts of the combatants raised an infernal game, while the
squares and lines, the galloping of horses mounted and riderless,
the mingled crowds of wounded and fugitives, the volumes of
smoke and flashing of fire …*

Macready and the 30th marched into that chaos, and passed some wounded of the 44th. The two battalions had fought alongside each other in Spain, and as the newcomers advanced, the wounded men of the 44th:

*Raised themselves up and welcomed us with faint shouts, 'Push
on old three tens, pay 'em off for the 44th, you're much wanted,
boys, success to you, my darlings.' Here we met our old Colonel
riding out of the field, shot through the leg; he pointed to it and
cried, 'They've tickled me again, my boys, now one leg can't laugh
at the other!'*

The wounded colonel was a Scotsman, Alexander Hamilton, and the surgeons decided to amputate the leg, but every time they readied for the operation they were called away to deal with a more urgent case and, in the end, they simply left the wounded limb alone. Hamilton walked on it until his death in 1838.

While Colonel Hamilton waited for the knife which never came, Macready was reinforcing the British line. They came up alongside the 42nd, and Macready remembers having to step over dead and wounded Highlanders:

> We reached [the 42nd] just as a body of lancers and cuirassiers had enveloped two faces of its square. We formed up to the left and fired away. The tremendous volley our square, which in the hurry of formation was much overmanned on the sides attacked, gave them, sent off those fellows with the loss of a number of men, and their commanding officer. He was a gallant soldier, and fell while crying to his men, 'Avancez, mes enfants, courage, encore une fois, Français!'

'Advance, my children, have courage, one more time, Frenchmen!' No one knows how many cavalry charges were made by the French. Some accounts of the battle list four, others five, six or seven, and the truth is no one knows, and probably did not know even when they were on the battlefield. Quatre-Bras was a confusing fight. There was no vantage point for either side to gain an impression of what was happening in the cauldron where men fought, suffered and died. Wellington's troops arrived all afternoon and he fed them into the fight where British line opposed French columns, and British lines were threatened by the ever-present cavalry and so formed square which made them an easy target for the efficient French artillery that was smothering the farmland with thick skeins of smoke. Wellington needed to reconnoitre the fighting for himself and was almost caught by Kellerman's cuirassiers, who had charged close to the crossroads. The Duke turned his horse, Copenhagen, and galloped towards the Gordon Highlanders, the 92nd, who were in four ranks just in front of the Nivelles road. The Duke bellowed at the Highlanders to duck, they crouched, and Copenhagen soared over their heads to carry his rider to safety. That was the closest the French came to the vital road, and the horsemen suffered for it, being slaughtered by the Highlanders' volleys. Over 250 of Kellerman's 700 men were dead or wounded, and the ferocious little general was himself unhorsed. He tried to rally his men, but they had taken enough and retreated. Kellerman grabbed the bridles of two horses and ran between them as they rode back through the red-coated squares that kept firing at them.

Lines and squares. British infantry made a line two ranks deep, though if there was cavalry around they would sometimes double the line and so make four ranks. If a battalion was in four ranks then usually only the first two ranks fired, while the men behind reloaded the muskets and handed them forward. A British line invariably defeated a French column, even one containing three, four or five times its number, simply because every British musket could fire and only the outer ranks of the French could return the musketry, but the line was horribly vulnerable to cavalry. If horsemen managed to reach the open flank of the line they would swiftly reduce it to a panicked mob, but if the battalion had formed square then it was the cavalry who became vulnerable. It is a deadly game of paper, scissors and stone.

A square (which was often an oblong) had four ranks. The front rank was kneeling and did not fire their muskets; instead they rammed the butts of their muskets into the ground and held them out with fixed bayonets to make a hedge of blades, augmented by the second rank which crouched with fixed bayonets. The two inner ranks could fire over the heads of the men holding bayonets. Horsemen thus faced a formidable and usually insurmountable obstacle. There was no open flank to attack, instead they had to charge into a wall of steel from which bullets were flying. A horseman takes up at least a yard of space and, if he is facing an average-sized British battalion of around 500 men, then only sixteen or seventeen horsemen can be in the front rank of the charge and they are faced with at least 200 men, half of whom are firing muskets at very close range. No wonder that cavalry rarely broke a square. It had happened. The King's German Legion broke two French squares at Garcia Hernandez in Spain, but it was only achieved through sacrifice. It is thought that the first square broke when a dying horse and man skidded into its face and drove a hole into the French ranks through which the following horsemen galloped. Once inside, of course, they could attack the rear of the ranks, and at Garcia Hernandez the first square broke apart in panic and ran to the second, clawing at it to find safety, and so shattered its cohesion, and the deadly horsemen rode into the panic with the survivors of the first square. A third square, seeing the danger, used their musketry to keep both panicked fugitives and exultant horsemen at bay.

So cavalry prayed to find infantry in line, because that would give them an easy victory, and at Quatre-Bras that prayer was answered. It happened when Wellington's line of infantry was suffering and defeat looked not just possible, but likely. The 42nd and 44th, like many other battalions, were running low on ammunition. The cavalry might be seen off, but as soon as the French horsemen disappeared from view the artillery opened up on the tight British squares, while hordes of French skirmishers shot from the cover of the trampled rye. The 42nd began the day with 526 men, but ended with just 238. The rest were killed or wounded. The battalion was too hurt to form a single square and so the Highlanders and the Essex men joined together.

On the British left the 95th Rifles were being pushed relentlessly backwards, while still more Frenchmen now assaulted the Bossu Wood on the right. Fortuitously new troops arrived and Wellington could reinforce the beleaguered Riflemen and send three more battalions to hold the ground beside the Bossu Wood. One of these was the 69th, a Lincolnshire battalion, which formed square close to the 42nd and 44th, but on this right flank they were supposedly under the command of Slender Billy, the 23-year-old Prince of Orange, and he decided the three newly arrived battalions would be more effective in line. He ordered them to redeploy. There were protests from the battalion officers, but Slender Billy would have his way and so the 69th, the 33rd and the 73rd spread into line.

The order to form line came when Kellerman's cuirassiers were still rampaging among the British units. They saw the redcoats' vulnerability and attacked. The 73rd was close enough to the Bossu Wood to scramble for cover among the thick undergrowth, the 33rd just had time to form square, but the 69th was marooned in the centre of the field and was caught by the horsemen. Lieutenant Frederick Pattison, of the 33rd, described what happened in a letter to his brother:

> *The ground through which we had to advance was much undulated, and in full crop of rye, which in that rich and luxuriant country grows exceedingly high, and on this account obstructed observation. As we advanced the leading company of our regiment … observed the French cavalry advancing to the charge. Orders were then given to form square … the enemy perceiving we were prepared for them, instead of advancing, made a movement to the left, broke in upon the open columns of the 69th Regiment, which being on a low part of the field had not observed them.*

The 69th was destroyed, its King's Colour was captured, and only a few of its men managed to reach the safety of a nearby square. Losing a colour was a terrible disgrace. For some men the flags had an almost mystical significance. William Miller was an officer in the 1st Foot Guards and was mortally wounded at Quatre-Bras. His dying wish was to see the colours for the last time, so the Regimental Colour was brought to where he lay dying and, an eyewitness said, 'his countenance brightened, he smiled'. Men fought like demons to protect the flags and Ensign Christopher Clarke of the 69th killed three cuirassiers in his successful attempt to save the Regimental Colour, but he took twenty-two separate sword cuts in the fight. He survived and later joined the 42nd Highlanders.

The 33rd had almost as hard a time as the 69th. They were in square because of the presence of the cavalry, but they were also in clear view of a French gun battery. Lieutenant Pattison saw his company commander cut in two by a roundshot, 'and poor Arthur Gore's brains were scattered upon my shako and face'. George Hemingway was a private in the battalion and, two months after the battle, he wrote to his mother:

> The enemy got a fair view of our regiment at that time, and they sent cannon shot as thick as hail stones. Immediately we got up on our ground and seen a large column of the French cavalry, named the French cuirassiers, advancing close up on us, we immediately tried to form square to receive the cavalry, but all in vain, the cannon shot from the enemy broke down our square faster than we could form it; killed nine and ten men every shot; the balls falling down amongst us … and shells bursting in a hundred pieces … had it not been for a wood on our right, about 300 yards, we should have every man been cut in pieces with the cavalry, and trampled upon by their horses.

The 33rd, which had been the Duke's old regiment, made it to the wood where some cuirassiers were foolish enough to follow, and now it was the redcoats' turn to kill and, in the tangling trees, they cut down their pursuers.

The destruction of the 69th and capture of their flag was the high point of the battle for the French. They had been advancing on both flanks and steadily destroying the British centre, but still more troops were arriving from Brussels and the Duke at last had sufficient men and artillery. He decided it was time to attack, but first a stone house beside the main road had to be cleared of its French garrison. Colonel Cameron, of the 92nd Highlanders, was itching to get rid of that garrison and had repeatedly asked the Duke's permission to attack the house. 'Take your time, Cameron,' the Duke had answered, 'you'll get your fill of it before night.' Now Wellington released the Scotsmen. A regimental history records the words of one Highland soldier:

> It was hot work then. They were in the hoose like as mony mice, and we couldna get at them wi' our shot when their fire was ca'in' doon mony a goot man among us, but ... oot o' that they had to come, or dee where they were, so we ower the hedge an' through the garden 'til the hoose was fair surrounded, an' they couldna get a shot oot where we couldna get ane in. In the end they were driven oot, an' keepit oot. Ay, but the French were brave men, an' tried again and again to take it from us, but they only got beaten back for their pains, and left their dead to fatten the garden ground.

The flanks of the British position were stiffened by the newly arrived reinforcements which included the Guards Division which had marched from Nivelles. As they neared Quatre-Bras they:

> met constantly waggons full of men, of all the various nations under the Duke's command, wounded in the most dreadful manner. The sides of the road had a heap of dying and dead, very many of whom were British.

That is from the recollections of Robert Batty, who was an Ensign in the 3rd battalion of the 1st Foot Guards. He was twenty-six, old for an Ensign, which was the lowest commissioned rank in the British army, but Batty had been in uniform for only two years. He had been studying medicine at Caius College, Cambridge, but left the university to fight in Spain and was now marching towards the Bossu Wood where the heavy French column was driving back the tired defenders. The 600 men of the 1st Foot Guards were on the right of the British line and advanced close to the wood until they saw the French.

> The moment we caught a glimpse of them we halted, formed, and having loaded and fixed bayonets, advanced ... at this instant

our men gave three glorious cheers, and though we had marched
fifteen hours without anything to eat and drink, save the water
we procured on the march, we rushed to attack the enemy.

The Frenchmen were trying to capture the Bossu Wood, so the British Guards went into the trees which, Batty recalls:

were so thick it was beyond anything difficult to effect a passage
… they contested every bush and at a small rivulet running
through the wood they attempted a stand, but could not resist us
… our loss was most tremendous and nothing could exceed the
desperate work … the French infantry and cavalry fought most
desperately and after a conflict of nearly three hours (the
obstinacy of which could find no parallel, save in the slaughter it
occasioned), we had the happiness to find ourselves complete
masters of the road and wood.

The cavalry Batty mentions were not in the wood, no horsemen could hope to negotiate the tangled undergrowth and low branches, but the Guards were also fighting off men in the fields to the west where the Black Watch, the 44th and 69th, and all the other battalions had been fighting and dying.

But, as evening descended, the Duke's reinforcements had arrived and, with them, wagonloads of new ammunition. It was time to go from the defensive to the attack, and the Duke ordered his thickened line forward. The French resisted for a while, then retreated all the way back to where they had started that morning and Gemioncourt, the great farm which dominated the battlefield, was again in allied hands. The French were in some disarray. One anonymous French eyewitness wrote that:

the crowd of Cuirassiers and wounded troops surging to the rear
of the army sowed panic there; the equipment teams, the
ambulance men, the canteen people, the servants, the whole

crowd of non-combatants who follow the army, fled precipitately, carrying with them all they met, across the fields and along the road to Charleroi which was soon jammed. The rout was complete and spread quickly, everyone was running away in total confusion and shouting 'Here comes the enemy!'

The panic was premature. Ney had been frustrated, but his forces were still intact and they had, at least, succeeded in denying Blücher any British aid. 'We were only too happy to have prevented the English from going to the aid of the Prussians,' said Captain Bourdon de Vatry, an aide-de-camp to Napoleon's brother, Jérôme, who had commanded part of Ney's forces. De Vatry was at supper with Marshal Ney and Jérôme Bonaparte when a messenger arrived demanding that Ney march to the Emperor's support. The message, of course, came far too late, and Ney could not obey anyway because he had failed to capture the vital crossroads.

Darkness fell late on 16 June. It was midsummer and the sun did not set till 9 p.m., and full darkness was a full two hours later. It had been a long day that had begun so well for Napoleon and, though he had not achieved all his objectives, he was still in the driving seat. He had almost succeeded in splitting his enemies, and had driven the Prussians back in retreat. Ney had attacked far too late, and so never had a chance to lead his men eastwards and fall on the Prussian flank, but he had succeeded in keeping Wellington busy all afternoon and evening. The Duke had promised to go to Blücher's aid, but only if he was not attacked, and he had been attacked. So at nightfall, as Ney dined at a table made from a plank balanced on two barrels, the French were still in a commanding position.

Wellington had won his battle, at least in terms of frustrating the French objective. He had held the crossroads and denied Ney the chance of swinging eastwards and falling on the flank of the Prussians. That was no small victory. If Ney, or even d'Erlon, had attacked the Prussian right then the battle of Ligny could have ended in the utter rout of Blücher's army. That had not happened. The Prussian army had been battered, but it was still intact and still very much a viable fighting force, yet the cost to the Duke had been high. Over 2,200 British casualties, another 1,100 from the Hanoverians and Brunswickers, including the Duke of Brunswick, who had died from a bullet to the head, and approximately 1,200 Dutch. French losses were slightly fewer, about 4,400 killed or wounded as against Wellington's 4,500.

The Duke had held the crossroads against what, for most of the day, had been a far superior force, yet now, as the sun finally set, the crossroads offered the allies no advantage at all because, instead of leading to the Prussians, the Nivelles road now led to Napoleon's victorious forces. Wellington had still not heard what happened at Ligny, but late on that Friday evening he received a confused report that the Prussians had suffered a defeat. He sent an aide towards Ligny to discover what he could, and the man returned to say that all he had seen in the failing light were French vedettes, cavalry groups set as sentries. It was plain that Napoleon had driven the Prussians back, though to where, or how far, or in what condition, Wellington did not yet know.

Even so, whether the defeat was massive or minor, it was obvious what the Emperor would do now. He would use the Nivelles road to fall on Wellington's flank. The campaign's objective was in the Emperor's grasp. The British, after all, were the paymasters of the new coalition opposing France. Knock them out of the war and it was conceivable that the coalition would fall apart.

All Napoleon had to do was march at dawn.

Clockwise from top | *Quatre-Bras where the battle was fought, by James Rouse. The Duke of Brunswick was killed on the left, near the wood.* | *'The Death of Frederick William, Duke of Brunswick-Wolfenbüttel at the Battle of Quatre Bras', by Johann Friedrich Matthai.* | *General François Étienne de Kellerman. When Kellerman arrived at Quatre-Bras he was immediately ordered by Ney to charge the enemy, an order Kellerman questioned, as he only had 700 cuirassiers under command, but Ney insisted. 'Partez!' he shouted. 'Mais partez donc!' Go! Go now!*

CLOCKWISE FROM TOP LEFT | *The Prince of Orange, 'Slender Billy', by Matthew Dubourg, was an active, if wayward presence at Quatre-Bras and Waterloo: his orders led to heavy losses for a British brigade at Quatre-Bras.* | *'Voltigeurs, Cents-Suisses', by Eugene Titeux, 1815. Élite French skirmishers, they were useful for weakening an enemy line before the column attacked. 'Voltigeur' was derived from vaulter, or gymnast, because the ideal skirmisher was an agile, quick-moving man.* | *'The 28th Regiment at Quatre Bras', by Lady Butler. Private Thomas Patton was an Irishman in the 28th, a Gloucestershire regiment, and at Quatre-Bras they were in square and had been ordered to hold their fire. Enemy horsemen had surrounded the square, but were making no effort to break the red-coated ranks; it was a stand-off, but then Patton recalled how a French officer, he thinks he was a general, 'came over our bayonets with his horse's head and encouraged his men to break into our square.'*

From top | 'Battle of Quatre-Bras: Sir Thomas Picton Ordering the Charge of Sir James Kempt's Brigade', engraving by George Jones, published 1816. | 'The 7th Queen's Own Hussars under Sir Edward Kerrison, charging the French at Quatre-Bras', by Denis Dighton, 1818.

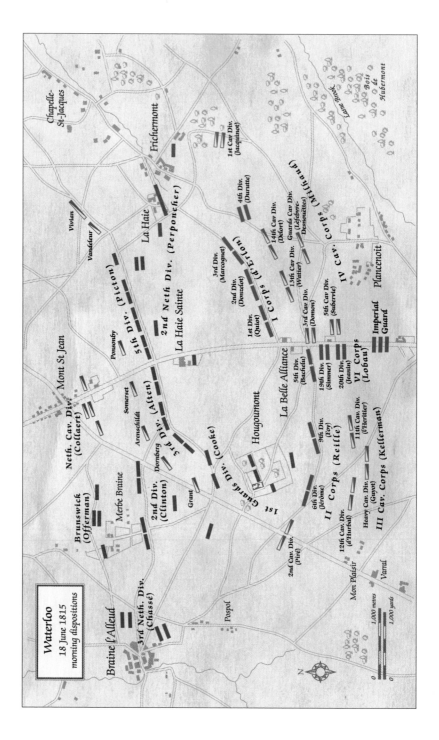

Waterloo
18 June 1815
morning dispositions

Chapelle-St-Jacques
Frichermont
Mont St Jean
La Haie
Vivian
Vandeleur
La Haie Sainte
Pomsonby
5th Div. (Picton)
2nd Neth Div. (Perponcher)
Neth. Cav. Div. (Collaert)
Somerset
Arentschildt
3rd Div. (Alten)
Dornberg
Merbe Braine
Brunswick (Offerman)
2nd Div. (Clinton)
Grant
1st Guards Div. (Cooke)
Hougoumont
La Belle Alliance
5th Div. (Bachelu)
19th Div. (Simmer)
20th Div. (Jeanin)
VI Corps (Lobau)
9th Div. (Foy)
II Corps (Reille)
11th Cav. Div. (l'Heritier)
III Cav. Corps (Kellerman)
6th Div. (Jérôme)
2nd Cav. Div. (Piré)
12th Cav. Div. (d'Hurbal)
Heavy Cav. Div. (Guyot)
Mon Plaisir
Varral
Pospol
1st Cav Div. (Jacquinot)
4th Div. (Durutte)
14th Cav Div. (Delort)
Guards Cav Div. (Lefebvre-Desnouëttes)
13th Cav Div. (Watier)
IV Cav. Corps (Milhaud)
3rd Div. (Marcognet)
2nd Div. (Donzelot)
1st Div. (Quiot)
I Corps (d'Erlon)
3rd Cav Div. (Domon)
5th Cav Div. (Subervie)
Imperial Guard
Plancenoit
Bois de Hubermont
Lasne Brook
Braine l'Alleud
3rd Neth. Div. (Chassé)

N

1,000 metres
1,000 yards
0
0

CHAPTER FIVE

Ah! Now I've got them,
those English!

SATURDAY, 17 JUNE. IT HAD CLOUDED over during the night and
the dawn was unseasonably chilly. Wellington had three hours'
sleep in the village of Genappe, just north of Quatre-Bras, but he
was back at the crossroads shortly after 3 a.m. 'Ninety-Second,' he said
to some bivouacking Highlanders, 'I will be obliged to you for a little
fire,' and the soldiers dutifully made a campfire beside which the Duke
brooded as he waited for more reports about the fate of his Prussian
allies. He was dressed in white breeches and half-boots, a dark blue
tailcoat and a white neckcloth, with his usual cocked hat. He always
dressed plainly for battle. Many officers liked to wear their gaudiest
uniform, none more so than Horatio Nelson, who had made himself
conspicuous on HMS *Victory*'s deck with his braided coat and jewelled
decorations, but Wellington invariably wore the plain coat. His men
knew who he was, he needed no gilded frippery.

The sun rose about half past four that morning, and shortly after,
the Duke might have noticed a distraught woman wandering with
three small children through the army's bivouacs. She was certainly
noticeable, because Martha Deacon was nine months pregnant. She

had travelled to Quatre-Bras the day before, presumably riding with her children on a supply wagon. Her husband, Thomas Deacon, was an officer, an Ensign with the 73rd, another Highland battalion. Now she had lost him. All she knew was that he had been wounded in the final advance the previous evening. He had been walking beside Sergeant Thomas Morris when a musket ball had killed the man on Morris's other side. The ball had struck the man in the forehead, killing him instantly. 'Who is that?' Deacon had asked. 'Sam Shortly,' Morris said, and glanced at his officer. 'You are wounded, Sir.'

'God bless me, so I am,' Deacon responded. One arm had been broken by a musket ball. He dropped his sword and made his way to the rear in search of Martha and their children, whom he had left with the 73rd's baggage guard, but though he looked till past nightfall he could not find her. At dawn, faint with loss of blood, he was put aboard one of the wagons carrying the wounded back to Brussels.

Martha, clothed only in a dress of black silk covered by a light shawl, kept looking for Thomas. Eventually she found someone who knew of her husband's fate, but by then there was no transport northwards and so, with her three children and despite being heavily pregnant, Martha Deacon walked the 22 miles to Brussels. She walked through a rainstorm so fierce that the Duke declared he had not even known its like in India, yet she kept on walking. The journey took the little family two days, but did have a happy ending. Martha found Thomas recovering in Brussels and next day she gave birth to a baby girl. They christened the child Waterloo Deacon.

The Prussians were also awake early. Marshal Blücher, bruised and battered, had snatched a few hours' sleep in the hamlet of Mellery, not far from Ligny. He was discovered there by his staff, and in the early morning there was a discussion about what the Prussians should do next. Gneisenau, who so mistrusted the British, suggested a retreat east towards the Rhine and Prussia, but such a movement would take Blücher's army still farther away from his British–Dutch allies, and Blücher, unlike Gneisenau, both liked and trusted Wellington. The debate was brief. Gneisenau, clever and opinionated as he was, nevertheless understood that his commander had an instinctive talent for warfare and so yielded to Blücher's demand. The army would not go eastwards, but north to Wavre.

This was, perhaps, the most crucial decision of all those four days. The allies had lost the easy communication that had been offered by the Nivelles road, but there were still country lanes that connected Wavre to the Brussels highway. Those lanes were not paved, and they twisted through fields and woodlands, they crossed rivers and streams, but by going north to Wavre instead of retreating eastwards, Blücher was keeping alive the possibility of uniting his forces with Wellington's army. It was a brave decision. Blücher must have known that the French would send a force to harry his retreat and attempt to block any move west towards Wellington, and by going to Wavre he made his own chances of a safe withdrawal eastwards far more difficult, but he was not nicknamed Marshal Forwards for nothing. Wellington might not have come to his aid the previous day, but the old warhorse would not abandon his ally yet.

And so the Prussians marched north. The Captain of a Westphalian cavalry squadron remarked that the mood of the troops was grim. It had begun to rain and some of the new saddles became swollen with the damp and the riders developed saddle sores, so he ordered them to dismount and lead their horses. The road was difficult, the weather appalling and the troops miserable, but then they encountered Marshal Blücher on the roadside and the mood changed instantly owing to the:

cheerful spirit and freshness of our seventy-four year old Field Marshal. He had his bruised limbs bathed in brandy, and had helped himself to a very large schnapps and now, though riding must have been very painful, he rode alongside the troops exchanging jokes and banter with them and his humour spread like wildfire down the column. I only glimpsed the old hero, though I should dearly have liked to express to him my pleasure at his escape.

It is hard to imagine the Duke of Wellington exchanging 'jokes and banter' with his men. It was not his style. More than once he stopped men from cheering him because, he said, if you let them cheer you today then tomorrow they will jeer at you. He was not loved as Blücher was, nor worshipped like Napoleon, but he was respected. He could be sharply witty; long after the wars were over some French officers pointedly turned their backs on him in Paris, for which rudeness a woman apologized. 'Don't worry, Madame,' the Duke said, 'I've seen their backs before.' He had learned to hide his emotions, though he would openly weep for the casualties his battles caused, and he possessed an explosive temper which he had also learned to control. His men might see the temper, rarely the emotions, but if he was cold towards them he also had confidence in them, and they in him. As Private William Wheeler of the 51st, who served Wellington in the Peninsular War and at Waterloo, wrote:

> *If England should require the service of her army again, and I should be with it, let me have 'Old Nosey' to command. Our interests would be sure to be looked into, we should never have occasion to fear an enemy. There are two things we should be certain of. First, we should always be as well supplied with rations as the nature of the service would admit. The second is we should be sure to give the enemy a damned good thrashing. What can a soldier want more?*

Wellington would have liked that praise. But now, on the morning after the fight at Quatre-Bras, he was probably unsure whether he would be able to give Napoleon a 'damned good thrashing'. He was waiting for news from Blücher as he paced beside the fire the Highlanders had made for him. He was alone for at least an hour, deep in thought, sometimes chewing abstractedly on a switch lopped from a tree, but then Lieutenant-Colonel the Honourable Sir Alexander Gordon, one of the Duke's aides, brought Wellington the news he needed to hear. Blücher's army, though wounded, still lived and had gone towards Wavre. North to Wavre, not east towards Prussia. 'Old Blücher has had a damned good licking,' the Duke growled to an officer of the Coldstream Guards, 'and gone back to Wavre, eighteen miles. As he has gone back, we must go too. I suppose in England they will say we have been licked. I can't help it; as they are gone back, we must go too.'

So the orders were sent to prepare for the retreat to the position Wellington had reconnoitred the previous year, the ridge of Mont St Jean above the unremarkable valley where the rye grew tall. The Duke might fear that the British public would interpret the retreat as an admission of defeat, but there was no danger that the French public would see the events of 16 June as anything but a victory. Napoleon made certain of that, sending a despatch to *Le Moniteur Universel*, the official newspaper, describing Ligny and Quatre-Bras as two further victories to add to the Empire's roll of honour. The published report prompted jubilation in Paris.

The first duty of the day for the British was to rescue their wounded, many of whom had lain all night where they fell. Cavalrymen placed injured men on horses, and those too weak to stay in the saddle were carried away on blankets. Doubtless some French wounded were rescued too, though priority was given to the British and Dutch, who were carried back to Brussels on wagons and, doubtless, in agony.

The French tended their wounded far better than their enemies, or at least attempted to, mainly through the influence of Dominique Jean Larrey, Chief Surgeon to the Imperial Guard. Larrey realized that treating men as soon as possible after they were wounded produced far better results than leaving them to suffer, and so he invented the 'flying ambulance', a lightweight vehicle, well-sprung, with a swivelling front axle to make it manoeuvrable on a battlefield crowded with corpses and wreckage, and with a floor which could be rolled out of the rear to make an operating table or to help load the wounded. He often performed surgery on the battlefield, but preferred to establish a central casualty station to which his ambulances would bring the wounded, while the British, in contrast, used their bandsmen to carry men to the rear where surgeons in blood-soaked aprons waited with saws, knives and probes. A skilled surgeon, and Larrey was very skilled, could amputate a leg in less than a minute. There was no anaesthetic, apart from the dulling effects of alcohol, and no antiseptics other than vinegar or spirits of turpentine. Larrey preferred operating while the patient was still in shock, and he had discovered that the recovery rate of men thus treated was much higher, though men with abdominal wounds stood very little chance of survival no matter how soon they received surgery. Most British casualties had to wait a long time before they received medical help, and many of the men wounded at Quatre-Bras were not to see a surgeon until they had reached distant Brussels, while Larrey was operating very close to the battlefield. Napoleon said of him that 'he was the most honest man and the best friend to the soldier I ever knew'.

It took the British until midday to rescue their wounded, and meanwhile Wellington gave careful instructions for the army's withdrawal. The infantry had to go first, but 'in such a manner as should prevent the enemy from observing what we were about'. Lieutenant Basil Jackson was sent to give the order for withdrawal to General Picton:

> *I found [him] at a farm-house a short distance along the Charleroi chaussée, [he] gave me a surly acknowledgment of the order; he evidently disliked to retire from a position he had so gallantly held the day before, and no wonder!*

What Jackson did not know, what no one except Picton and his servant knew, was that the irascible Welsh General had been struck by a musket ball the previous day. The ball had broken two of his ribs, enough to make any man surly, but Picton concealed the wound because he did not want anyone trying to persuade him to leave the army. He was in a bad mood anyway, forced to ride a trooper's horse because his groom had taken fright and fled with his horses.

Wellington had over 30,000 men and 70 guns at Quatre-Bras and needed to withdraw them the 8 miles to the ridge at Mont St Jean. He considered halting his army closer to Quatre-Bras, at a low ridge just north of Genappe, but he decided the ground at Mont St Jean was more favourable for defence. He knew he could be attacked at any moment. There was already desultory fighting as the advance picquets of both armies fired at each other, and that crackle of muskets and rifles could quickly grow into the full-throated roar of battle. And the Duke had to withdraw along a single road, the *chaussée*, which must carry all his guns and wagons. Infantry might be able to march through the fields on either side of the road, but they would be obstructed by thick crops, hedges, ditches, walls and thickets. In short this withdrawal would be a difficult and dangerous manoeuvre, but it had to be done and, once the wounded had left, the army got under way. The infantry and most of the artillery went first, while the cavalry and the lighter artillery stayed behind as the rearguard. Wellington wanted the retreat done calmly and, as if to demonstrate his unconcern, he lay down in a pasture and put a newspaper over his face and pretended to sleep. Yet he must have been concerned, because every moment meant there were fewer and fewer men at Quatre-Bras, and those who remained were increasingly vulnerable to an enemy attack.

Except none came.

Astonishingly, Marshal Ney did nothing. His troops were bivouacked around the village of Frasnes, less than three miles south of the crossroads, yet they were given no orders to assault the dwindling forces to their north, not even to scout the fields where they had fought so grimly the day before. There was some skirmishing as the advanced French picquets fought against their opposite numbers, but Ney ordered no general attack. It was during this sporadic exchange of fire in the dawn of Saturday, 17 June that Edward Costello, the Rifleman, recorded a sad moment as the 95th withdrew from the positions they had held through the previous day. Not all the women who accompanied the army had stayed in Brussels and many, like Martha Deacon, had accompanied their men. Costello's company retreated along a pathway to the Nivelles road. The track, he said:

*was partially protected by a hedge from the enemy's fire, when
one of my companions heard the cries of a child on the other side;
on looking over he espied a fine boy, about two or three years of
age, by the side of its dead mother, who was still bleeding
copiously from a wound in the head, occasioned, most likely, by a
random shot from the enemy. We carried the motherless, and
perhaps orphan child by turns to Genappe, where we found a
number of women of our division, one of whom recognised the
little fellow, I think she said as belonging to a soldier of the First
Royals.*

Yet though the picquets on either side exchanged fire, the French
seemed oblivious to Wellington's withdrawal. Marshal Ney somehow
thought this Saturday would be a day to rest his troops and so, under
towering black clouds that slowly came from the north to cover the sky,
the British and Dutch slipped away until, by 2 p.m., only the rearguard
of cavalry and horse artillery was left.

Ney's inactivity was unforgivable. His task that morning had been
to make Wellington's life difficult by attacking again, because Wellington
would then have been forced to leave troops at Quatre-Bras to fight off
the French attacks, and those troops would have been threatened by an
attack coming from Ligny. In truth Wellington was in a very precarious
position, exposed to his south and east, and with only the single road
as his means of escape northwards. He could, of course, have withdrawn to Nivelles, but that would have taken him further from the
Prussians, and the Duke was not thinking about abandoning their joint
campaign. So Ney had a prime opportunity to trap Wellington, but
instead he did nothing. Napoleon, when he discovered the British withdrawal, publicly shamed Ney by saying in front of him and others, '*On
a perdu la France!*' – You've lost France! – but the Emperor's own
behaviour on that Saturday morning was scarcely better.

Napoleon slept late and woke in an affable mood. He insisted on
touring the Ligny battlefield, as if luxuriating in the victory he had won
the previous day. He assumed Wellington, like Blücher, was in retreat,

and he was in no evident hurry to pursue either army. He did send cavalry patrols eastwards to find the Prussians, and those horsemen sent back reports that Blücher's men were fleeing east in disorder. In fact those disordered troops on the road to Namur were Rhinelanders who had deserted the Prussian army. Blücher was not on the Namur road, he was going north, travelling to Wavre.

Then Napoleon heard that Wellington's army, far from retreating, was still at Quatre-Bras. The report astonished him. Could Wellington really be that stupid? But he saw his opportunity and sent orders for Ney to hold Wellington in place while the Emperor brought 69,000 men to fall on the Duke's exposed left flank. Meanwhile Napoleon detached a quarter of his army, 33,000 men under Marshal Grouchy, and ordered them to pursue the Prussians.

This was the morning when Napoleon could have won the campaign. He had Ney's men close to Wellington and the rest of his army within an hour's march of the British–Dutch forces. If Napoleon had attacked at dawn Wellington would surely have been doomed, but the Emperor had let the morning go to waste, and when he did reach Quatre-Bras in the early afternoon he found the last units of the British–Dutch army just leaving, undisturbed by Ney's troops, who were cooking meals in their bivouacs. '*On a perdu la France!*' he had snarled at Ney, but the Emperor had been almost as lackadaisical as the Marshal. The French, on that Saturday morning, should have pursued Blücher's Prussians and attacked Wellington without delay, but they did neither. Worse, they still did not know where the Prussians were, and they had given Wellington time to retreat in safety.

Napoleon ordered a pursuit, sending cavalry and horse artillery to chase Wellington's men, but now nature intervened. The heavens opened. Those dark clouds rumbled with thunder, were split by lightning and down came the rain. Such rain! This was the storm Wellington reckoned worse than any he had experienced in monsoon India, a sustained cloudburst that turned the fields to mud and ran the red dye in the coats of the British infantry, leaking it onto their white trousers to turn them pink. But those infantry were well on their way to Mont

St Jean. It was the cavalry and the horse artillery who had to hold the French pursuit at bay.

It is time to meet Cavalié Mercer again, the gunner officer whose troops received the news of Napoleon's escape from Elba 'with unfeigned joy ... all eager to plunge into danger and bloodshed, all hoping to obtain glory and distinction'. Mercer left one of the best and most famous accounts of the Waterloo campaign, and his troop of horse artillery was one of those that had to hold off the French pursuit. Just before the rain came, though, he had his first glimpse of Napoleon:

> *I had often longed to see Napoleon, that mighty man of war, that astonishing genius who had filled the world with his renown. Now I saw him and there was a degree of sublimity in the interview rarely equalled. The sky had become overcast since that morning, and at this moment presented a most extraordinary appearance. Large isolated masses of thundercloud, of the deepest, almost inky black, their lower edges hard and strongly defined, lagging down, as if momentarily about to burst, hung over us ... while the distant hill lately occupied by the French army still lay bathed in brilliant sunshine ... when a single horseman, immediately followed by several others, mounted the plateau.*

Mercer had glimpsed the Emperor, who was riding his white mare, Désirée. Napoleon, seeing the British rearguard escape, threw his cavalry forward. The fiercest of the fighting was around Genappe, the village just three miles north of Quatre-Bras. The French lancers pursued British hussars and were counter-charged by the Life Guards. Mercer's troop, like the other gunners, found vantage points from which to fire shells at the enemy cavalry before limbering up and galloping on. One of the artillery units was a rocket troop, a new weapon that Wellington thought only good for frightening horses. He had first encountered rockets in India, where they had been used by the enemy, and then again in Spain, where Colonel William Congreve's rockets were first deployed, and Captain Mercer was fascinated by his first sight of the new-fangled weapon:

> *The rocketeers had placed a little iron triangle in the road with a rocket lying on it. The order to fire is given, portfire applied; the fidgety missile begins to sputter out sparks and wriggle its tail for a second or so, and then darts forth straight up the chaussée. A gun stands right in its way, between the wheels of which the shell in the head of the rocket bursts; the gunners fall right and left; and those of the other guns, taking to their heels, the battery is deserted in an instant. Strange; but so it was.*

It was strange, possibly, because that first rocket was accurate; thereafter every rocket flew wild, some even turning in their flight to threaten the British. The Duke would happily have rid himself of the rocket troop, but they had the patronage of the Prince Regent and so he was stuck with them.

The rain dampened the pursuit. Once the army was through the cramped streets of Genappe, where a narrow bridge carried the highway across the River Dyle, they left the French behind, though Captain Mercer had a close shave in the village. Lord Uxbridge, second in command to Wellington and the commander of all the British–Dutch cavalry, demanded that Mercer and his guns follow him down a narrow side alley only just wide enough to let the guns pass. Mercer was at a loss to know what Uxbridge wanted, but obeyed, then suddenly, as they emerged into the fields beyond the village, enemy cavalry appeared just 50 yards ahead:

> *The whole transaction appears to me so wild and confused that at times I can hardly believe it to have been more than a confused dream, yet true it was; the general-in-chief of the cavalry exposing himself amongst the skirmishers of his rear-guard, and literally doing the duty of a cornet! 'By God, we're all prisoners' (or some such words), exclaimed Lord Uxbridge, dashing his horse at one of*

*the garden banks, which he cleared, and away he went, leaving us
to get out of the scrape as best we could.*

There was no room for the horses dragging the guns to wheel
around, so Mercer had to unlimber his guns and turn them by hand.
Miraculously the enemy cavalry did not interfere with this laborious
process and Mercer led his battery back to the village centre, where he
discovered Lord Uxbridge assembling a rescue party.

And on they went in the pouring rain. The artillery and the wagons
used the road, the cavalry retreated through the fields to the east of the
highway and the infantry to the west. A Nassauer officer, Captain
Friedrich Weiz, reckoned the staff work was 'exemplary', the retreat was
done efficiently, despite the weather and the French pursuit. The British
were to lose fewer than a hundred men during the journey to Mont St
Jean, the French probably about the same. One of the French casualties
was Colonel Jean Baptiste Sourd, who commanded a battalion of lancers.
Sourd had risen from the ranks, been made a Baron of the Empire, and
Napoleon had just offered the Colonel another promotion, an offer Sourd
had not yet answered. Now, at Genappe, the forty-year-old Colonel
Sourd was badly cut up, probably by the Life Guards, and had to go back
to the casualty station where Larrey, the Chief Surgeon, decided that his
right arm had to be amputated. Sourd lay on the table, and while Larrey
cut and sawed and tied off arteries and sewed a flap of skin over the
stump, the Colonel dictated a letter to the Emperor:

> *The greatest favour you can do me is to leave me in command of
> the regiment I hope to lead to victory. I refuse the rank of general
> if the great Napoleon will forgive me, because the rank of Colonel
> is sufficient.*

Then Sourd signed the letter with his left hand before remounting
his horse and galloping after his men, who still followed the British rearguard. His wound healed and Sourd was to survive until 1849. The
Colonel had been injured in the cavalry fight which occurred in

Genappe, a fight which left a deep impression on many British observers. The British cavalry was armed with swords or sabres, but the French had lancers. Those lancers filled the road between the small town's houses, presenting an almost impenetrable hedge of blades with no open flank that could be attacked. Britain's 7th Hussars were ordered to charge the French, who were now too close to the retreating British–Dutch forces for comfort. Sergeant Major Cotton remembered that the lancers were 'awkward customers to deal with':

> When our charge first commenced, their lances were erect, but upon our coming within two or three horse's lengths of them, they lowered the points and waved the flags, which made some of our horses shy.

The flags he speaks of were pennants attached just behind the lance's slender steel blade. The attack by the 7th Hussars failed. They suffered badly, then suffered again when they tried a second assault, and the survivors were then pursued by a mixed group of lancers and cuirassiers, which was only stopped by a charge of the Life Guards, heavier cavalry, who got past the long lance blades and hacked at the French with their big swords. The lance was an effective weapon, especially in pursuit, but its weakness was that if an enemy managed to dodge the blade then the lancer was effectively defenceless. Nevertheless the British were so impressed by the performance of the French lancers that, after the wars, they formed their own lancer regiments.

The Life Guards stopped the immediate pursuit, but the pouring rain did most to help Wellington's men escape. 'The tracks were so deep in mud', Hippolyte de Mauduit, the Imperial Guardsman, remembered, 'that we found it impossible to maintain any order in our columns.' Lieutenant Jacques Martin, a French infantry officer, described the chaos:

> A storm, such as I had never seen, suddenly unleashed itself on us … in a few minutes the road and the plain were nothing more than a swamp which became ever more impassable because the

*storm persisted for the rest of the day and the whole night. Men
and horses sank into the mud up to their knees. The growing
darkness stopped troops from seeing each other, battalions
mingled and every soldier marched as best as he could and where
he could. We were no longer an army, but a crowd.*

The French pursuit turned into a struggle against weather and mud.
Most of the infantry marched through the fields, leaving the paved road
for the gunners, and men found their own paths, trying to avoid the
trampled mud of the men who went before, and they spread out so
much that some men did not rejoin their units till morning. And still
it rained. Then, as evening fell, the leading French cavalrymen breasted
a small rise in the highway and were met by sudden shell fire. It was
dusk, the sky unnaturally dark with heavy clouds, the rain pelting
down, and there, in the gloom, were sudden flashes of fire and over the
wide wet valley came the shells, leaving tiny traces of smoke from their
fuses, and the muzzle flashes showed all along a ridge to the north. The
shells exploded, doing little damage, and some did not explode at all
because the soaking wet ground extinguished their burning fuses, and
then the gunfire ended as suddenly as it had begun.

Till now the British guns had fired from close to the highway, but
the leading French cavalry had seen these new flashes all along a ridge
which was now wreathed in smoke that drifted through the heavy rain.
They knew what that smoke meant. It meant the guns had left the road
and were emplaced along a ridge the enemy intended to defend. The
British had decided to make a stand and the pursuit was over. Ahead of
the French was the Duke of Wellington and his army.

Offering battle at a place called Mont St Jean.

*   *   *

Four hundred years before, near a village called Azincourt, an English
army had waited to do battle with the French, and on that October night
it had rained and rained and the sky had echoed with thunder. It had
been a drenching rain and next morning, as the rain at last ended, the
field where the English offered battle was a quagmire of mud. It was that

mud, more than the English arrows or English valour, which defeated the French men-at-arms who, laden with fifty or sixty pounds of plate armour, had to wade through knee-deep mud to reach their opponents. The thick mud tired them so that when they reached Henry V's line they were hacked down in a merciless display of butchery.

And on Sunday, 18 June 1815, the ground in the valley south of Waterloo would be muddy. It was an omen.

The Emperor either did not know the history, or else decided that rain on the eve of a battle was no omen at all. He had made mistakes over the last two days, but he was still supremely confident. General Foy remembered Napoleon's prediction:

The Prussians and English cannot possibly join each other for another two days after such a battle as Fleurus [Ligny] and given the fact that they're being pursued by a considerable number of troops. We shall be only too glad if the English decide to stay because the battle that is coming will save France and be celebrated in world history!

That is quite a change from 'On a perdu la France!', but that savage remark had been made in a fit of anger when Napoleon realized how Ney had let slip an opportunity. Yet despite that missed chance, Napoleon still had good reason to be confident. So far as he knew the Prussians were retreating eastwards, pursued by Marshal Grouchy, while Wellington had foolishly offered battle.

I shall have my artillery fire and my cavalry charge, so as to force the enemy to disclose his positions, and when I am quite certain which positions the English troops have taken up, I shall march straight at them with my Old Guard.

Napoleon was rather prone to making such dismissive statements, and his tactics on Sunday, 18 June would not be quite so simple as he predicted, but they would still be indicative of confidence. The French had good sources of intelligence from among the French-speaking Belgians, and the Emperor must have known that Wellington's army was a fragile coalition, while his own army was full of battle-tested veterans. Napoleon's fear, that night, was that Wellington would slip away in the darkness and so deprive France of a great victory. 'The rain fell in torrents,' Napoleon recalled in his memoirs:

> Several officers who had been sent out on reconnaissance and some spies who returned at half past three, confirmed that the English–Dutch troops were not moving ... two Belgian deserters, who had just left their regiment, told me their army was preparing for battle and no retreat was happening, that Belgium was praying for my success and that the English and Prussians were both equally hated there ... The enemy commander could do nothing more contrary to the interests of his cause and his country ... than to stay in the positions he had occupied. He had behind him the defiles of the Forest of Soignes and if he were beaten any retreat would be impossible ... The day began to dawn. I returned to my headquarters well satisfied with the great error which the enemy commander was making ... the British oligarchy would be overthrown by it! France, that day, was going to ride more glorious, more powerful and mightier than ever!

Napoleon's headquarters that night were in a farmhouse, Le Caillou, just south of the wide valley where his enemies waited. He had a restless night, which is hardly surprising, and very early on the morning of Sunday, 18 June, he received a despatch from Grouchy that should have disturbed him. The message said that the Prussians, instead of retreating eastwards, had gone north to Wavre, which meant that Blücher's forces were within a few hours' march of the rain-soaked valley beneath Mont St Jean, yet the Emperor did not seem alarmed and was not to respond to Grouchy until mid-morning. He had, after all, despatched a large part of his army to keep the Prussians busy. Those 33,000 men were sent to prevent Blücher linking up with Wellington, and the Emperor was confident he could prevent such a junction. He was interested only in the troops that faced him, the British–Dutch army, and because Napoleon had never fought a pitched battle with British troops, he asked his generals for their opinions. It was at breakfast in Le Caillou that Marshal Soult told Napoleon, 'Sire, in a straight fight the English infantry are the very devil,' an opinion that irritated Napoleon, as did General Reille's gloomy comment that well-posted British infantry was *inexpugnable*, impregnable. Napoleon's riposte is famous:

Because you've been beaten by Wellington you consider him to be a good general! And now I tell you that Wellington is a bad general, that the English are bad soldiers, and that this affair will be over before lunch!

Napoleon has been mocked for that statement, as he has for his derisory comment that Wellington was nothing but a 'sepoy General', but as Andrew Roberts points out in his fine book *Napoleon and Wellington*, what else was the Emperor to say on the morning of battle? His task was to raise morale, not praise the enemy's strengths. He knew Wellington's reputation and knew his generals were in awe of the Duke, and so he belittled his opponent with scorn. And, almost certainly, he believed himself to be the better commander. 'There are ninety chances in our favour,' he told his generals. He had once said that 'battles should not be fought if one cannot calculate at least a seventy percent chance of victory'.

So did his confidence come from sickness? That may seem a strange question, but it has been suggested Napoleon was suffering from acromegaly, a rare hormonal disorder which, among other things, provokes over-optimism. It has also been suggested that Napoleon was suffering from piles, constipation, cystitis or epilepsy, all of which are offered as explanations of his lethargic behaviour that June. He was certainly tired, but so were virtually all the senior officers involved in the campaign. The late Sir John Keegan worked out that Wellington had no more than nine and a half hours' sleep in the three days leading to the battle of Waterloo, which was probably less than the Emperor.

Much of the argument about Napoleon's illnesses smacks of excuses, though there is little doubt that he was not as energetic as he had been in his youth. Colonel Auguste-Louis Pétiet was on Marshal Soult's staff and had many opportunities to observe Napoleon.

> *Napoleon's stoutness had increased. His head had become enlarged and more deeply set between his shoulders. His pot-belly was unusually pronounced ... it was noticeable that he remained on horseback much less than in the past ... I found it hard to keep my eyes off this extraordinary man upon whom Victory had for so long showered her gifts. His stoutness, his dull white complexion, his heavy walk made him appear very different from the General Bonaparte I had seen at the start of my career during the campaign of 1800 in Italy when he was so alarmingly thin that no soldier in his army could understand how, with so frail a body and looking so ill as he did, he could stand such fatigue.*

Yet, tired or not, the Emperor was eager for battle. His fear, during the night, had been that Wellington would retreat further, but dawn confirmed their presence. The night before, seeing their campfires light the rainy sky, the Emperor had exulted, '*Ah! Je les tiens donc, ces anglais!*' Ah! Now I've got them, those English!

And so he had.

*   *   *

The British–Dutch headquarters was in the little town of Waterloo, where the Quartermaster's department had chalked names on doors to show where men were billeted. 'His Grace the Duke of Wellington' was written on the front door of a comfortable house on the main street (it is now a museum) where the Duke spent much of the night writing letters. He had about three hours' sleep. The rain kept falling.

He wrote to the British Ambassador to the Kingdom of the Netherlands, Sir Charles Stuart, who was in Ghent, 'Pray keep the

English quiet if you can. Let them all prepare to move, but neither be in a hurry or a fright, as all will yet turn out well.' He also wrote to Lady Frances Webster, the 22-year-old friend he had met in the Brussels park. At the top of the letter he wrote 'Waterloo, Sunday morning, 3 o'clock June 18th 1815':

> *My dear Lady Frances, we fought a desperate battle on Friday, in which I was successful, though I had but very few troops. The Prussians were very roughly handled, and retired in the night which obliged me to do the same to this place yesterday. The course of the operations may oblige me to uncover Bruxelles for a moment, and may expose that town to the enemy; for which reason I recommend that you and your family should be prepared to move to Antwerp at a moment's notice. I will give you the earliest information of any danger that may come to my knowledge; at present I know of none.*

It was all very well for the Duke to counsel against panic, but it had already started. Rumours spread fast and those rumours said the British–Dutch had been defeated, the Prussians were fleeing, and that Napoleon was advancing unstoppably towards Brussels. Tupper Carey was an Assistant Commissary-General, and had been sent towards Brussels in search of supplies.

> *I had hardly proceeded a mile when suddenly a panic seemed to have seized every one at the cry of the enemy being at hand. It seemed ridiculous to me, who had just arrived from the front, where all was quiet ... Never did I witness a scene of such confusion and folly. To add to its bad effects, it was raining hard, and we were in the Forest of Soignes. The servants got rid of their baggage, let it drop on the ground, then, jumping on their animals, galloped off to the rear ... The peasantry, carrying provisions in the country waggons, cut the traces of the harness and ran away with the horses, abandoning the waggons.*

It was scarcely better in Brussels. Rumours of Wellington's defeat spread and English visitors were desperate to find transport out of the city. John Booth, an English civilian, was in the city that night and left an account of the confusion:

The scuffle that took place to get at the horses and carriages it is impossible to describe; the squabbling of masters and servants, ostlers, chambermaids, coachmen, and gentlemen, all scolding at once, and swearing at each other in French, English and Flemish ... words were followed by blows ... one half of the Belgic drivers refused either to go themselves, or let their beasts go, and with many gesticulations called upon all the saints and angels in heaven to witness, that they would not set off, no, not to save the Prince of Orange himself; and neither love nor money, nor threats, nor intreaties, could induce them to alter this determination. Those who had horses, or means of procuring them, set off with the most astonishing expedition, and one English carriage after another took the road to Antwerp.

Antwerp lay directly to the north of Brussels and the roads to the port were good, as was the canal system. Lucky travellers could get a berth on a barge and be served fine meals in a luxury cabin while draught horses pulled them smoothly northwards, but by 17 June the barges had either left Brussels or been commandeered by the British army to serve as floating ambulances to carry the wounded to Antwerp's wharves. Rumours of a great British defeat at Quatre-Bras reached Antwerp with the refugees, causing more panic. Similar rumours had infected the French on the evening of Quatre-Bras where 'everyone was running away in total confusion and shouting "Here comes the enemy!"' Ned Costello, the Rifleman, wrote, 'It is curious to observe that, in the rear of an army in battle, confusion and uproar generally exists while all in front is order and regularity. Many people imagine the reverse.'

The Duke was displaying order and regularity. At some time that night he received an assurance that the Prussians would march to his aid next morning, and that assurance was all he needed. His concern that night was that Napoleon would turn his right flank, thus cutting him off from a retreat to Ostend, and to guard against that eventuality Wellington posted 17,000 men in the village of Hal. Those troops would play no part in the battle because Napoleon never tried to manoeuvre Wellington out of his prepared position, he just attacked head-on, but that rainy night Wellington had no way of knowing what the Emperor planned. The Duke's second in command, the Earl of Uxbridge, asked Wellington what he planned for the morning and received a very dusty response. 'Who will attack first tomorrow,' the Duke demanded, 'I or Bonaparte?'

'Bonaparte,' Uxbridge replied.

'Well, Bonaparte has not given me any idea of his projects, and as my plans will depend upon his, how can you expect me to tell you what mine are?'

Wellington had not wanted Uxbridge to be his second in command and leader of the British cavalry. It has frequently been suggested that this was because Uxbridge had eloped with the wife of Wellington's youngest brother, Henry. It was a major scandal. Wellington would have preferred Lord Combermere as his cavalry leader. Sir Stapleton Cotton, as Combermere had been called in 1812, had led the British cavalry at the battle of Salamanca and had been a crucial part of that astonishing victory, but Uxbridge had royal patronage and that trumped a mere Duke's wishes. 'Lord Uxbridge has the reputation of running away with everybody he can,' a friend quipped to the Duke when the appointment was announced.

'I'll take good care he don't run away with me,' was Wellington's curt rejoinder. And on the night before the battle, doubtless feeling he had been too hard on Uxbridge with his put-down over his plans, he clapped his second in command on the shoulder. 'There is one thing certain, Uxbridge, that is that whatever happens you and I will do our duty.'

Uxbridge was, in truth, a talented cavalryman, but must have found being second in command to Wellington extremely frustrating. The Duke did not delegate. He had no Chief of Staff as Blücher and the

Emperor did. He was his own Chief of Staff and trusted no one to do his job half as well as he knew he could do it himself. Lord Uxbridge's question, about what the Duke planned, was entirely justified and deserved a considered answer, but Wellington did not want a discussion, and certainly he did not want to tempt Uxbridge to offer advice. He was the commander and that was that.

The tone of the letters he wrote that night, and the brusqueness with which he treated Uxbridge, betray that he was not as confident as Napoleon. Nor should he have been. He trusted only half his army to fight well, and that army would be beaten if the Prussians failed to arrive. The Czar might have called Wellington the conqueror of the world's conqueror, but he had yet to prove it, and he must have been assailed by doubt on that rain-soaked night. He was about to face the man universally reckoned to be the greatest soldier of the age, a man he had never met in battle, and a man often called a genius.

Yet Wellington knew he could not show nervousness. In the morning, as the rain cleared, he met his friend Álava, the Spanish ambassador to the Netherlands whose presence at Waterloo was solely out of loyalty to the Duke. Álava was worried that Wellington was not his usual confident self, but the Duke put his friend's mind at rest when he nodded across the valley to where the French were forming up for battle. 'That little fellow', he said of Napoleon, 'doesn't know what a licking he's in for!'

∗ ∗ ∗

Yet Napoleon would only be licked if the Prussians came. This is, perhaps, the most important thing to understand about the Waterloo campaign. There has been argument about who 'won' the campaign, as if the Prussians and the British were in competition for the honour, but the essential fact is that Wellington would never have made a stand at Mont St Jean unless he believed the Prussians would march to his aid, and Blücher would never have risked that march if he believed Wellington could not hold off the French attacks.

Gneisenau, Blücher's clever Chief of Staff, presented the argument for abandoning Wellington. Gneisenau has come in for a great deal of criticism, especially from British commentators, for urging a retreat eastwards, but he was being entirely responsible. He was pointing out the dangers to his mercurial, passionate commander. It was true that Gneisenau had a low opinion of British troops and believed Wellington to be untrustworthy, and those convictions doubtless coloured his views, but he was telling Blücher that Wellington might only pretend to make a stand, then slip away, leaving the Prussian army vulnerable. Napoleon could then turn on Blücher's men, giving Wellington time to save his army. Did Gneisenau believe that? Maybe not, but he was right to present Blücher with the possibility. The old Marshal had to make the decision and he needed to know what risks lay in a choice to help Wellington. And Gneisenau, when he had been temporarily in command of the Prussian forces while Blücher lay bruised in the village of Mellery, had made certain that the retreat was northwards. He had posted staff officers at crossroads to direct the men onto the lanes leading towards Wavre. He had kept his commander's options open.

Gneisenau, whatever his private opinions about his British–Dutch allies, did not press his objections. When Blücher decided he would march to Wellington's aid, Gneisenau put the plans into operation. A young staff officer in Blücher's army wrote later:

> Blücher had abandoned his natural line of retreat in order to maintain contact with the Duke of Wellington because he felt that the first battle had to some extent been bungled and he was therefore determined to fight a second. So he informed the Duke of Wellington that he would come to the duke's assistance with his whole army.

That young staff officer was Major Carl von Clausewitz, who went on to become one of the most celebrated writers on war. He had endured the retreat towards Wavre, an horrific journey in a darkness made dangerous by the torrential rain. He described in a letter to his wife how the troops had to struggle along a sunken road, always fearing a French pursuit: 'I believe my hair turned grey that night.'

Yet the French pursuit did not materialize. Grouchy had 33,000 men and 96 cannon with which to pursue the Prussians, but he did not know where to look; indeed there was so little evidence of French activity by dawn on 18 June that Blücher assumed Napoleon had detached no men to follow him. Despite the weather, despite the darkness and despite the defeat they had suffered at Ligny, the Prussian army was now just 12 miles from Wellington's. They were difficult miles, across streams and through steep hills, but Blücher had promised Wellington he would march, and so he would. 'I shall once again lead you against the enemy,' the old Marshal declared in his Order of the Day, 'and we shall defeat him, because we must!'

At Ligny the Emperor had set a trap for Blücher, hoping that Ney or d'Erlon would fall like a thunderbolt on the Prussian right flank. The trap had failed.

Blücher had hoped that Wellington would come to Ligny and so attack the French left flank, but that trap had also failed.

Now a third trap was set. Wellington was the bait, Napoleon the intended victim and Blücher the executioner.

It was dawn on Sunday, 18 June 1815.

FACING PAGE | 'The Duke of Wellington', by Sir Thomas Lawrence: dressed in plain dark blue tailcoat, white breeches and half-boots ... with his usual cocked hat. The Duke always dressed plainly for battle – his men knew who he was, he needed no gilded frippery.

CLOCKWISE FROM TOP | *The village of Genappe, where Wellington bivouacked the night after Quatre-Bras ... it was also where Napoleon's carriage was captured by a Prussian detachment after the final defeat at Waterloo.* | *'Study for a Portrait of Baron Dominique Larrey', by Paulin Jean Baptiste Guérin. Chief Surgeon to the Imperial Guard, Larrey realized that treating men as soon as possible after they were wounded produced far better results, and so he invented the 'flying ambulance', a lightweight vehicle, manoeuvrable on a battlefield crowded with corpses.* | *Larrey attending a wounded soldier at the battle of Hanau, October 1813.*

CLOCKWISE FROM TOP LEFT | *William Paget, Lord Uxbridge, by Sir William Beechey. Paget was Wellington's second-in-command who, awkwardly, had previously run off with the wife of Wellington's youngest brother. He was to lose his leg with almost the last cannon shot of the battle of Waterloo.* | *Portrait of Marechal Soult, Duc de Dalmatie, by Joseph Desire Court. Marshal Soult told Napoleon: 'Sire, in a straight fight the English infantry are the very devil.'* | *'The British Royal Horse Artillery, Rocket Troop', by William Heath. A new weapon that Wellington thought only good for frightening horses.*

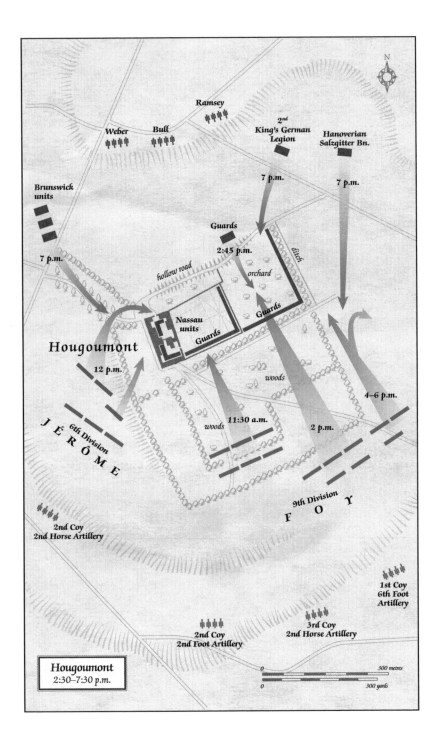

Ramsey

Weber   Bull

2nd
King's German
Legion

Hanoverian
Salzgitter Bn.

7 p.m.

7 p.m.

Brunswick
units

Guards

2:45 p.m.

7 p.m.

ditch

hollow road

orchard

Nassau
units

Guards

Guards

Hougoumont

Guards

12 p.m.

woods

J É R Ô M E

6th Division

woods

11:30 a.m.

2 p.m.

4–6 p.m.

9th Division

F O Y

2nd Coy
2nd Horse Artillery

1st Coy
6th Foot
Artillery

2nd Coy
2nd Foot Artillery

3rd Coy
2nd Horse Artillery

Hougoumont
2:30–7:30 p.m.

0   300 metres

0   300 yards

CHAPTER SIX

A cannon ball came from the Lord
knows where and took the head
off our right-hand man

T HE GENERALS HAD ROOFS over their heads, but for most of the troops the eve of battle was a nightmare of rain, mud and misery. Few had any shelter. William Gibney was a surgeon with the British cavalry, and he was luckier than some because he did at least have something to eat and drink:

There was no choice; we had to settle down in the mud and filth as best we could, and those having any provisions about them were fortunate. As I had obtained a bit of tongue (but whether cooked, or only smoked and salted, I know not) in the morning and had a thimble-full of brandy in my flask, I was better off than many. I looked about for a drier place to lie down … It was all mud, but we got some straw and boughs of trees and with these tried to lessen the mud and make a rough shelter against the torrents of rain which fell all night; wrapping around us our cloaks, and huddling close together, we lay in the mud.

He claimed to have slept 'like a top', but if so he was one of the few. Another cavalry surgeon, John Gordon Smith, remembered how his dragoons needed food, drink and fire:

Of the first our men had received a supply; the horses had also been, at least partially, cared for, but water! There was a draw-well close to the village, or hamlet of St Jean, and that was the only resource to which thousands of thirsty ones had access. The first attack upon it was the last; for snap went the rope, and down fell the bucket, to a depth from which it could not be recovered. Disappointed in the article of water, our attention was drawn to that of fire, in procuring of which we were eminently successful. The adjoining village furnished fuel in abundance. Doors, and window-shutters, furniture of every description, carts, ploughs, harrows, wheelbarrows, clock-cases, casks, tables etc etc were carried or trundled to the bivouac, and being broken up, made powerful fires, in spite of the rain. Chairs were otherwise disposed of. Officers were paying two francs each for them, and the men seemed, at first, to be able to keep up the supply. This, at last, failed, and for one, I was fain to buy a bundle of straw. In front of the field which the horses occupied, ran a miry cart-road (upon which the officers' fires were kindled) and by the side of this road was a drain, or shallow ditch. Here a party of us deposited our straw, and resolved to establish ourselves for the night, under cover of our cloaks; but such was the clayey nature of the bottom, that the rain did not sink into the earth, but rose like a leak in a ship, among the straw, and we were, in consequence, more drenched from below than from above.

The chairs, of course, were to keep officers' backsides out of the mud. The Duke of Wellington was fiercely opposed to the pillaging of civilians and he punished men severely for such thefts. His motive, beyond the preservation of discipline, was to prevent making unnecessary enemies. In Spain the French armies had incurred the hatred of almost all Spaniards by their rapacious behaviour, and the result had been the guerrilla war which had done as much as the formal fighting to defeat Napoleon's armies. When Wellington had invaded southern France in 1814 he had exercised savage control to keep his men from robbing the civil population, yet here, on the eve of battle, the soldiers were given leave to plunder. It was General Sir Frederick Adam, not Wellington, who permitted the behaviour. Second Lieutenant Richard Cocks Eyre, whose Rifle battalion had been at 'play' with French lancers near Mons two days before, says that on the evening of 17 June his men were 'like so many half drowned and half starved rats'. Then they received:

> *leave from General Adam who commanded our Brigade to plunder three farm houses ... The idea of a fire was a most consoling one! Chairs, tables, sofas, cradles, churns, barrels and all manner of combustibles were soon cracking in the flames, our fellows then proceeded to the slaughter of all the living stock the yard contained, and in less than an hour we had as delicious a breakfast of beef, pork, veal, duck, chicken, potatoes and other delicacies as I ever made an attack on.*

Second Lieutenant Eyre was lucky, some men did not even have the comfort of a fire, let alone a feast. Private Matthew Clay, a Guardsman, spent the night on the edge of a ditch, partially sheltered by a thick hedge. Other men slept in the open, using their knapsacks as pillows. There was little sleep for any. Thunder rolled across the dark that was occasionally split by lightning, and horses, picketed in the wet soil, broke loose and galloped in panic through the bivouacking troops. One of the horses that bolted belonged to Captain Johnny Kincaid, of the 95th Rifles. He had tied the horse's reins to one of his men's sword-bayonets (riflemen carried a bayonet with a sword handle and a 23-inch blade), rammed the blade into the earth and gone to sleep. He woke to find the beast gone and despaired of finding him, but after an hour the horse was discovered grazing between two artillery horses, the bayonet still tied to the reins. And all that night the rain went on falling, pelting down, soaking the ground, beating down the crops and flooding the ditches. Captain Mercer huddled with other officers:

> I know not how my bedfellows got on, as we all lay for a long while perfectly still and silent, the old Peninsular hands disdaining to complain before their Johnny Newcome comrades, and these fearing to do so lest they should provoke remarks as 'Lord have mercy on your poor tender carcass! What would such as you have done in the Pyrenees?' or 'Oho, my boy! This is but child's play to what we saw in Spain!' So all who did not sleep (I believe the majority) pretended to do so, and bore their suffering with admirable heroism.

It was worse for the French. At least Wellington's men had reached Mont St Jean in daylight and had time to plunder and break up furniture to feed their fires, but Napoleon's troops kept arriving through the first half of the night and the British, almost a mile away, heard the sound of wagon, gun and limber wheels rumbling on the Brussels highway. The gathering darkness meant the French had small opportunity to scavenge for fuel or food. Some of their cavalrymen slept on their horses' backs, or tried to sleep, and must have envied the British–Dutch fires glowing through the incessant rain.

One hundred and fifty thousand men had come to the valley and 150,000 men tried to sleep through that rain-swept darkness, knowing that in the morning there would be a battle. It is impossible to give the exact numbers, except for the artillery, but Napoleon's army had about 77,500 men with 246 guns. Wellington waited for him with around 73,200 men and 157 cannon. Blücher, with another 100,000 men and 240 guns, was 12 miles to the east. For the moment Blücher can play no part in the battle, but he has promised to send half his men and 134 guns to Mont St Jean. Napoleon, then, must defeat Wellington before those Prussian troops can arrive.

Napoleon's troops outnumbered Wellington's, though not by a great deal. The Emperor's real advantage was that his troops were, on the whole, better. Wellington had complete faith in his British and King's German Legion units, but the rest, about half of his army, was of dubious quality and of uncertain loyalty. Napoleon's second advantage was in the number and efficiency of his artillery. Napoleon was an artilleryman by training. The guns were his 'beautiful daughters', but the effectiveness of those daughters was going to be hampered by mud.

Just as the mud at Agincourt had slowed and wearied the French men-at-arms, so the mud of Waterloo would help Wellington's men. Napoleon liked to use his guns to batter an enemy, to weaken him at long range, just as he had torn apart the exposed Prussian infantry at Ligny. A battalion in line, square or column was an easy enough target, but at long range the gunners liked to 'graze' their roundshot. Grazing was a little like skipping a stone across a pond, except that the heavy roundshot would be aimed short of the target and would bounce once, twice or many times before striking home. It was, perhaps surprisingly, a more accurate method than shooting directly. If a gunner aimed to hit his target directly, without grazing the roundshot, then any small variation in the powder charge or in the missile itself could affect the flight, and a shot which went high would do no damage. A grazed shot kept low and hit home almost every time, but the mud slowed such grazing shots, even stopped them. The mud affected the shells too. Roundshot was solid, a shell was a hollow iron sphere packed with powder, and the ground at Waterloo was so soft that many of the shells buried themselves before exploding, or else the burning fuse was extinguished by the damp earth. Howitzers were cannon that fired in a high arc, enabling gunners to drop shells over intervening obstacles, or onto the hidden reverse slopes where Wellington liked to shelter his troops, and the howitzer shells were particularly prone to being engulfed by mud on landing.

Napoleon had around 53,000 infantry, almost the same number as Wellington, though again Wellington's troops were of varying quality. Artillery might hammer an enemy, and cavalry could destroy vulnerable units, but infantry were the battle-winners. It was the infantry that had to make the attacks which captured the enemy's ground and hold it. Cavalry might pierce deep into the enemy's territory, but as Kellerman had discovered at Quatre-Bras, once there they were horribly vulnerable to musket and cannon fire. To overwhelm infantry a general needed his own infantry, and here Napoleon really had no advantage. To break Wellington the Emperor's infantry had to advance across half a mile of open ground, all the while under the flail of the British–Dutch cannons, while their opponents could lie low till the last moment, and that last moment would be an infantry versus infantry firefight, fought at very close range. We have already seen how it was impossible to move men in line across open country. The French would have to advance in column, and they would be met by lines. The French, of course, would deploy into line when they reached the enemy, but they needed to cross the valley in column and a column was a fat target for an artilleryman.

As dawn came on that wet Sunday, the French could see an enemy waiting on the far ridge even though many of the British–Dutch troops were hidden on the reverse slope. Nevertheless, the shape of the battle-field was clear, and it was small. Waterloo is one of the most cramped battles ever fought; three armies struggling in three square miles.

The French centre was at the tavern called La Belle Alliance which stood where the highway crossed the southern ridge. A man standing by the tavern and looking north along the road would see the valley spread left and right in front of him. The ridges were not parallel, both were curved, with the northern ridge forming a semicircle facing south and the southern almost a mirror image, so that the wide valley formed a natural arena in the shape of a human eye. The eastern limit of that arena was marked by a scatter of stone buildings, some woods and, beyond those, broken countryside. Those small hills, cut with streams and by the headwaters of the River Lasne, were easily defended and difficult to attack, so the eastern edge of the battlefield was defined by that rougher country. There was a scatter of hamlets and big farmsteads on the margin of that rougher land: Papelotte, La Haie (not to be confused with La Haie Sainte), Smohain, Frichermont, all of them capable of being stout stone fortresses, so that flank, the British–Dutch left flank, was no place to try and manoeuvre around Wellington's forces. Behind the French lines, still on their right, was a large village called Plancenoit. Most Frenchmen probably gave Plancenoit very little thought. It was behind them, so unlikely to be a part of any battle against Wellington's men, but by day's end it would be a place of butchery.

Napoleon spent most of the day close to La Belle Alliance. Wellington was far more active than the Emperor, but when he had no business elsewhere he tended to stay near an elm tree which stood by the crossroads at the centre of the northern ridge. The distance from La Belle Alliance to that elm was three-quarters of a mile (1,400 metres), and from the crossroads east to Papelotte was again three-quarters of a mile. A minor road ran along the northern ridge's crest. The French could see the road's hedges, and between the French and that road was the wide valley with its tall crops of rye, barley and wheat. To an observer at La Belle Alliance that stretch of open country between the elm tree and Papelotte would appear as a long, gentle slope leading to the low crest of the ridge where Wellington's forces waited. An attack across that open ground was very possible.

A direct attack straight up the highway towards the elm tree was far more difficult, because halfway down the far ridge's gentle slope was the stoutly built stone farm of La Haie Sainte, and the French could plainly see that the enemy had put a garrison into that farm. Any attack on Wellington's centre would have to deal with the fortress of La Haie Sainte and with the green-jacketed riflemen who were in a large sandpit across the road from the farmhouse. The farm and the sandpit lay some 200 metres, a little more than 200 yards, in front of the ridge's crest.

To the left of La Haie Sainte was another stretch of open country, this one about two-thirds of a mile wide and another place where an attack would find few obstacles, though it would have to be funnelled between the garrison in La Haie Sainte and the defenders of the great complex of Château Hougoumont.

Hougoumont was a rich farmhouse built forward of Wellington's ridge. It was much larger than La Haie Sainte. There was a substantial house (the château), barns, a chapel, stables and other outbuildings, all surrounded by a high masonry wall. There was a walled garden and a hedged orchard. This was another formidable fortress, and here the two ridges came closest together, though the slopes between them were at their steepest. Hougoumont would be a tough nut to crack, but there was enough space between Hougoumont and La Haie Sainte for a major infantry assault.

Beyond Hougoumont, to the west, the country was more open. Napoleon would find it difficult to turn the British–Dutch left flank, the broken country beyond Papelotte was too easily defended, but Wellington's right flank, beyond Hougoumont, might have tempted him. If he sent an attack past Hougoumont, to the west, he could force Wellington to abandon his ridge and turn his army to face the new threat. Wellington feared such a manoeuvre and had placed most of his reserve troops in the village of Braine l'Alleud, which lay behind his right flank. Those troops could confront a flanking attack, but if all went wrong and Wellington was forced to retreat, he had another 17,000 men in the village of Hal, ten miles west of Waterloo, stationed there to provide a rearguard if his army was forced to retreat towards the sea. In the event those 17,000 troops would play no part in the day's fighting.

Napoleon had also detached part of his army, Grouchy's 33,000 men and 96 guns, to pursue the Prussians. Their job was to find the Prussians, engage them and so stop Blücher's men coming to Wellington's aid.

So, by dawn on Sunday, 18 June, the three armies are expecting battle. The rain stops at last, though there will be passing showers for much of the day and, though it is summer, it is still bitingly cold. Johnny Kincaid's riflemen, shivering beside the highway a little north of the elm tree, boil a big cauldron of water and throw in tea, sugar and milk; 'all the bigwigs of the army had occasion to pass,' he said, and 'I believe every one of them, from the Duke downwards, claimed a cupful.'

The French were no better off. Louis Canler, an eighteen-year-old infantryman, spent a bone-chilling night in the rain, but at least there was breakfast in the dawn. His company butchered a sheep and boiled it with some flour to thicken the broth, but they lacked salt for seasoning, so one of the men threw in a handful of gunpowder instead. The mutton, Canler recalled, 'tasted foul'.

Private Matthew Clay, the guardsman who had spent a miserable night beside a ditch in the orchard of Hougoumont, had much the same experience. At dawn, he said:

> we procured some fuel from the farm of Hougoumont and then lighted fires and warmed ourselves. Our limbs were very much cramped sitting on the side of the wet ditch the entire night. The Sergeant of each section gave a small piece of bread, which was about an ounce, to each man, and enquiry was made along the ranks for a butcher.

A pig was slaughtered and the carcass cut up. Clay received a portion of the pig's head, but though he scorched the meat, he found it inedible. Then he readied his musket. It was loaded, because Hougoumont's garrison had feared a night attack which never came, so he fired the weapon into a muddy bank. All along both ridges men were clearing their muskets. The powder could have become damp and none wanted a useless musket when the enemy came, so they fired their weapons to get rid of the overnight charge. Clay checked his ammunition, tightened his musket's doghead, the screw-driven vice which held the flint in place, then oiled the powerful spring and trigger. The damp had swollen the wood of some muskets, hampering the springs.

Clay, like every other redcoat, carried a Brown Bess musket, though in truth there was no such weapon. There were Land Pattern muskets, India Pattern muskets and New Land Pattern muskets, all carrying the nickname of Brown Bess. The basic musket was developed during the early years of the eighteenth century, a hundred years before Waterloo, and a soldier of Marlborough's army would have had no trouble using a New Land Pattern musket made in the early nineteenth century. The muskets were heavy, weighing a little over 10 lbs, and cumbersome, with a barrel length of either 39 inches or 42 inches, firing a ball three-quarters of an inch in diameter. It was possible to fire five shots in a minute, but that was exceptional, and the normal rate of fire was between two and three shots a minute, and even that was optimistic. As a battle progressed the touch-holes became fouled with burned powder and the barrels caked with powder residue, and the flints chipped and needed replacing. Nevertheless a British battalion of 500 men could expect to fire between 1,000 and 1,500 shots a minute. If fired at too great a range, say anything over 100 yards, most of those shots would miss because the smoothbore musket was notoriously inaccurate. Much of the inaccuracy was caused by 'windage', which is the difference between the barrel's interior width and the musket ball's width. This was usually about a twentieth of an inch, which made the ball easier (and thus quicker) to load, but the ball literally bounced as it sped down the barrel and the last bounce would dictate the direction of the flight. There were various tests made of a musket's accuracy, and a typical one was conducted by the Prussians, who discovered that a battalion firing at a target 100 feet wide and 6 feet high scored 60 per cent hits at 75 yards, 40 per cent at 150 yards and 25 per cent at 225 yards. Colonel George Hanger, who was an expert marksman, wrote in his book *To All Sportsmen*, published in 1814:

> *A soldier's musket, if not exceedingly ill-bored (as many are), will strike the figure of a man at 80 yards; it may even at a hundred; but a soldier must be very unfortunate indeed who shall be wounded by a common musket at 150 yards, provided his antagonist aims at him; and as to firing at a man at 200 yards with a common musket, you may as well fire at the moon.*

Estimates were made during the Napoleonic Wars of the musket's efficiency. At the battle of Talavera it was reckoned that in half an hour 1,300 French were either killed or wounded, but it had taken 30,000 musket balls to achieve that! 3,675,000 rounds were fired by Wellington's army at Vitoria and caused 8,000 casualties, which is one hit in every 459! At close range the results were much better, and the British especially were trained to wait until the enemy was very close before opening fire.

The French too were clearing their muskets. Their weapon, the Charleville musket, was about a pound lighter than the Brown Bess, and just as inaccurate. The bore was smaller, and this meant that French infantry could not use British cartridges which they might find on their dead or wounded enemies, while British troops could, and did, use scavenged French ammunition. French powder was of significantly worse quality than British, which led to quicker fouling of the barrel and touch-hole. The normal way to rid a barrel of caked powder was to swill it out with hot water, but urine was almost as effective.

Dawn found the soldiers of both armies cold, damp and stiff. 'If I look half as bad as you do,' Captain William Verner of the British 7th Hussars said to a fellow officer, 'then I must be a miserable looking fellow!' Sergeant Duncan Robertson of the 92nd Highlanders reckoned 'I never felt colder in my life,' but revived a little when the battalion was issued with a gin ration. 'Everyone was covered with mud,' Assistant-Surgeon Haddy of the 1st Life Guards recalled:

And it was with the greatest difficulty that the men managed to get fires lit, some breakfast cooked, and their arms cleaned and their ammunition dried. Several hours passed quietly, the weather improved and later the sun came out ... mostly we were waiting and still.

'We were ordered to bridle up and prepare for action,' Assistant-Surgeon William Gilbey of the 15th Hussars remembered:

This we did in darkness, wet, and discomfort, but a night spent in pouring rain, sitting up to the hips in muddy water, with bits of straw hanging about him, does make a man feel and look queer

on first rising. Indeed, it was almost ludicrous to observe the
various countenances of us officers, as, smoking cigars and
occasionally shivering, we stood around a watch fire giving out
more smoke than heat. It was tedious work waiting for orders. We
were anxious to be put into motion, if it were only to circulate the
blood, for both horses and men were shaking with cold.

The Duke of Wellington left his quarters in Waterloo at 6 a.m. and rode the short distance to the ridge of Mont St Jean, pausing along the way to scrounge that mug of hot tea from Kincaid's riflemen. Once at the ridge he rode along the crest, inspecting the positions. He ordered more loopholes hacked through the big exterior wall of Hougoumont. Müffling, the Prussian liaison officer, was worried that the Duke had put so few men into the big château with its wide gardens, orchard and farm buildings. 'Ah you don't know Macdonell,' the Duke answered, 'I've thrown Macdonell into it.' Lieutenant-Colonel James Macdonell was a Scotsman, thirty-four years old, who had transferred to the Coldstream Guards in 1811. His task that Sunday was to defend Hougoumont with 1,500 guardsmen and 600 Dutch–German allies.

And so all along the ridge men tried to dry their uniforms and their ammunition, they snatched what small food they could find – some lucky soldiers discovered a plot of potatoes and dug them up – they cleaned their muskets, and they waited.

And they waited.

And still the French attack did not come.

* * *

Napoleon made the decision. His gunners declared the ground was too wet for their artillery. The big cannon would recoil with every shot and dig themselves into the morass and then it would be a fearful struggle to get the heavy guns back out of the sucking mud and pointing correctly again, and so the Emperor decided he would wait two or three hours and let the ground dry. There would still be time enough to destroy Wellington's army. Marshal Soult, the Emperor's Chief of Staff, suggested that it would be better to attack sooner for fear that the

Prussians might be coming, but Napoleon scorned the idea. The Prussians had been beaten, had they not? They could not possibly recover in time to assist Wellington and, besides, was not Marshal Grouchy occupying them?

The Emperor did not waste the hours as the ground dried. He knew the value of psychological warfare and so he deliberately set out to overawe the army waiting to his north. The tale is best told by one of Wellington's men, a corporal in the Royal Scots Greys. John Dickson was on picquet duty, posted on the crest of the ridge, just behind the hedged road that ran along the ridge's summit, and so some yards ahead of his regiment which was formed on the reverse slope, and he had a splendid view of the French display.

> *It was daylight, and the sun was every now and then sending bright flashes of light through the broken clouds. As I stood behind the straggling hedge and low beech trees that skirted the high banks of the sunken road on both sides, I could see the French army drawn up in heavy masses opposite me. They were only a mile from where I stood, but the distance seemed greater, for between us the mist still filled the hollows. There were great columns of infantry, and squadron after squadron of Cuirassiers, red Dragoons, brown Hussars, and green Lancers with little swallow tail flags on the end of their lances. The grandest sight was a regiment of Cuirassiers dashing at full gallop over the brow of the hill opposite me, with the sun shining on their steel breastplates. It was a splendid show ... No one who saw it could ever forget it.*
>
> *There was a sudden roll of drums along the whole of the enemy's line, and a burst of music from the bands of a hundred battalions came to me on the wind ... Then every regiment began to move. They were taking up position for the battle.*

They were also trying to overawe the British–Dutch army. To an extent it worked, some observers said that young untried troops stared pale-faced and trembling at the serried glory of France that was being paraded in the fitful sunlight, but others, veterans of the Peninsula, had seen it all before.

And still they waited. Nine o'clock, ten o'clock. Both armies had stood to their arms, the bands were playing, no one moved. Napoleon was still waiting for the ground to dry, though he took care to send new orders to Marshal Grouchy. Those orders were drawn up by Marshal Soult, and they were intended to make certain that Blücher had no chance of interfering with the day's great battle. The document was headed 'In front of the farm of Caillou, 18th June, 10 am', and it seemed Grouchy was still unsure exactly where the Prussians were, because Soult has to tell him that reports have finally arrived confirming that at least part of Blücher's army is heading for Wavre:

> *The Emperor directs me to tell you that at this moment his Majesty is going to attack the English army, which has taken position at Waterloo ... Thus his Majesty desires that you direct your movements on Wavre in order to draw near to us, place yourself in touch with our operations, and link up your communications with us, driving before you those portions of the Prussian army that have taken this direction and may have stopped at Wavre, where you should arrive as soon as possible. You will follow the enemy's column on your right, using some light troops to observe their movements and gather up their stragglers. Inform me immediately about your dispositions and your march, also about any news of the enemy, and do not neglect to link up your communications with us. The Emperor desires to have news from you very often.*

The order is worth quoting at length because it is almost impenetrable nonsense, and Grouchy, instead of asking for elucidation, seized on the single command to direct his movements towards Wavre. What Napoleon seemed to have wanted was for Grouchy to position his army between Blücher and the field of Waterloo. That would have drawn

Grouchy nearer to Napoleon, in which case the order to drive 'before you those portions of the Prussian army that have taken this direction' makes little sense, because Grouchy would merely be herding those Prussians towards Wellington. If Blücher had withdrawn to Wavre, and the document does not make it clear that the French were certain of this, then Grouchy should shadow them by keeping their 'column on your right', and that does make sense because, by keeping the Prussians to his right, to the east of him, Grouchy would be placing himself between Blücher and Napoleon. But Grouchy is also ordered to march to Wavre 'as soon as possible'. By marching directly on Wavre, which was the option Grouchy chose, the Prussians were not on his right but to his front and, increasingly, way off to his left. Between Wavre and Mont St Jean was a steep-banked defile through which the River Lasne flowed, and Grouchy's 33,000 men and 96 guns could have delayed an army ten times their size for hours at that obstacle. Yet presumably the French did not know of this defile, so did not ask Grouchy to defend it. Instead he was expected to direct his movements on Wavre, where he should arrive as soon as possible, and also drive the enemy before him, keep the enemy on his right, and draw near to Napoleon, and how was he to do all those contradictory things at once? Grouchy, who was already some miles east of Napoleon, decided his job was to march north to Wavre, and so he did, and that meant the country lanes and the deep Lasne valley between Wavre and Mont St Jean were undefended.

But what did it matter? Napoleon was certain that the Prussians could not join Wellington for at least two days, he believed he had nine chances in ten of winning the battle, and at last, close to eleven in the morning, the ground was reckoned firm enough to let the cannons fire.

And so it begins. You might think, with so many memoirs of the battle, so many eyewitnesses who were to record their memories of that dreadful day, that we would know exactly how and when the battle commenced, but some say it was a British cannon that fired first, and others that it was the French, and no one can agree on the time that one or other of those guns fired. The best estimate is that it was about twenty minutes past eleven, and that the cannon on the left of

Napoleon's line fired first. And once they did, the rest of the Emperor's beautiful daughters opened fire, wreathing the ridge of La Belle Alliance with thick powder smoke. Johnny Kincaid and his riflemen had taken post in the sandpit just across the road from La Haie Sainte, which was garrisoned by fine King's German Legion troops. His position, well forward of the British–Dutch line, gave him a splendid view of the battle's first moves. He saw a mass of blue-coated French infantry advancing through the woods towards Hougoumont, then the guns opened fire. 'A cannon ball came from the Lord knows where,' he said, 'and took the head off our right-hand man.' In front of him now were 'innumerable specks' which he recognized as artillery pieces. Those specks vanished behind their own smoke as the cannonballs rumbled overhead to strike the ridge's top.

We saw Buonaparte himself take post at the side of the road, immediately in our front, surrounded by a numerous staff; and each regiment, as they passed him, rent the air with shouts of 'Vive l'Empereur!', nor did they cease after they had passed; but, backed by the thunder of their artillery, and carrying with them the rubidub of drums, and the tantarara of trumpets, in addition to their increasing shouts, it looked, at first, as if they had some hope of scaring us off the ground.

It was, Kincaid said, 'in singular contrast to the stern silence reigning on our side'.

But the stern silence was over. The battle had begun.

* * *

Blücher decided to send his IV Corps to Wellington's aid first, which made sense because that part of his army had not been involved in the defeat at Ligny. It was battle-ready, unwounded, but, awkwardly, farthest away from Mont St Jean. It marched at dawn and almost immediately it ran into problems because a baker lighting his oven in Wavre managed to set his house and shop on fire. The only road wide enough to take the guns and ammunition wagons ran past the burning house.

The town's two fire engines, manual pumps, were dragged to the scene, and Prussian soldiers assisted in extinguishing the flames, but the fire delayed the march by at least two hours because the inferno was too hot to allow the ammunition wagons to pass safely.

The delay meant that the second Corps of Blücher's men to march were forced to wait while General von Bülow's IV Corps marched past. Blücher, meanwhile sent a messenger to Baron von Müffling, the liaison officer who was in close attendance to Wellington: 'I request your lordship to tell the Duke of Wellington, in my name, that, ill as I am, I intend to put myself at the head of my troops.' Blücher was still suffering from the fall from his horse at Ligny, but, as he wrote later, 'I would rather have been tied to my horse than miss the battle.' His Chief of Staff, von Gneisenau, was much more guarded, and added a cautionary note to the despatch asking von Müffling whether, in his opinion, Wellington really meant to fight or simply wanted Napoleon to turn on the arriving Prussians and use that distraction as a cover for his escape.

Once out of Wavre the roads to Mont St Jean were atrocious, mere country lanes that twisted across the hilly landscape. A local shepherd guided the troops, but the march was inevitably slow and difficult. 'Hollow tracks cut into deep defiles had to be negotiated,' Lieutenant-Colonel von Reiche, a staff officer, recalled:

> On each side were almost impenetrable woods so that we had no opportunity of avoiding the road. Progress was very slow, especially as at many places men and horses could only pass in single file and artillery moved only with enormous trouble. As a result the columns became extremely stretched and, wherever the ground permitted, the front of the column had to halt to give the rearmost men time to close up.

And ahead was the desperately difficult and steep ravine of the River Lasne, a place where a small body of French troops could have stopped an army in its tracks. But Blücher's cavalry patrols had already crossed the ravine and discovered it unguarded. The road to Waterloo was open.

And late morning, just after Blücher himself left Wavre to ride westwards, the sound of gunfire rolled across the hills.

Eight miles south of Wavre, Marshal Grouchy was finishing a late breakfast when he heard the guns. He abandoned his dish of strawberries and took his staff into the garden, where they listened to the distant sound. Some, perhaps suspecting they were hearing thunder, went on all fours and put their ears to the ground. It was gunfire they were hearing right enough, and it was coming from the west. General Gérard urged the Marshal to turn about and march towards the sound, but the Marshal dismissed the suggestion. 'It is merely an affair of the rearguard,' he responded, supposing that Wellington was retreating from Mont St Jean just as he had retreated from Quatre-Bras the day before. Gérard, who was an able and experienced soldier, insisted they should march towards the sound of gunfire, but Grouchy adamantly refused. Gérard was having a bad campaign. He commanded Napoleon's 4th Corps and it had been by his recommendation that General Louis-Auguste-Victor Bourmont was given a brigade in that Corps, and Bourmont, a Royalist, had deserted as soon as the French crossed the frontier. He had ridden to the Prussians, taking whatever he knew of Napoleon's intentions with him. Now Grouchy ignored Gérard's excellent advice. Grouchy had been ordered to 'direct your movements on Wavre', and so, breakfast over, he obeyed. He kept his troops marching north.

While 12 miles to the west the long day's killing had begun.

FROM TOP | *The French centre was at the tavern called La Belle Alliance, aquatint by James Rouse. A man standing by the tavern and looking north along the road would see the valley spread left and right in front of him.* | *Every other redcoat carried a Brown Bess musket, though in truth there was no such weapon: there were Land Pattern muskets, India Pattern muskets and New Land Pattern muskets, all carrying the nickname of Brown Bess. An expert marksman wrote: '... as to firing at a man at 200 yards with a common musket, you may as well fire at the moon.'* | *A French Infantry carbine, for officers, corporals and fouriers of the voltigeurs.*

ABOVE | '17th June 1815, 7 O'Clock', by John Lewis Brown. On the eve of the battle, Napoleon was still supremely confident. General Foy remembered Napoleon's prediction: 'We shall be only too glad if the English decide to stay because the battle that is coming will save France and be celebrated in world history!'

RIGHT | General Baron von Müffling, the Prussian liaison officer who was in close attendance to Wellington, was later promoted to Field Marshal. For a time he was commander of the allied garrison that occupied Paris, then he was appointed chief of the general staff of the Prussian military. He died in 1851.

Above | *Hougoumont, the aftermath: the disposal of the dead, aquatint by James Rouse. A visitor to the battlefield ten days after the fight saw the funeral pyres at Hougoumont: 'The pyres had been burning for eight days and by then the fire was being fed solely by human fat. There were thighs, arms and legs piled up in a heap and some fifty workmen, with handkerchiefs over their noses, were raking the fire and the bones with long forks.'*

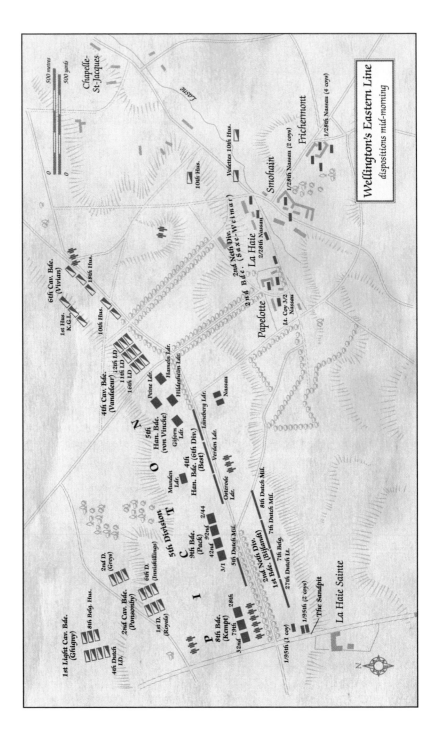

Wellington's Eastern Line
dispositions mid-morning

CHAPTER SEVEN

The Big Boots don't like
rough stuff!

S OME PEOPLE HAVE WONDERED why the Duke of Wellington did not fortify his low ridge top with earthworks, especially with bastions that could have protected his artillery from the Emperor's much larger number of cannon. It would have been difficult to make such bastions during the drenching rainstorms of Saturday night, but not impossible. Yet the Duke ordered no such earthworks, probably because the very last thing he wanted was to encourage Napoleon to manoeuvre around his position. The Duke wanted to be attacked head-on. In a straight infantry-versus-infantry fight the Duke had total confidence in both his redcoats and in his King's German Legion battalions. He had, as he told someone later, 'just enough of them', but too many of his infantrymen were untried and inexperienced, and expecting such troops to leave the comfort of their reverse slope and manoeuvre in open country under cannon fire and in the face of Napoleon's veterans was to invite panic and disaster. He feared that open right flank beyond Hougoumont and so he did nothing to make the ridge itself more formidable. He wanted an attack straight up the *chaussée*, a head-on fight.

Napoleon wanted to destroy Wellington's army, and he described his proposed tactics simply enough:

I shall have my artillery fire and my cavalry charge, so as to force the enemy to disclose his positions, and when I am quite certain which positions the English troops have taken up, I shall march straight at them with my Old Guard.

That was disingenuous. What he really planned was to weaken Wellington's line before he launched massive, hammer-blow attacks that would crash through the Duke's centre, which meant he was doing exactly what Wellington wanted him to do. The Emperor had declared it would all be over by lunch, but then he had waited to allow the ground to dry, so it would all be over by teatime instead.

So how to weaken the British–Dutch centre? First there were the guns, the great guns that could tear battalions into ragged ruin just as they had shattered the exposed Prussian infantry on the slopes above Ligny. Wellington placed most of his infantry behind the crest, which reduced the effectiveness of the bombardment, but the Emperor also planned a diversionary attack that would be pressed hard enough to persuade Wellington to reinforce the British–Dutch right wing at the expense of his centre. That meant attacking Hougoumont, the complex of buildings on Wellington's right flank, the fortress which Baron von Müffling feared was inadequately garrisoned. Napoleon reckoned that if he threatened to capture Hougoumont then Wellington would have no choice but to take troops from the ridge top to reinforce the garrison. Once those reinforcements had left the ridge then the real attack, the overwhelming attack, could be launched across the valley to capture Mont St Jean.

So the battle begins at Hougoumont, pitting Lieutenant-Colonel James Macdonell, a Coldstreamer, against His Majesty Jérôme I, by the Grace of God, King of Westphalia, Prince of France, Prince of Montfort, and he would have been none of those things had he not also been Napoleon's brother. He was the youngest of the family, but like all

Napoleon's siblings he had risen to unimaginable heights thanks to his brother's patronage. Joseph, the oldest child, became King of Spain, Lucien was Prince of Canino and Musignano, Elisa was Grand Duchess of Tuscany, Louis had been King of Holland, Pauline was the Princess Borghese, Caroline the Queen Consort of Naples, and Jérôme, briefly King of Westphalia, was now a General of Division in his brother's army. Relations between the two were often fraught, because Jérôme was a spendthrift wastrel. He was thirty-one years old in 1815, but his troubles with his brother began much earlier when, aged nineteen, he had met and married an American, Elizabeth Patterson from Baltimore. The marriage drove Napoleon into a fury. He needed his siblings to marry for dynastic reasons, not for something as trivial as love, and so he forbade Elizabeth to enter France and insisted his brother divorce her. Elizabeth, or Betsy as she was known, retreated to London, where her son, Jérôme Napoleon Bonaparte II, was born in Camberwell. The British, of course, were more than happy to shelter Betsy and use her story to embarrass the Emperor. 'You have much ambition,' Napoleon had written to Jérôme in 1809:

> some intelligence, a few good qualities, but are spoiled by stupidity, by great presumption, and have no real knowledge. In God's name keep enough wits about you to write and talk with propriety.

Four years later, after the reverses of the disastrous Russian campaign in which Jérôme had failed miserably, the Emperor let loose a much more damning judgment:

> You are hateful to me. Your conduct disgusts me. I know no one so base, so stupid, so cowardly; you are destitute of virtue, talents and resources.

Yet family loyalty overrode such judgments, and Jérôme had been entrusted with the leadership of the largest division of infantry in his brother's army, the 6th Infantry Division, with nearly 8,000 men, though 1,000 of those had been lost at Quatre-Bras. Now Jérôme had something to prove. He wanted to show his brother that he was not base, cowardly and spoiled by stupidity and, ordered to attack Hougoumont, he was determined to capture it.

Nothing wrong with that, except the capture of Hougoumont was not what Napoleon wanted. He wanted it besieged, and the siege should be fierce enough, and last long enough, to persuade Wellington to reinforce the château's garrison with troops from the ridge. Only when the siege had achieved that aim of weakening Wellington's line could it be captured, but Jérôme had other ideas. He would take Hougoumont! Jérôme's immediate superior was General Reille, an experienced soldier who had risen from the ranks and who, at Waterloo, had responsibility for most of Napoleon's left wing. It had been Reille who incurred the Emperor's wrath by offering his opinion that well-posted British infantry were well-nigh impregnable, and now Reille had to attack that infantry, and he began by ordering Jérôme to occupy the valley just south of Hougoumont's wood and then to push a strong line of skirmishers up into the trees.

The wood was a large stretch of mature trees, mostly oak, that grew to the south of the walled complex of Hougoumont. There were wild raspberries in the sparse undergrowth and forget-me-nots bright along the wood's edges. The ground rose steeply through the trees, so that any attack would be uphill into the face of the wood's defenders, 600 skirmishers from Hanover and from the Dutch–German Nassauers. The wood and the steep slope above from where the French began their attacks were also in range of the British–Dutch artillery posted on the high ground above the château.

It was late morning. Napoleon had originally wanted to begin the battle at 9 a.m., but he had waited for the ground to dry so it was after 11 a.m. when Jérôme's men advanced to capture the wood. General Reille's orders were specific enough, threaten Hougoumont, but neither Napoleon nor Reille wanted a major brawl that would suck in too many French troops. The main French effort would be against Wellington's left and centre, not against his right, but Jérôme wanted his victory, and when the first French troops discovered that the German skirmishers were formidable opponents, Jérôme fed in more men. General Foy, who commanded another division under Reille, called the wood a 'death-trap'. To reach it the French had to cross a stretch of open ground that was under artillery fire, and once in the wood they faced muskets and rifles. The defenders had the advantage of the high ground and had little need to expose themselves except when shooting. The French struggled up the hill to be shot back down again, and soon their wounded were being carried back across the valley. Captain de Vatry, one of Jérôme's staff officers, heard the men complaining that there were no more ambulances:

> This is what happened ... most of [the drivers] had never heard gunfire before, they became nervous under the fire of the English batteries, unharnessed the horses or cut the traces and galloped away.

Marshal Ney, who had been given charge of the day's attacks, sent a staff officer to discover what happened at Hougoumont, and there followed another misunderstanding. The aide was appalled when he discovered French infantry cowering behind trees and begging for help, and so he urged Jérôme to throw in his whole division, over 7,000 men. Jérôme hardly needed the encouragement. He sent in all his troops and then begged Reille for more. The fight for Hougoumont, far from draining Wellington's army of reserves, was now soaking up inordinate numbers of French infantry. But numbers counted, and as the thousands of blue-coated Frenchmen climbed through the bullet-scarred trees they inevitably pushed the defenders out of the wood. The fight had been going for about an hour and now, sometime after midday, Jérôme's men faced the real fortress itself, Hougoumont.

The complex of Hougoumont is perhaps best envisaged as three rectangles superimposed on each other. The largest rectangle was an apple orchard protected by a ditch and a hedge. The French, attacking from the south, could gain access to the orchard, but once inside they encountered the second and far more formidable rectangle, the walled formal garden. The garden must once have been the pride of Hougoumont, a lovely space of parterre flower beds cut by walks shaded by hornbeams and cherry trees. More important to Colonel Macdonell was that the formal garden was protected to the west by buildings, and to the south and east by a brick wall that was seven feet high. He constructed platforms behind the wall so that men could shoot over the coping, and the wall itself was loopholed. The third rectangle is the buildings to the west of the garden, and these really were formidable. The buildings were contiguous, so that they presented a solid wall of masonry. To the south, facing the French attack, were a gardener's house, a storeroom and, between them, a big arched gateway that had been closed and barricaded. The walls of those buildings were again loopholed, as were the buildings that faced west, the chief of which was a great barn. On the opposite side of the rectangle were cowsheds and stables that backed onto the formal garden, while in the centre of the rectangle was the château itself, a substantial and comfortable house with high windows from which men could shoot over the roofs of the other structures. A small chapel stood next to the house. The main farmyard was between the barn and the cowsheds and the main entrance to the whole complex was on the north side of that yard. This is the famous north gate which was to see one of the battle's most celebrated incidents.

A lane ran alongside the great barn separating the walled buildings from a small kitchen garden that was protected by a hedge and a fence. The whole complex of orchards, gardens, hedges, brick walls and stone buildings was, in the words of Lieutenant-Colonel Alexander Woodford, a Coldstreamer, 'well calculated for defence':

> *The dwelling-house in the centre was a strong square building, with small doors and windows. The barns and granaries formed nearly a square, with one door of communication with the small yard to the south; and from that yard was a door into the garden,*

*a double gate into the wood ... and another door opening into
the lane to the west. There was also another carriage gate at the
North West angle of the great yard.*

As the French emerged from the oak wood they faced this formidable range of walls and buildings. Immediately to their front they saw
the gardener's house, its windows spitting musket fire, while to its
right were 200 metres of the formal garden's high brick wall. The
distance from the wood's edge to the wall was about 30 yards, and it
was in that space that Jérôme's men died and suffered. One of the first
to be killed was General Bauduin, the commanding officer of Jérôme's
1st Brigade. Many of the German troops who had defended the wood
had now joined the garrison inside Hougoumont's walls, and one of
them, Private Johann Leonhard, fought from behind the loopholed
garden wall:

*We had scarcely taken up position at the loopholes when masses
of French came from the wood, all intent on capturing the farm,
but they were too late! The shower of balls that we loosed off on
the French was so terrible that the grass was soon covered with
French corpses. Their retreating and advancing went on!*

The Dutch–German troops who had defended the wood needed
to retreat into the complex of buildings. As there was no available
entrance facing the trees, they ran around the wall, and their under-
standable haste gave rise to the accusation that they had panicked and
run. Several British officers wrote scornfully that the Dutch troops
fled, but the evidence indicates that they joined the Guardsmen in the
formal garden which was now under siege as the French made desperate efforts to scale the wall. Jérôme's men charged repeatedly and were
repeatedly thrown back by muskets flaring from loopholes or from
the upper floors of the buildings. One of the German troops inside
the compound described the defenders' fire as 'murderous', and
because the range was so short, the musket fire was accurate. Thick

powder smoke wreathed the buildings and the upper wood, and the French, desperate to capture this great bastion, sent in yet another brigade of infantry. This was ghastly work. The French had not brought artillery to break down the walls, nor were they supplied with ladders to escalade the defences, yet still they charged. One French infantryman remembered the 'dead, dying and wounded lying in heaps'. Lieutenant-Colonel Francis Home of the 3rd Guards, the Royal Scots, described the slaughter in front of the wall as 'immense', and said that the French wounded, lying in those heaps, repeatedly asked him to 'order his men to fire upon them and put them out of their misery'. A battery of six British howitzers was also targeting the upper wood, shredding the oak trees with shrapnel and shell fragments that added to the carnage.

Over 9,000 French infantry were now trying to evict James Macdonell's defenders. Unable to scale the garden wall, the French tried to surround the buildings, sending men to the left and the right. The château was hard-pressed, but reinforcements came from the ridge above. Not from Wellington's centre, which was Napoleon's hope, but from the Guards battalions immediately behind the château. Wellington himself despatched some of those reinforcements with the words, 'There, my lads, in with you and let me see no more of you.' Two companies of Coldstreamers charged down the hill and, with fixed bayonets, scoured the French away from the eastern flank, then joined the garrison inside the walls. Other companies were sent down later until, according to Lieutenant-Colonel Home, 'the whole of the 3rd Regiment and eight companies of the Coldstream were employed in or near Hougoumont. The whole force employed there at any one time never exceeded 1,200 men', and those 1,200 men (to whom we should add the surviving Nassauers) were tying down at least 9,000 Frenchmen.

Private Matthew Clay, the guardsman whose inedible breakfast had been a scorched scrap of pig's head, was one of the men defending the small hedged kitchen garden that lay across the lane from the great barn. The garden was hardly defensible against the huge number of

Frenchmen who now tried to assault Hougoumont, and so the defenders were ordered back behind the walls, but Clay and another guardsman, 'a very steady and undaunted old soldier', managed to get separated from their company during this brief retreat. They were forced to stay outside the walls, where they exchanged shots with the enemy skirmishers:

> I unwisely ascended the higher part of a sloping ground on which the outside wall of the farm was built. I thought I would be able to single out the enemy's skirmishers ... but I very quickly found that I had become a target for them because my red coat was more distinctly visible ... I continued to exchange shots with the enemy across the kitchen garden, but they, having the advantage of the fence as a covering, their shots freely struck the wall in my rear ... my musket, now proving defective, was very discouraging but looking on the ground I saw a musket which I immediately took possession of in exchange for my own one. The new musket was warm from recent use and proved an excellent one.

After some minutes Clay noticed that a gate leading into the farm's yard was open and the two redcoats made a dash for it, reaching safety just after a number of Frenchmen had been killed in the gateway:

> the gates were riddled with shot holes ... in its entrance lay many dead bodies of the enemy. One which I particularly noticed appeared to be a French officer, but they were scarcely distinguishable, being to all appearance as though they had been very much trodden upon and covered with mud.

That French incursion through the gates was probably the first of two. Most accounts of the battle reckon that only one French assault succeeded in entering the walled compound, but Clay saw two and his account is reinforced by the memoirs of the German defenders. The struggle for Hougoumont is fierce and unrelenting, and it will last most of that long day, but for now we can leave besiegers and besieged because the great guns at the centre of Napoleon's line have opened fire, heralding the first major attack on Wellington's ridge. Hougoumont is by no means secure, the French will bring artillery to bear on the walls and there will be a savage crisis during the afternoon, but as the thunderous percussion of Napoleon's cannon fills the sky Macdonell's men are holding firm.

While in the centre of the Emperor's line the great guns are recoiling, spewing thick smoke into the valley and pounding Wellington's ridge with roundshot and shell. And the Peninsular veterans on that ridge recognized another sound, the *pas de charge*, the sound of drummers beating out the rhythm of assault, and a sound which announces that one of the greatest infantry attacks of the whole Napoleonic Wars is about to be launched.

* * *

The sound of Napoleon's guns pounded the air above the fields of Mont St Jean, and the same noise was rattling windows in Paris. A single cannon was firing from Les Invalides, the military hospital built by Louis XIV which also served as a retirement home for disabled veterans. There was no shot or shell loaded in the cannon; it was firing a salute, smothering the great parade ground with thick powder smoke. 'The gun at Les Invalides is firing!' remembered Émile Labretonnière, a student of mathematics. 'Do you hear it?' he asked the friend who shared his Paris apartment:

> 'It must be a great victory!' We got up at once and ran off to make enquiries. The gun was celebrating the victory the Emperor had gained over the Prussians at Ligny on June 16th. We went to the Café des Pyrénées to read the bulletin. We were wild with joy! The gun at Les Invalides brought back memories of the triumphs which had stirred our childhood. We were drunk with pride ... I remember the enthusiasm with which a student from Grenoble named Rousseau told us that Wellington had been captured and Blücher killed!

Emile had watched the army leave Paris in early June and had been hugely impressed. He described the departing troops as 'superb' and he believed they were 'so full of ardour' that they had to be invincible. He was elated at the news of Ligny, while the Royalists in Paris were downcast and spreading rumours that tried to undermine the Emperor's achievement. But that Sunday morning the gun at Les Invalides contradicted the Royalists' gloom, it told of victory, and Emile, like most Parisians, could not wait to hear of the Emperor's ultimate triumph. 'At last,' he wrote excitedly, 'the fight was on!'

He was right.

* * *

Napoleon and Wellington used their artillery differently. For a start the Emperor had far more guns at Waterloo, 246 cannon against Wellington's 157, and on the whole those guns were heavier. The French and Prussians both deployed 12-pounder cannon, while the heaviest British pieces were 9-pounders. The Emperor had trained as an artilleryman and he put great faith in his guns. He liked to assemble them in a Grand Battery and use them as an offensive, as against a defensive, weapon. At Wagram, in 1809, Napoleon had torn the heart out of an Austrian army with a Grand Battery of 112 guns. Now at Waterloo he concentrated 80 guns in another Grand Battery.

The French guns were defensive as well, of course, but Napoleon knew that any enemy position needed 'softening' before his troops assaulted. That was the job of the Grand Battery, to break apart enemy formations before his infantry or cavalry attacked them. Those assault troops would come under fire from the enemy artillery, so another task of Napoleon's guns was counter-battery fire, trying to destroy or disable the enemy's cannon.

Wellington chose not to concentrate his guns in a Grand Battery, instead scattering them along the whole of his line, where they were positioned to fire at any French assault. Essentially the British–Dutch guns are used defensively, and they were absolutely forbidden to engage in counter-battery fire. If an artillery unit started a duel with an enemy battery then they were likely to draw fire from other enemy guns and, inevitably, suffer from shattered wheels or broken carriages, rendering the cannon useless until repairs could be made. Captain Mercer discovered this for himself when he disobeyed orders and opened fire on a French battery that was annoying him:

> I ventured to commit a folly, for which I should have paid dearly, had our Duke chanced to be in our part of the field. I ventured to disobey orders, and open a slow deliberate fire at the battery, thinking with my 9-pounders soon to silence his 4-pounders. My astonishment was great, however, when our very first gun was responded to by at least half-a-dozen gentlemen of very superior calibre, whose presence I had not even suspected, and whose superiority we immediately recognised … I instantly saw my folly, and ceased firing, and they did the same – the 4-pounders alone continuing the cannonade as before. But this was not all. The first man of my troop touched was by one of those confounded long shots. I shall never forget the scream the poor lad gave when struck. It was one of the last they fired and shattered his left arm to pieces.

Mercer was indeed lucky the Duke did not see his attempt at counter-battery fire. Later in the day, when Wellington did see one of his batteries try the same thing, he ordered the arrest of the battery commander. And right at the beginning of the day, when the French paraded their troops as they waited for the ground to dry, another British battery commander saw Napoleon reviewing his army on the far ridge. Wellington happened to be close by and the commander asked permission to try a shot that might kill the Emperor and was very tartly told that the commanders of armies had better things to do than fire at each other. Permission denied. The British–Dutch guns were there to defend the ridge, not assault the enemy's position, let alone assassinate Emperors.

Napoleon did use his guns offensively, and around 1 p.m. in the afternoon he ordered the Grand Battery to start its bombardment of Wellington's position. Half the battery was the big 12-pounder cannons, the rest either 8-pounders or 6-inch howitzers. Mercer spoke of being attacked by 4-pounders, but the French had none, so his assailants were either 6-pounders, the smallest French calibre at Waterloo, or perhaps 5½-inch howitzers. The howitzers would prove deadly that day because of their ability to fire over obstacles, in this case the ridge which sheltered the majority of Wellington's troops.

The Grand Battery was on the right of Napoleon's position, the guns positioned well forward on the slope facing the British–Dutch army. Their target was the left side of Wellington's ridge, from La Haie Sainte across to the smaller fortress of Papelotte, and their job was to wear the defenders down with roundshot and shell. In letter after letter, diary after diary, soldiers of the era talk of the horror of such bombardments. The infantry could only suffer as the great missiles ripped into their ranks and the shells exploded, but that was why Wellington always tried to post his men on a reverse slope. It did not wholly shelter them, but it did mitigate much of the Grand Battery's effect.

The range was short, between 650 and 870 yards (600 and 800 metres), and the guns were huge. A 12-pounder weighed almost 2 tons and needed a crew of fifteen men who had to reposition the monster after each firing because of the massive recoil. A well-trained crew could fire two shots a minute, though that was rare and, in the muddy conditions of Waterloo, almost impossible to maintain. Mark Adkin, in his indispensable book *The Waterloo Companion*, reckons that the Grand Battery fired around 4,000 roundshot and shells at the eastern section of Wellington's ridge in the half-hour before the infantry attacked. That sounds like a considerable weight of metal, but the target area was wide, deep, and much of it was hidden from the gunners. Those reverse slopes protected the British–Dutch infantry, though the protection they offered was certainly not complete. Lieutenant-Colonel Francis Home, before being sent to reinforce Hougoumont's garrison, was positioned on the right of the ridge, above the château, and other French guns were also cannonading that part of Wellington's line. For a time those guns did little damage – 'they had not gotten our range,' Home said, 'and firing rather high, their shot flew over us' – but gradually the French gunners adjusted the elevating screws on their cannons and the shots began to land among the redcoats who had been ordered to lie down. One round-shot 'dreadfully lacerated' Lieutenant Simpson, 'he however remained perfectly sensible and aware of his situation. His only request then was to be put out of his pain but lived till evening.'

If Wellington had not sheltered his troops, if, like Blücher at Ligny, he had kept them visible to the French gunners, the slaughter would have been gruesome, but the French artillerymen could only guess where the infantry was concealed and try to skim the ridge top in hopes that their roundshot would land among their enemies. 'The gunners were standing in line,' a French officer wrote of the Grand Battery,

> *inserting the charges, ramming them home and swinging the slow matches to make them burn more fiercely … Behind them stood the captains of the guns, nearly all of them elderly and they gave their orders as if on parade. Eighty guns fired together, drowning out every other sound. The whole valley was filled with smoke. A second or two later the clear calm voices of the captains could be heard again; 'Load! Ram! Arm! Fire!' This continued without break for a half an hour. We could scarcely see our comrades while across the valley the English had also opened fire. We could hear the whistle of their cannon balls in the air, the dull thud when they struck the ground and that other sound as muskets were smashed to matchwood and men hurled twenty paces to the rear, every bone crushed.*

Accuracy was difficult. The artillery was not rifled, so windage affected every shot, and then there was the smoke. There was little wind that day, so the smoke lingered in the damp air and after the first shot it is doubtful that the French gunners could see their targets at all clearly, but they knew the range and the gun captains would check the barrel's elevation before each shot. In 1835 the British tested artillery from the Napoleonic Wars and discovered that at 600 yards they struck their target almost nine times out of ten, though accuracy dropped off sharply as the range lengthened. The test targets were board fences that simulated infantry in line, which is a generous test, and against a smaller target, such as a single field gun, accuracy was much harder to attain. But if a roundshot did find its target the damage could be horrific. At Waterloo one French 12-pounder ball, 4¾ inches in diameter, killed or wounded twenty-six men in one strike. Fortunately for the British–Dutch forces most of the Grand Battery's cannonade was frustrated by Wellington's use of the reverse slope.

There were roughly 15,000 British–Dutch–German troops in the area that was bombarded by the Grand Battery, but nearly all of them were concealed behind the crest of the ridge. The French knew they were there, even if they could not see them. They could see some officers and skirmishers ahead of the battalions, and there were plenty of men in Napoleon's army who knew Wellington's habit of posting men out of sight, but the few men in sight, along with the artillery posted on the forward slope, were small and difficult targets. Napoleon's artillerymen wanted to weaken the defenders' line, and that was almost impossible for the cannon, though howitzers, by dropping their shells just beyond the crest, were more dangerous.

The noise was huge. Eighty guns, even if only firing once a minute, would fill the air with a percussive pounding, and other guns besides those in the Grand Battery were joining the cacophony. Smoke thickened in front of the blackened muzzles, and blast flattened the rye in great fans in front of each cannon. One soldier described the sound of the roundshot going overhead as being like the noise of a heavy barrel of ale being rolled across a wooden floor above his head; indeed the noise was so deafening that some men thought another huge thunderstorm had broken across the Belgian countryside.

The bombardment was, as an officer of the 92nd said, 'horrendous', but casualties were few. The infantry were either lying down, or sitting, and the thick mud helped. Howitzer shells buried themselves, muffling the effects of the explosion, and one Hanoverian officer noted that 'the number of casualties would have been much higher had not the rain softened the soil so that the cannon balls lost much of their lethal force that they could have kept by bouncing off hard soil.' Yet some shots found targets. Captain Friedrich Weiz reported that the allied artillery suffered severely:

Three guns of a recently arrived battery were smashed before firing a single shot, and one of this battery's caissons blew up just as it was passing near the front of the 1st battalion. With the caisson ablaze its horses panicked and hauled it straight towards the large artillery park from where it had come. A huge disaster was averted when some dragoons rode up in a hurry and, while racing alongside, stabbed and brought down the horses.

The veterans in the allied ranks had seen and heard such cannonades before, though rarely with such intensity, but the noise, the smoke and the screams of wounded men and horses had an effect on troops new to combat. And one brigade seems to have been especially affected, Bylandt's Brigade of Dutch and Belgian battalions. Most histories of Waterloo recount that they were mistakenly left on the forward slope and so suffered extraordinary casualties that eventually broke them so that they fled, but in fact they had been withdrawn from their forward position and were posted just behind the ridge's crest. In front of them was the road which ran along the ridge, and that road had thick hedges. Lieutenant Isaac Hope, the officer who described the cannonade as 'horrendous', said that the hedges 'afforded [Bylandt's men] no shelter from the enemy's fire, yet concealed them from their view'.

In front of the road, on the forward slope, the British guns were entirely exposed to the French cannonade. There were thirty-four guns there, served by around a thousand men. A thousand sounds a lot, but in addition to the gun crews who loaded, fired and repositioned the cannon, men were needed to bring ammunition from the caissons parked to the rear. Those men were exposed to the enemy's fire, but continued their own bombardment, which was aimed, not at the smoke-wreathed Grand Battery, but beyond it to where d'Erlon's Corps was assembling for their assault. Eighteen thousand French infantry were on the far ridge, and the Dutch–British guns were shooting into their thick ranks.

The heaviest British guns were 9-pounders, but they were supplemented by 6-pounders and by howitzers. The British tended to use their howitzers as cannon, firing on a fairly flat trajectory, while the French often elevated a barrel as much as 30°. At Waterloo the British howitzers were not needed to lob shells over obstacles because the French did not use Wellington's reverse-slope tactic, so the howitzers were firing directly at the infantry beyond the swirling clouds of smoke. The British guns were firing a mix of shells, roundshot, and Britain's 'secret' weapon, the spherical case-shot.

The French knew all about spherical case, but never managed to duplicate it. It was the invention of Henry Shrapnel, a Royal Artillery officer, and was simply a shell designed to explode above the enemy and shower him with musket balls. When it was good it was very good, but when it was bad it was horrible. In 1813, in the Peninsula, a single shrapnel round killed every horse and man of a French gun crew, but the friction between the musket balls and the powder inside the case was sometimes so intense that the case-shot exploded inside the gun barrel. That problem was not to be solved for half a century, but fortunately for the gunners it did not happen frequently and Shrapnel's spherical case-shot was reliable enough. It was only effective if the gunner cut the fuse to the right length, a skill that also applied to shells. A shell was simply a round iron ball filled with gunpowder that was ignited by a fuse. The fuse was a length of cord which protruded from the shell and was lit by the gun's firing. Cut a fuse too short and the shell would explode in mid-air, doing no damage; cut it too long and the shell would land with its fuse spitting sparks, and a brave man could extinguish it. Cut to the right length, and that length depended on the distance of the target from the gun, the shell would explode and scatter fragments of its casing for up to twenty yards. All the gunners at Waterloo were experts at cutting fuses, but many men on both sides reported that the shells were rendered less effective because of the mud. Major Jean-Baptiste

Lemonnier-Delafosse, a staff officer, was on the French left, a long way from where the Grand Battery was firing at the British ridge. He was watching the fight at Hougoumont and just behind him was a brigade of carabiniers, heavy cavalry who, like the cuirassiers, wore breastplates and had big thigh-length riding boots. The hill where Lemonnier-Delafosse was posted was under fire from the British–Dutch guns above Hougoumont, and many of their shots fell among that cavalry. 'To escape their range,' Lemonnier-Delafosse recalled:

> this brigade moved to the left which made General Foy laugh, 'Ha! The Big Boots don't like rough stuff!' We received the cannon balls standing firm. They smothered us in mud and the soaked ground, by conserving the tracks of their paths, looked like a field rutted by cart wheels. This was lucky for us because many of the projectiles buried or muffled themselves while rolling along the muddy soil.

The cannonade over Hougoumont is a reminder that the battle of Waterloo was not a series of discrete events like the acts of a play. The battle is often described that way, with Act One the assault on Hougoumont and Act Two the attack by d'Erlon's Corps, but of course the two events coincided. While d'Erlon's Corps is threatening Wellington's left there is also smoke, gunfire and death on Wellington's right. The Duke is assailed by all this. He can see little because of the smoke, and almost nothing of what happens at Hougoumont is visible because a swell of land hides the château from his command position on the ridge. French roundshot and shell are flying near him, and the noise is pounding the eardrums, not just the noise of guns and exploding shells, but screams from the wounded, drummers on the far ridge and, on both ridges, the regimental bands playing. One officer described the air as 'undulating' from the passage of the shells and roundshot, and already that air was heating from the blast of the great guns. In time it would be described as like walking into an oven. The Duke's great gift was to remain calm in this turmoil, to filter out what was unthreatening and to concentrate on what was essential. He knows that a great attack is about to be launched on his left and he has ridden along that part of the ridge to inspect the troops who will be attacked, but he is content to let General Picton, who commands that wing, deal with the threat. He knows and trusts Picton, just as he trusts Macdonell in Hougoumont. He is watching the far ridge, using his telescope, trying to read what Napoleon intends, but he is also turning that spyglass to the east.

And so is Napoleon, because both men are waiting for reinforcements. Wellington knows he needs Blücher's troops, indeed he would never have made this stand on Mont St Jean's low ridge if he did not have the Prussian's promise to come to his aid. Napoleon is looking for Grouchy's Corps, those 33,000 men with their 96 guns who will give him an overwhelming edge in numbers and so lead to victory over the man who carries the impertinent description of the conqueror of the world's conqueror.

And far off to the east, from whence help will come to one side or the other, troops are visible.

* * *

Those troops are 6 miles away and the day is overcast, sometimes showery. The Duke of Wellington reckoned he put on and took off his cloak fifty times that day as rain swept across the battlefield. Even on a clear day it would have been difficult to see who those far troops were, but on that rainy, smoke-shrouded day it was impossible. All that could be seen were horsemen in dark uniforms coming from a wood. But Napoleon already knew who they were.

They were Prussians, the advance guard of von Bülow's Corps, and Napoleon knew because one of his cavalry patrols had captured a Prussian officer who had been carrying a message to Wellington. The messenger was brought to Napoleon and told the Emperor that the Prussian army had spent an undisturbed night at Wavre, where they had seen no French troops. 'We suppose they have marched on Plancenoit,' the messenger said, meaning that the Prussians had assumed that Grouchy, instead of pursuing them, had turned back to join Napoleon. Plancenoit was the big village behind Napoleon's right wing.

Napoleon would already have realized that Grouchy had done no such thing. Grouchy had sent a message early that morning, and the message was almost as confused as the orders Napoleon had despatched to Grouchy:

> *Sire, all the reports and information confirm the fact that the enemy is retiring on Brussels, either to concentrate there or to give battle after joining Wellington … fortunately the weather in the night was so wretched that they cannot have advanced very far … I am going to start immediately for Sart-à-Walhain from where I shall proceed to Corbais and Wavre.*

In other words Grouchy had no real idea where the Prussians were, or what they were doing, and he was moving north under the impression that they were marching from Wavre towards Brussels. He was certainly in no position to stop Blücher marching to Mont St Jean. Napoleon must have known all this. The Prussians were coming to Wellington's help, they were in sight, and Grouchy was still marching on Wavre. But the Emperor's reply to Grouchy, dictated to Marshal Soult, was astonishingly complacent:

> *Your movement from Corbais to Wavre agrees with His Majesty's arrangements. Nevertheless the Emperor requests me to tell you that you must keep manoeuvring in our direction and seek to draw near to our army before any corps places itself between us. I do not point out any particular direction to you.*

Once again the meaning is, at best, opaque. The Emperor approves of Grouchy taking his troops north towards Wavre, but at the same time suggests he manoeuvres westwards to prevent Blücher's men from joining Wellington. But before the despatch was sent Marshal Soult added an urgent and more cogent postscript:

> *A letter which has just been intercepted tells us that General Bülow is to attack our right flank. We believe we can see that*

corps ... Therefore do not lose a minute to draw nearer to us and crush Bülow who you will catch in the very act.

'Do not lose a minute to draw nearer to us.' That is clear enough, an instruction for Grouchy to hurry west towards the Emperor's battle and attack the Prussians as they close on Napoleon's right wing, but that despatch did not reach Grouchy until late in the afternoon, by which time he was fighting the rearguard that Blücher had left in Wavre. Grouchy's 33,000 men and 96 guns were winning a victory, but it meant nothing because the real battle, the deciding battle, was happening to their west.

Grouchy will be no help to Napoleon. It is unclear when the Emperor realized that those 33,000 men were not coming to support him, but it should have been obvious from around 1 p.m. The Prussians are in sight and Grouchy is not. Napoleon now faces a dilemma. He has Wellington's army in front of him, but he must have known that a heavy force of Prussians was approaching to his right. He will be greatly outnumbered, yet he still insisted that he had a good chance of winning the battle. 'This morning we had ninety chances of winning,' the Emperor told Soult, 'we still have sixty.' A more prudent general might have thought of disengaging and retreating southwards, then looking for another chance to divide the allies, but Napoleon believed he had victory in his grasp. All he needed to do was shatter Wellington's line, put the British–Dutch to panicked flight, then turn to face the new enemy. Blücher's men were still far away, the vanguard about 6 miles distant, but the rest had to be in columns of march strung along narrow country lanes. It would take a long time for those columns to reach Mont St Jean and even more time for the arriving troops to arrange themselves for a fight. The Emperor believed he had enough time, but nevertheless he sent 3,500 cavalry, 7,000 infantry and 28 guns to make a new line facing east that could defend his right flank against any Prussian assault. The battle has scarcely begun and Napoleon's plan is to attack the British head-on, yet already 9,000 men are tangled in the fight at Hougoumont, and now more men are being sent to the opposite flank. The Emperor had hoped to force Wellington to send reinforcements to Hougoumont, thus weakening the centre of his line, but instead it is the French who are using up their reserves to reinforce their flanks.

Yet even so, in the early afternoon, Napoleon still reckons he can destroy Wellington's army before the Prussians get involved, and the immediate instruments of that destruction are the four attack columns of d'Erlon's Corps.

The cannons of the Grand Battery ceased firing because 18,000 infantrymen were marching through the gun line. The cannon would not start firing again until those infantry had descended into the valley and it was safe to fire over their heads, but that would take some time, because the battalions had filed through the guns and now they had to form their attack columns. Sergeants shouted, officers checked the dressing of the ranks, and the British–Dutch roundshot ripped through files and the shells cracked apart in gouts of flame and vicious scraps of casing.

Then they were ready. The drums began again, beating the *pas de charge*, the Eagles flew bright above the tricolour flags, the guns of the Grand Battery readied to open fire again, and the four mighty columns marched to the attack.

FACING PAGE, CLOCKWISE FROM TOP | 'View from Mont St Jean of the Battle of Waterloo, 1816'.
The sound of Napoleon's guns pounded the air above the fields of Mont St Jean. | *An 1817 aquatint,*
'Delineated under the inspection of Officers who were present at that memorable Conflict', showing
the intensity of the battlefield. | *'Portrait of Count Jean-Baptiste Drouet d'Erlon', by Ary Scheffer:*
d'Erlon's superior numbers and crack troops came within a whisker of breaking Wellington's army. |
Portrait of Jérôme Bonaparte, by François Joseph Kinson. Jérôme wanted to show that he was not
base, cowardly and spoiled by stupidity and, ordered to attack Hougoumont, he was determined to
capture it.

OVERLEAF | 'The Battle of Waterloo', by Denis Dighton. *French hussars and Polish lancers fighting*
British infantry.

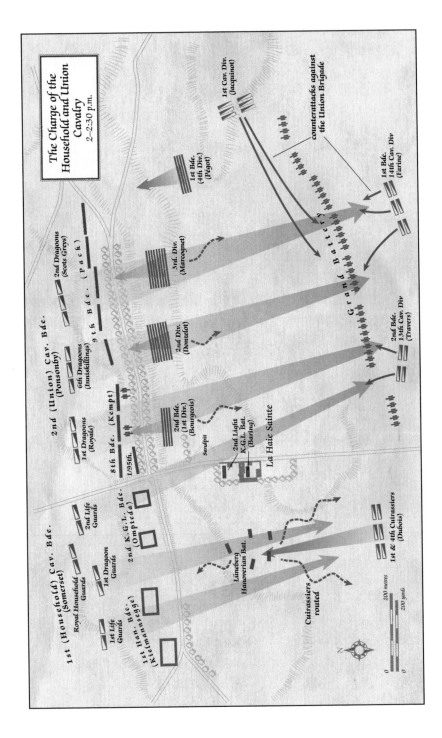

The Charge of the Household and Union Cavalry
2–2:30 p.m.

1st (Household) Cav. Bde. (Somerset)
1st Life Guards
Royal Household Guards
2nd Life Guards
1st Dragoon Guards
2nd K.G.L. Bde. (Ompteda)
1st Han. Bde. (Kielmansegge)

2nd (Union) Cav. Bde. (Ponsonby)
1st Dragoons (Royals)
6th Dragoons (Inniskillings)
2nd Dragoons (Scots Greys)

8th Bde. (Kempt)
1/95th.
9th Bde. (Pack)

Lüneberg Hanoverian Bat.
2nd Light K.G.L. Bat. (Baring)
La Haie Sainte
Sandpit
2nd Bde. (1st Div.) (Bourgeois)
2nd Div. (Donzelot)
3rd. Div. (Marcognet)

1st Bde. (4th Div.) (Pégot)

1st Cav. Div. (Jacquinot)

counterattacks against the Union Brigade

G r a n d   B a t t e r y

1st Bde. 14th Cav. Div (Farine)
2nd Bde. 13th Cav. Div (Travers)

Cuirassiers routed
1st & 4th Cuirassiers (Dubois)

N

0   200 metres
0   200 yards

180

CHAPTER EIGHT

Those terrible grey horses, how they fight!

GENERAL JEAN-BAPTISTE DROUET, COUNT d'Erlon, had something to prove. His escapades on 16 June, when he had marched his 1st Corps from one battlefield to the other and had engaged the enemy on neither, had infuriated Napoleon. But all that would be forgiven and forgotten if he broke through Wellington's line. And by chance his great attack would be launched against the weaker half of the Duke's position.

Wellington's concern for his right flank had persuaded him to make that wing almost twice as strong as the eastern side, and so his strongest forces and most of his guns were all west of the great highway to Brussels, and d'Erlon's Corps was now attacking the eastern side. There were 18,000 infantrymen marching in the four columns, and again it is worth remembering that 'column' is a misleading word. It suggests an elongated formation with the narrow end aimed like a spear at the enemy's line, while in truth it was much more like a brick advancing sideways, and d'Erlon's assault was made by four such bricks, each one a division of French infantry. They did not advance together, but in echelon, with General Quiot's 1st Division leading the way on the left.

Quiot's men were marching close to the highway, indeed some of them straddled the road, and those men would attack the King's German Legion garrison in La Haie Sainte as well as the ridge beyond. They were protected by 800 cuirassiers, heavy cavalry, who rode on their left flank. Quiot's Division would strike Wellington's line first, quickly followed by the 2nd, 3rd and 4th Divisions one after the other. The 2nd was just to Quiot's right, and so on to the 4th Division, which would assault the eastern end of the ridge with some men attacking the strong farmstead of Papelotte. Thus the assault covered the whole of Wellington's eastern line from La Haie Sainte to Papelotte. More cavalry rode on the outer flank of the 4th Division.

In all there were thirty-three French battalions marching across the valley, and waiting for them were seventeen allied battalions: five from the Dutch army, four Hanoverian and, crucially, eight experienced British battalions. The statistic is misleading because French battalions were usually smaller than British, around 550 men as against 650, but the French do have an advantage in total numbers. Four of the attacking battalions were drawn into separate fights on the flanks, either to assault La Haie Sainte or Papelotte, but the vast majority of d'Erlon's Corps were aiming for the bare hilltop that stretched for three-quarters of a mile between those two makeshift fortresses.

It looked like a bare hilltop. True, there were those allied guns on the forward slope, but beyond those cannon all that the attacking infantry could see were the hedges lining the road which ran along the ridge's summit. The hedges were no great obstacle. Captain von Rettburg, of the King's German Legion artillery, recorded that sections of the hedges had been cut down to allow guns and troops to pass through. Between the hedges was the shallow sunken road, then the gentle reverse slope where most of the defenders waited, either lying flat or sitting to avoid the roundshot skimming the ridge's crest.

Typically a French battalion in column would be two companies wide and nine ranks deep, which meant there were about sixty men in each rank, but for this assault d'Erlon ordered his four divisions to form their columns in an unusual configuration. Each battalion would be in line, a normal three-deep French line, and then the battalions would be stacked one behind the other to form a gigantic rectangle. Thus General Marcognet's Third Division had eight battalions in line, making 24 ranks, three for each battalion. The Division went into battle about 4,000 strong, so each of the 24 ranks had approximately 160 soldiers. In truth the ranks were slightly shorter because the eight battalions sent their skirmishers forward to scour ahead of the column, but those light troops would rejoin their battalions when the clash came at the ridge's crest. Twenty-four ranks containing between 150 and 160 men each form a massive column, and such a formation was unusual, though not unknown. Why did d'Erlon choose it? Like many other French officers at Waterloo, he had faced British infantry in the Peninsula, and he knew that the two-deep British line gave the redcoats a wide frontage and allowed every musket to be used against the head of the column, which could only offer a sparse reply because most of the men were deep inside the formation and unable to fire.

So how could a column defeat such a line? One answer was to hope that the line had been weakened by artillery and by skirmishers, but the reverse slope had taken away much of the artillery's effectiveness and the French skirmishers had to deal with the British–Dutch skirmishers, so d'Erlon must have known his men would have to face those lethal British lines. The answer to the problem was to combine line and column. The column's leading battalion was already in line, a French line three ranks deep, and every man in that line could use his musket, while the following battalions could be marched sideways, like sliding doors, to extend the line to left and right. French doctrine insisted that a column should always deploy into line at the moment of attack, but that deployment was often a moment of weakness, especially when faced by disciplined troops in a wider line who could fire inwards from their flanks, and this unusual formation seemed to promise a solution. The leading battalion, after all, did not need to deploy, but could use its volley fire to shelter the succeeding battalions as they spread wider.

But before that theory could be put to the test they had to reach the crest of the British ridge, and to do that they needed to cross the wide valley under fire from the allied artillery. The British and Dutch guns on the forward slope were being offered an unmissable target, and their solid roundshot slashed through French ranks, shrapnel exploded overhead and, as the French struggled further forward, they were hit by canister.

Canister was the most effective anti-personnel weapon available to Napoleonic armies. It was simple and nasty, merely a tin can filled with musket balls. There were two types, heavy and light, the difference being in the weight of the balls inside the can. When a round of canister was fired the can split apart at the gun's muzzle and the musket balls spread out, turning the cannon into a giant shotgun. Gunners frequently double-shotted their weapons, firing canister and a roundshot together. Canister was a short-range weapon, useless above 600 yards, while the British generally reserved its use until the range had shortened to about 350 yards, at which distance the cone of spreading balls would be just over 100 feet wide. Some, of course, were wasted in the air or on the ground, but at short range, against massed formations, canister was a fearsome weapon. D'Erlon's Corps was fortunate that there were only thirty-six allied cannon facing them and some of those had already been disabled, but those that remained did immense damage to the French. Captain von Rettburg, the King's German Legion gunner officer, watched as his 9-pounders tore huge holes in the nearest French column. That column was to his right, so he could fire across the huge formation and he saw how the French lost cohesion as their ranks were mowed down by roundshot and canister. The death those guns delivered was savagely effective, but they were too few to check the advance of the great columns. A rough estimate would suggest that the allied guns were able to deliver about 600 rounds, either roundshot, shell, spherical case or canister, at the advancing French.

Captain Pierre-Charles Duthilt was an officer in the 45th Regiment which had the dubious honour of being the leading battalion in General Marcognet's column, the third to march forward. 'Our turn came,' he wrote:

*and the order to attack was greeted with a fervent shout of Vive
l'Empereur! The four columns moved down the slope … with
ported arms. We were to climb the opposite slope where the
English held the ridge and from where their batteries blasted us.
The distance was not great and an average person on foot might
have taken no more than five or six minutes to cover the ground,
but the soft, rain-soaked earth and the tall rye slowed our
progress considerably. As a result the English gunners had plenty
of time to destroy us.*

Louis Canler, the young conscript whose breakfast had been
flavoured with gunpowder, was in the 28th Regiment of the Line in the
1st Division, the one closest to the highway. He saw d'Erlon position
himself at the centre of the columns and heard the General shout,
'Today you must conquer or die!'

*The shout of Vive l'Empereur came from every mouth in reply to
this brief speech and with the drummers beating the charge the
columns moved off … At that moment the enemy batteries which
had only sent cannon-balls and shells decimated our columns
with canister. We had scarcely gone one hundred paces when the
commander of our second battalion, Marins, was mortally
wounded. The Captain of my company, Duzer, was struck by two
balls. Adjutant Hubaut and Eagle-bearer Crosse were killed … at
the second discharge of the English guns the grenadiers'
drummer, Lecointre, lost his right arm.*

Lecointre kept beating his drum with his left hand until he collapsed
from loss of blood, though he survived the battle. Like all the French
drummers he was beating the *pas de charge*, the rhythm that always
accompanied French attacks. A young British officer remembered the
rhythm as 'the rum dum, the rum dum, the rummadum dummadum,
dum, dum', followed by a pause in which the massed troops would
shout '*Vive l'Empereur!*' Captain Johnny Kincaid, waiting with his rifle-

men in the sandpit which lay close to La Haie Sainte, remembered the rattle of those ominous drums, backed by the blare of trumpets and punctuated by shouts of 'Vive l'Empereur', and over it all was the deafening pounding of the big guns. This was the cacophony of battle. It was as if, Kincaid reckoned, the French had hopes 'of scaring us off the ground' by noise alone.

The French officers, Canler remembered, were forever shouting 'Close ranks!'

> The third discharge reduced the frontage of our battalion to that of a company. The dreadful command of 'Close ranks!' was heard again. This command, far from bringing dread or despair to our hearts, encouraged a totally opposite effect. It boosted our courage and inspired not only the idea of victory but of avenging our unfortunate comrades who were dying in front of us.

Canler reckoned it took the column twenty minutes to cross the wet, rye-thick ground, a walk that Captain Duthilt supposed should only take five or six minutes, yet slow as the advance was, Duthilt still felt that the French were hurrying too much, risking indiscipline, because of the fervour they felt:

> The haste and enthusiasm were becoming dangerous because the soldiers still had a long march before meeting the enemy and were soon tired out by the difficulty of moving on the heavy, churned soil which tore off gaiter straps and even took off shoes. There was soon disorder in the ranks, especially as the head of the column came within range of the enemy fire.

It took fifteen or twenty minutes to cross the valley, and for all that time the columns were being raked by roundshot, by shell and by canister, but still they marched, uphill now, though the slope was gentle. A battle was already being fought ahead of the columns where the skirmishers of both sides were shooting at each other, but as the huge columns closed on the ridge's crest the French skirmishers fell back to join their parent battalions. They had driven back the allied skirmishers, but did not cross the crest to fire on the troops beyond. That would be the job of the great columns.

The allied gunners deliver a last blast of canister to rip bloody holes in the approaching ranks, then the gunners abandoned their cannon and ran back to shelter with the infantry beyond the crest. One British gunner sergeant panicked and spiked his gun by hammering an iron nail into the touch-hole for fear that the enemy would capture and use the weapon. The allied guns are quiet now, and then the French cannon cease fire for fear of hitting their own infantry, who are now almost at the ridge's top. On the left French troops have succeeded in driving the King's German Legion riflemen out of La Haie Sainte's orchard and into the farm buildings, where a small battle like that fought at Hougoumont flares up. La Haie Sainte is surrounded by a high stone wall, but it has few loopholes. Nevertheless the German garrison holds a much larger number of enemy at bay. Slender Billy, the Prince of Orange, sees the farm threatened and sends a Hanoverian battalion to help and, just as at Quatre-Bras, he insists the battalion forms line. The battalion advances on the right of the main road, the opposite side from where the columns are nearing the hilltop, but that flank of the French is covered by 800 cuirassiers. The Hanoverians see the cavalry too late and are destroyed, their colour lost.

But the fight at La Haie Sainte is not the crucial battle. The Germans inside are besieged, but the French, though they surround the farm, have no means of escalading the walls or forcing the stout gates. The barn doors are missing, but the Legion has barricaded the entrance and keep the French at bay. On the other flank the defenders of Papelotte are driven out by sheer weight of numbers, but again that is not crucial. Victory will come only if the columns reach the crest and pierce the Duke's line.

The guns of the Grand Battery have stopped firing and their huge clouds of gun smoke slowly drift eastwards to clear the view across the valley. And the French see victory. They see the mass of blue uniforms reach the crest. Behind them are great swathes of bloodied rye and innumerable bodies, some dead, some crippled, some crawling back towards the silent guns, but the Eagles are flying high on the British ridge. A French staff officer glanced at Napoleon to see his reaction. 'Satisfaction could be seen written on his face, all was going well and there is no doubt that at that moment he thought his battle was won.' Marshal Soult believed the same thing and, while watching the slowly unfolding events on the valley's far side, even found time to write a swift letter to a friend in Paris saying that the battle was going excellently and promised a fine hope of victory.

But Soult had fought the Duke of Wellington before and he should have known better.

* * *

Young Louis Canler survived the crossing of the valley. He had seen men killed and maimed, but he was untouched. The climb to the crest was difficult because the soil was so wet and the trampled rye stalks so tangling, and as he neared the hedge which marked the summit the strap of his right gaiter broke. The gaiters helped keep his shoes on and now his right foot came out of his shoe. He bent down to pull the shoe out of the mud and at that moment a musket ball slammed through his shako, making a hole through the metal plate stamped with his regiment's number. The ball grazed his scalp and blew out of the back of the shako. If his shoe had not been stuck in mud he would have been dead.

That musket ball probably came from a soldier in Bylandt's Brigade, the Dutch troops who were posted behind the hedges. Or possibly it was fired by any of the Dutch–British skirmishers who had retreated to the crest where the hedges lined the sunken road. The French had halted momentarily, not out of fear of what waited beyond the hedges, but because the time had come to deploy into line. The column had done its job of getting a mass of men across the valley, but now it was firepower that would win the day, and that needed a line formation.

That sounds like a disciplined manoeuvre, going from column to line, but in truth it was frenetic. The French were suddenly aware that troops waited beyond the crest; those troops were standing now.

Musketry came from the Dutch battalions who were lining the hedge. The leading French battalions returned the fire. Captain Duthilt, who was three hundred yards east of young Canler, says they 'rushed' on the enemy. 'We chased them with the bayonet,' he says, 'and crossed the hedges ... we were on the plateau and shouted victory.'

The shout was premature, even though the French assault had driven off most of Bylandt's Brigade. Those Dutch soldiers had been placed further forward than the rest of the defenders, they had lined the hedges and suffered more from the cannonade. They exchanged volley fire with the French for a moment, then broke, fled and were jeered by the redcoats as they ran. One Dutch battalion stayed to fight it out, and most of the fugitives were rallied in the rear and went back to the crest when the action was over. The Brigade was largely made up of inexperienced soldiers who had fought bravely at Quatre-Bras, but the long cannonade and the assault of the vast French columns broke their nerve. That was one effect of columns. They might have limited firepower, but their very size made them terrifying to inexperienced soldiers.

Yet behind the crest were some very experienced soldiers, men who had fought French columns before, men in red coats led by the irascible Welshman, General Picton. Captain Mercer had met Picton the evening before, but had not recognized him:

> He was dressed in a shabby old drab greatcoat and a rusty round hat. I took him at the time for some amateur from Brussels (of whom we had heard there were several hovering about) and thinking many of his questions rather impertinent was somewhat short in answering him, and he soon left us. Imagine my astonishment on learning soon after that this was Sir Thomas Picton!

Picton had exchanged the rusty round hat for a top hat. He was on horseback, watching the French who had managed to get past the hedges and roadway. It was now that Picton ordered his redcoats forward. They were in line, of course, and overlapped the disordered

French columns. Lieutenant James Kerr-Ross of the 92nd Gordon Highlanders describes advancing to the crest of the ridge where:

> we encountered a strong column of French infantry forming on the top of our position, whose leading files gave us their fire which our men did not return, but advanced steadily to the attack, and when we got within a very short distance of the enemy (at perhaps not thirty yards) they broke up and ran back in great confusion. Our fire was now very destructive.

That was classic British infantry work: not to waste inaccurate musket fire at long range, but get close and stay steady and then let the practised volley fire do its deadly work. Picton saw the French recoil and recognized the chance. 'Charge!' he shouted. 'Charge, Hurrah!' and was immediately killed by a musket ball that pierced his forehead. His presentiment beside the Welsh grave had been sadly accurate.

Yet so had his final impetus. The redcoats went forward with fixed bayonets and the French were checked, though not before there was some hand-to-hand fighting. One of the British battalions was the 32nd, from Cornwall. It was closest to the crossroads, just north of La Haie Sainte, and the French closed on the battalion. One of the colour bearers was a lieutenant who was suddenly confronted by a French officer who:

> seized the staff, I still retaining a grasp of the silk (the colours were nearly new). At the same moment he attempted to draw his sabre, but had not accomplished it when the covering Colour-Sergeant, named Switzer, thrust his pike into his breast, and the right rank and file of the division, named Lacy, fired into him. He fell dead at my feet.

The Colour-Sergeants were there to do just that, protect the colours, and they were armed with a weapon that would not have been out of place at Agincourt, a spontoon, a nine-foot spear with a cross-piece to prevent the blade penetrating an enemy's body too far. This was not mercy, but practicality. One British officer at Waterloo watched an enemy lancer trying to pull his weapon from the body of a British dragoon and the man needed several hard tugs to free the blade and was vulnerable while he did that. The cross-piece was meant to prevent the blade being trapped by a corpse.

Lieutenant Scheltens was in the Dutch–Belgian battalion that did not flee with the rest of Bylandt's Brigade. 'Our battalion opened fire as soon as our skirmishers had come in,' and that must have been perilously close to the ridge top because:

Captain Henri l'Olivier, who commanded our grenadier company, was struck on the arm by a musket ball of which the wadding, or cartridge paper, remained smoking in the sleeve of his tunic.

There was fighting all along the ridge top now. Some redcoat battalions, just like Lieutenant Scheltens's men, were giving volley fire at a murderously close range. The volleys rippled along the battalions, a company firing, then reloading and waiting their turn. The French had not deployed properly. They were meant to widen into a line that would overlap their opponents, but the volleys whipped in from the flanks and drove men back. Other redcoats were using bayonets, stabbing the 17-inch blades at undisciplined Frenchmen. Men were screaming, shouting, the drums still beating, trumpets blaring, muskets hammering as thousands of men contested the ridge top. The redcoats had the momentary advantage, and Captain Duthilt thought that was caused by his men's enthusiasm, which had:

caused our ranks to fall into confusion and in our turn we were assailed with the bayonet by new enemies. The struggle recommenced and a dreadful mêlée followed. In this bloody confusion the officers did their duty by trying to restore some order ... for troops in disorder can do nothing.

Duthilt was faced by the 92nd, who were using their bayonets to drive the French back while off to their right Captain Johnny Kincaid had been forced out of his sandpit and had retreated to the ridge top by the crossroads, where his riflemen were firing at the nearest column. Sir James Kempt had taken over command from Picton and he shouted to Kincaid, wanting an assurance 'that I would never quit that spot'. Kincaid gave his word to the general, then immediately regretted it because:

> *glancing my eye to the right, I saw the next field covered with the cuirassiers, some of whom were making directly for the gap in the hedge where I was standing.*

French cavalry threatened, French infantry was on the ridge's crest and Marshal Soult was surely justified in thinking that victory was imminent. Duthilt's men might have been in disorder, but there were more battalions stacked behind his and sheer weight of numbers would push the redcoats back. And those redcoats were in line, and infantry in line was red meat to cavalrymen, as the cuirassiers had already proved on the Hanoverians whose slaughtered bodies lay thick close to La Haie Sainte. The British battalions would have to form square and, while that would protect them from cavalry, it would make them horribly vulnerable to French infantry volleys. Scissors, paper, stone.

And then the cavalry charged.

Only it was the British cavalry.

* * *

Baron Simon Bernard was an aide to the Emperor. A clever man in his mid-thirties, he was an engineer by training and a soldier by choice. He had distinguished himself at the battle of Leipzig, but after Napoleon's first abdication he had sworn his loyalty to King Louis XVIII and been promoted to General. Napoleon's return from Elba had prompted another change of allegiance and General Bernard was once again an aide to the Emperor.

Now, as the sounds of battle rose to a crescendo, he rode eastwards with a light cavalry regiment. The day's small wind was out of the west, so the noise of cannon and the crackling of muskets – some men said it sounded like dry thorns burning – was carried to the horsemen as they probed the tangled countryside east of the battlefield.

After a while General Bernard dismounted. The cavalry stayed hidden in woodland as he went further east on foot. Among Bernard's many skills was map-making, so he knew how to read countryside and he kept himself concealed by low ground, by hedgerows and trees. After a while he reached the edge of the Lasne defile and crouched there. The river beneath him was swollen by the rains, but he was more interested in the soldiers he could see crowding the defile's far side. He used his spyglass.

He had hoped to see blue uniforms, and he did. He knew the Prussians were advancing through this difficult countryside, but he had still hoped to see evidence of Grouchy's men on the river's far side, but instead he saw that the coats were the darker blue of Prussian infantry. The troops across the defile also wore rolled-up blankets slung over their left shoulders, and no army except the Prussian did that. The good news was that the river's defile had steep, high banks that were slippery with mud. There was no easy road for the Prussian artillery, just an obstacle that would give the enemy engineers a nightmare. There was time, then, but not much.

He went back to his horse and rode to give Napoleon the news.

General Bernard was to survive the day unscathed, but his change of allegiance from Louis XVIII to the Emperor meant he would be banished from France, so eventually he emigrated to the United States, where his engineer training was put to good use. He built Fort Monroe in Virginia and helped design the Chesapeake and Ohio Canal.

But for now he has to tell the Emperor that the Prussians are desperately close to the French right flank, which means the British–Dutch must be broken, or else it will become a battle of three armies.

And on the crest of the British ridge the Eagles are flying high.

* * *

Perhaps the most famous painting of Waterloo is Lady Butler's magnificent picture showing the charge of the Royal Scots Greys. The painting is called *Scotland Forever!* and now hangs in Leeds Art Gallery, but the picture, splendid though it is, is entirely misleading. It was painted sixty-six years after the battle and Lady Butler used her husband's army connections to arrange for the regiment to charge at her while she sat at her easel. The big grey horses are at full gallop, led by an officer brandishing his sword, and the mass of men come straight towards the eye. It is the enemy's view, and it is terrifying.

So was the real charge, but where Lady Butler shows the horsemen galloping on flat ground, the British heavy cavalry had to negotiate the sunken road, the hedges and the redcoats before they could close with the enemy. Four regiments made the charge. No one seems certain who ordered the counter-attack by the heavy cavalry, it was either Wellington or, more likely, Lord Uxbridge, but the timing was perfect. The Household Brigade attacked down the main road, and then, going from west to east, the Royals, the Inniskilling Dragoons and on the left flank the Royal Scots Greys. The English, the Irish and the Scots. They were all heavy horsemen, mounted on big horses and carrying the brutal Heavy Cavalry Pattern sword, a straight-bladed weapon that could thrust or hack. Light cavalry carried the sabre, a slashing weapon, but heavy cavalry were the shock troops of a battlefield, using weight, reach and strength to break the enemy. One thousand three hundred such cavalrymen went into the fight. They came in two lines from behind the redcoats, who had to move hurriedly aside to let the horsemen through and some redcoats were trampled, while others grabbed hold of stirrups and went with the cavalry, and they charged the whole width of the ridge, the westernmost on the highway, and so along to the crest above Papelotte. The shock, the surprise, was total.

John Dickson, who remembered watching Napoleon's army parade in the early morning shafts of sunlight, was a Corporal in the Royal Scots Greys. His regiment, all mounted on white (i.e. grey) horses, was behind the 92nd, those Scots who had fought so hard at Quatre-Bras. He heard Sir Denis Pack, the brigade commander, appeal to the 92nd, 'You must advance! All in front of you have given way!' He meant the battalions of Bylandt's Brigade who had fled, and so the Highlanders fixed bayonets and advanced through the beech and holly hedge, crossed the road and

delivered a volley at twenty paces into the French, and it was just then
that Dickson heard the order, 'Now then, Scots Greys, charge!'

*At once a great cheer rose from our ranks ... I dug my spurs into
my brave old Rattler and we were off like the wind ... after
rearing for a moment, she sprang forward, uttering loud
neighings and snortings and leapt over the holly hedge at a
terrific speed. It was a grand sight to see the long line of giant
grey horses dashing along with flowing manes and heads down,
tearing up the turf about them as they went. The men in their red
coats and tall bear-skins were cheering loudly, and the
trumpeters were sounding the 'charge'. Beyond the first hedge the
road was sunk between high, sloping banks, and it was a difficult
feat to descend without falling; but there were very few accidents
... All of us were greatly excited and began crying 'Hurrah!
Ninety-Second! Scotland for ever!' as we crossed the road ... we
heard the Highland pipers playing ... and I clearly saw my old
friend Pipe-Major Cameron standing apart on a hillock coolly
playing 'Johnny Cope, are you wauking yet?' in all the din ... I
rode in the second rank. As we tightened our grip to descend the
hillside among the corn, we could make out the feather bonnets
of the Highlanders, and heard the officers crying out to them to
wheel back by sections. A moment more and we were among
them. Poor fellows! Some of them had not time to get clear of us,
and were knocked down ... They were all Gordons, and as we
passed through them they shouted, 'Go at them, the Greys!
Scotland for ever!' My blood thrilled at this, and I clutched my
sabre tighter. Many of the Highlanders grasped our stirrups, and
in the fiercest excitement dashed with us into the fight. The
French were uttering loud, discordant yells. Just then I saw the
first Frenchman. A young officer of Fusiliers made a slash at me
with his sword, but I parried it and broke his arm; the next
second we were in the thick of them. We could not see five yards
ahead for the smoke ... The French were fighting like tigers ... as*

*we were sweeping down a steep slope on the top of them, they
had to give way. Then those in front began to cry out for 'quarter'
throwing down their muskets and taking off their belts. The
Gordons at this rushed in and drove the French to the rear. I was
now in the front rank, for many of ours had fallen.*

The Royal Scots Greys charged at the eastern end of the ridge. The
French had advanced their great columns in echelon from the west, so
the division attacked by Dickson and his comrades had still not reached
the summit, nor would they now because the big horses were cutting
bloody channels into the French ranks and putting them to rout. Young
Louis Canler was in the column closest to the Brussels highway, the
column which had led the echelon attack. He had suffered the bombardment of the allied guns as his battalion crossed the valley and seen the
drummer keep beating his drum despite losing his right arm. His
column did reach the summit of the ridge, and the men thought that
was enough to give them victory, but no sooner had they reached the
sunken road than they were attacked by the Royals, an English heavy
cavalry regiment. Canler comments that there was no time to form
square and so his unit was broken.

And that was the great disadvantage of the formation the French had
chosen to use. A column made of successive battalions in line looked
magnificent and, given the chance, might have spread into a formidable
line to give devastating volley fire, but it would take a battalion in a three-
rank line a lot of time to form square, and they would be hampered by
the battalions in front and behind while they did. There was neither space
nor time to form square. Major Frederick Clarke, who charged with the
Scots Greys, reckons the enemy was trying to form square, but 'the first
and nearest square had not time to complete their formation, and the
Greys charged through it.' So the British heavy cavalry drove into the
panicking columns and Canler tells what happened:

*A real carnage followed. Everyone was separated from his
comrades and fought for his own life. Sabres and bayonets*

slashed at the shaking flesh for we were too close packed to use our firearms.

Canler was at the back of the column, but the horsemen hacked their way through and split the battalions apart. Canler suddenly found himself alone and did the sensible thing, he surrendered. Infantry had come with the horsemen and they took his weapons and his knapsack, which held all his belongings. The French knapsacks were much prized as plunder; they were better made and more comfortable than the British issue.

Off to the east, where Corporal Dickson is riding Rattler into the enemy, Captain Duthilt is trying to rally his men who, he thought, had become disorganized because of their enthusiasm.

Just as I was pushing one of my soldiers into the rank I saw him fall at my feet because of a sabre cut. I whirled round. English cavalry was forcing their way into our midst and cutting us to pieces. Just as it is difficult, if not impossible, for the best cavalry to break infantry who are formed in squares ... so it is true that once the ranks have been broken and pierced then resistance is useless and nothing remains but for the cavalry to slaughter at almost no risk to themselves. This is what had happened. Our poor men stood up and stretched out their arms, but they could not reach far enough to bayonet those cavalrymen mounted on powerful horses and the few shots fired in this chaotic mêlée were just as fatal to our own men as to the English. And thus we found ourselves defenceless against a merciless enemy who, in the intoxication of battle, sabred even our drummers and fifers. That is where our eagle was captured.

Duthilt's 45th Regiment of the Line is being destroyed by the Royal Scots Greys, one of whom is Sergeant Charles Ewart, a particularly powerful man. He graphically described his capture of the Eagle. It must have occurred fairly late in the fight between the 45th and the

Scots Greys, because he mentions the presence of a lancer, so it is probable that Ewart spurred down the slope and caught the colour party of the French regiment as it tried to escape back across the valley, by which time French cavalry had ridden to attempt a rescue.

> *It was in the first charge I took the Eagle from the enemy; he and I had a hard contest for it; he thrust for my groin, I parried it off, and I cut him through the head; after which I was attacked by one of their Lancers who threw his lance at me, but missed the mark by my throwing it off with my sword by my right side; then I cut him from the chin upwards, which cut went through his teeth. Next I was attacked by a foot soldier, who, after firing at me, charged me with his bayonet; but he very soon lost the combat, for I parried it, and cut him down through the head; so that finished the contest for the Eagle. After which I presumed to follow my comrades, Eagle and all, but was stopped by the General saying to me, 'You brave fellow, take that to the rear; you have done enough till you get quit of it,' which I was obliged to do … I took the Eagle into Brussels, amidst the acclamation of thousands of the spectators who saw it.*

Ewart was rewarded with a commission, and to this day there is a pub named for him on Edinburgh's Royal Mile. Napoleon, watching from the far ridge, is supposed to have said, 'Those terrible grey horses, how they fight!'

The Royals also captured an Eagle, this one from the 105th Regiment, which was ahead of Louis Canler's battalion. Captain Kennedy Clark described the incident. His squadron, he said:

> *had advanced 200 or 300 yards beyond the second hedge, and the first line of French infantry had been broke, I perceived, a little to my left, an enemy's 'Eagle' amongst the infantry, with which the bearer was making every exertion to get off towards the rear of the column. I immediately rode to the place calling out to 'Secure*

the colour!' and at the same time, my horse reaching it, I ran my sword into the officer's right side, who carried the 'Eagle', who staggered and fell forwards but I do not think he reached the ground, on account of the pressure of his companions.

A Corporal, Francis Stiles, who was following Kennedy Clark, managed to grasp the Eagle's flag and ride away with it.

Not all the cavalrymen did as well as Ewart or Stiles. Private Hasker was a stocking weaver who had joined the cavalry. He was a Methodist and, charging at the cuirassiers, he crossed swords with an enemy, but neither he nor the Frenchman wanted to fight to the death so they rode away from each other. The Frenchman had rather impressed Hasker by yelling his war cry, presumably '*Vive l'Empereur!*' and Hasker thought he should have a war cry too, but all he could think of on the spur of the moment was 'The sword of the Lord and Gideon!' So he shouted that aloud, and just then his horse stumbled and fell:

Before I had well recovered my feet, one of the cuirassiers rode up and began slashing at my head with his sword. I soon fell down with my face to the ground. Presently a man rode by and stabbed at me with a lance. I turned around and was then stabbed by a sword by a man who walked past me. Very soon another man came up with a firelock and bayonet and, raising both his arms, thrust his bayonet (as he thought) into my side near my heart ... one of my fingers was cut off and there I lay bleeding from at least a dozen places, and was soon covered with blood. I was also at that time plundered by the French soldiers of my watch, money, canteen, haversack and trousers, notwithstanding that the balls from the British army were dropping on all sides.

Poor Hasker spent the rest of the day and all the following night where he fell. Eventually he was rescued and managed to clamber onto a wagon which took him to Brussels where, at last, his wounds were treated.

But the assault of the British Heavy Cavalry threw d'Erlon's great attack into utter disarray. The great columns had been broken apart and the horsemen were riding among the scattered men slashing with their swords, while the British infantry had come down from the crest to pillage and take prisoners. Lieutenant Scheltens, the Belgian officer whose captain had musket wadding smoking in his jacket sleeve, helped gather in the captives:

> One French battalion commander had received a sabre cut across his nose which was now hanging down over his mouth. 'Look,' he said to me, 'what they do to us!' The poor fellow might have suffered far worse. I gave protection to two French officers in this débâcle. They gave me the masonic sign, so I had them taken to the rear where they were not, as usually happens, searched and robbed.

The French had come tantalizingly close to victory on the ridge top. The massive columns had been checked by the infantry fire, but the disparity in numbers must have counted in the end, except the British cavalry had streamed across the crest and driven deep into the panicking ranks. In the minutes after the charge there was chaos. Horsemen were still attacking isolated Frenchmen, other French infantrymen were retreating as fast as they could and, though no one mentions it, they must have formed rallying squares to protect themselves as they returned the way they had come. 'Hundreds of the infantry threw themselves down and pretended to be dead while the cavalry rode over them,' Kincaid recalled. 'I never saw such a scene in all my life!' The cuirassiers who had threatened Kincaid were driven back by the Household Cavalry, who charged at the same time as the Scots Greys, Inniskillings and Royals. 'Charge' is too strong a word, because their path was across the road, through the hedges, across ditches and, as Captain William Clayton remembered, 'the ground presented a surface of mud ... which, soon after the commencement of the action became so deep ... as to render it very difficult, when advancing to the charge, to push our horses into a trot.'

Nevertheless around 800 heavy cavalry of the Household Brigade charged a similar number of cuirassiers. The French had the advantage of wearing breastplates and of carrying swords with blades that were six inches longer than the British, while the British had a slight advantage in numbers, the downward slope and surprise. The sound of heavy cavalry fighting heavy cavalry was like 'tinkers at work' one officer recalled. The French were forced back and some were unlucky enough to be trapped in the sunken road beside La Haie Sainte, where they found their retreat blocked by an abatis, a crude but effective barricade made of heavy branches, and those men, crammed together and unable to extricate themselves, were ruthlessly slaughtered. The carnage continued till some French infantry, still clinging to La Haie Sainte's orchard, fired down at the British cavalry. Those French infantry retreated soon after, leaving the King's German Legion still in control of the isolated farm.

British–Dutch infantry were shepherding around 3,000 prisoners to the rear, stripping them of weapons and possessions. On the right of the French advance the easternmost column had attacked the farm of Papelotte, but they now withdrew as the other columns retreated. The great attack on Wellington's centre-left had come so close to success, but was now routed, and the survivors of d'Erlon's Corps trudged, limped or crawled back across the valley.

While off on Wellington's right the crisis had come at Hougoumont.

And the British cavalry, elated by their victory, decided to win the battle all on their own.

OVERLEAF | *Lady Elizabeth Butler's splendid, though entirely misleading, 'Scotland Forever' painted in 1881: 'They were all Gordons, and as we passed through them they shouted, "Go at them, the Greys! Scotland for ever!" My blood thrilled at this, and I clutched my sabre tighter. Many of the Highlanders grasped our stirrups, and in the fiercest excitement dashed with us into the fight. The French were uttering loud, discordant yells. Just then I saw the first Frenchman. A young officer of Fusiliers made a slash at me with his sword, but I parried it and broke his arm; the next second we were in the thick of them.'*

CLOCKWISE FROM TOP | *42nd Highlanders at Waterloo, 1815.* | *Thomas Picton, by Sir Martin Archer Shee: Picton was seriously wounded at Quatre-Bras, two of his ribs being broken by a musket ball – he died leading his men to charge at Waterloo.* | *A damaged cuirass of the 2nd French Carabiniers.*

ABOVE | 'The Fight for the Standard', by Richard Ansdell, which now hangs in the Great Hall of Edinburgh Castle, depicting Sergeant Charles Ewart's capture of the French Eagle: '... then I cut him from the chin upwards, which went through his teeth. Next I was attacked by a foot soldier, who, after firing at me, charged me with his bayonet; but he very soon lost the combat, for I parried it, and cut him down through the head; so that finished the contest for the Eagle.'

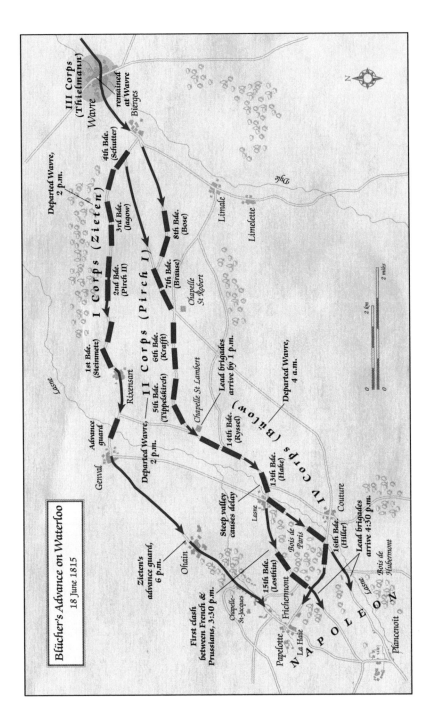

Blücher's Advance on Waterloo
18 June 1815

III Corps (Thielmann)

Wavre

remained at Wavre

Bierges

4th Bde. (Schutter)

Departed Wavre, 2 p.m.

I Corps (Zieten)

3rd Bde. (Jagow)

2nd Bde. (Pirch II)

8th Bde. (Bose)

7th Bde. (Brause)

Dyle

Limale

Limelette

Chapelle St-Robert

1st Bde. (Steinmetz)

II Corps (Pirch I)

6th Bde. (Krafft)

Rixensart

Lasne

Advance guard

5th Bde. (Tippelskirch)

Genval

Departed Wavre, 2 p.m.

Chapelle St-Lambert

14th Bde. (Ryssel)

Lead brigades arrive by 1 p.m.

IV Corps (Bülow)

Departed Wavre, 4 a.m.

13th Bde. (Hake)

Zieten's advance guard, 6 p.m.

Ohain

Steep valley causes delay

Lasne

Couture

First clash between French & Prussians, 3:30 p.m.

Chapelle-St-Jacques

15th Bde. (Losthin)

Frichermont

Bois de Paris

16th Bde. (Hiller)

Lead brigades arrive 4:30 p.m.

Papelotte

La Haie

NAPOLEON

Bois de Hubermont

Lasne

Plancenoit

N

0 2 km

0 2 miles

CHAPTER NINE

We had our revenge!
Such slaughtering!

H IS NAME WAS LEGROS and his nickname *l'Enfonceur*. He was
a Sous-Lieutenant in one of the infantry battalions besieging
Hougoumont and he was a big man, some described him as
'gigantic'. He had risen through the ranks and was about to write his
name in history.

The north gate of Hougoumont faced towards the British-held ridge.
A lane led down to the gate, and still does, though the walls either side
of the present gateway are much lower than they were in 1815. The gate
opened inwards, and was left unbarred for much of the time because
that was the best route whereby ammunition and reinforcements could
reach the hard-pressed garrison which, by mid-afternoon, is under fire
from three sides.

And sometime that afternoon the gigantic *l'Enfonceur* led a group
of about thirty or forty infantrymen and forced the north gate open. He
carried a pioneer's axe. The pioneers served the engineers of the army
as labourers and they had big axes to cut down trees, but in the hands
of a man like Legros it was also a lethal close-quarters weapon. It is not
quite certain whether *l'Enfonceur* found the gate open or whether he

broke it down. Some accounts claim he smashed through a panel of the gates with his axe, but it seems more likely that a French attack drove some British skirmishers out of the ground to the château's east and those skirmishers retreated through the gate and did not have time to close it. Sous-Lieutenant Legros burst into the courtyard, followed by his men and a single drummer boy.

The situation was desperate for Macdonell. The ferocity of Legros's attack was clearing the big courtyard, and if more French troops managed to get through the gate then the defenders would be gutted from the inside. And those French reinforcements were coming.

Macdonell realized that the most important task was not to kill Legros and his companions, but to close the gates so that no more Frenchmen could enter. He led a small group of men past the intruders and together they forced the big gates shut. They heaved against the pressure from outside, some men shot through the slowly closing gap, and they ignored Legros's men who were fighting behind them. Other defenders shot from windows and doorways, pouring musket fire into the invaders. Then, finally, the gate was closed and barred and Macdonell and his men turned on Legros. All the French, except for the drummer boy, were killed.

The Duke of Wellington famously said that a man might as well write the history of a dance as write the story of a battle; too much is happening at once in a swirl of colour, noise and confusion. Few battles have been studied so closely, researched so comprehensively or written about so often, yet still there are mysteries. Was Legros's attack coincident with the assault of d'Erlon's Corps? Or was it later? Were the Coldstream Guards actually garrisoning Hougoumont when the French first attacked? Captain Moritz Büsgen was an officer in one of the Dutch Nassauer battalions, and in his description of the fight at Hougoumont it would appear that Macdonell had been ordered out of the buildings before the attack commenced and that Büsgen's men took over their abandoned positions; 'from the existing defence preparations ... it was obvious that this post had already been occupied,' Büsgen wrote. One historian suggests that Slender Billy ordered the British

Guards out of Hougoumont, which he was certainly stupid enough to do, but it is almost inconceivable that Macdonell would have obeyed, knowing as he did the trust that the Duke had placed in him. Büsgen also mentions a French incursion around 3:30 p.m., this one through a side gate, which no one else records. When Matthew Clay, the young guardsman who had been stranded outside the walls, retreated safely through the gates he saw:

> Lieutenant-Colonel Macdonell carrying a large piece of wood or the trunk of a tree in his arms. One of his cheeks was marked with blood and his charger lay bleeding a short distance away. With this timber he was hurrying to bar the gates against the renewed attack of the enemy which was most vigorously repulsed.

Clay probably did not carry a watch and he does not attempt to say what time he made his bolt for safety and saw Macdonell carrying the baulk of wood, but he does talk of another French incursion later, and that second invasion seems to be referring to Legros's men because Clay notes that a drummer boy was the only survivor. It was Clay who lodged the boy safely in an outhouse. He reckons the gates were forced by artillery, which no one else mentions, though sometime in the afternoon the French did bring artillery to join in the fight for the château.

It seems probable that there were two French incursions into Hougoumont, both of which were defeated, just as it seems likely that the garrison was composed of both British and Dutch troops, though to read the eyewitness accounts is to risk confusion. The problem stems from patriotism. British accounts stress British achievements and rarely offer credit to allies other than the King's German Legion, while Dutch, Hanoverian or Nassauer accounts carry a similar bias in favour of their own exploits. One source for what happened in Hougoumont is the unpublished memoirs of Private Johann Leonhard, a Nassauer; like Büsgen he contends that it was the Nassauers who garrisoned the farm and there is no mention of any British Guards in the repulse of the attacks coming from the wood:

*We had hardly taken up position at the loopholes when masses of
French came out of the wood ... but too late! A shower of balls
that we loosed off ... was so terrible that the grass in front was
soon covered with French corpses ... we were attacked four times
... but each time the French were again repelled.*

That seems clear enough: the Nassauers defeated every French
attack. Captain Büsgen says much the same, though he allows that
some Coldstreamers were sent 'in support of the battalion under my
command', which suggests that Büsgen commanded the garrison. But
against that we have the memoirs of George Evelyn, a British Guards
officer, who recollects that 'the French attacked with a much superior
force and the Dutch instantly gave way and fled'. Lieutenant-Colonel
Francis Home, second in command to Macdonell, writes that the
British occupied the château on the evening of the 17th and were not
reinforced by any Nassauer troops until 11 a.m. on the day of the battle;
'these at first might be 600 strong,' he writes dismissively, 'but after the
first hour there was not one of them to be seen; they had all vanished
... and were never seen afterwards excepting a few stragglers.' Who
was right? The suspicion is that the truth lies somewhere in between.
Macdonell certainly commanded the garrison, but it is also certain
that Dutch troops were still fighting when Legros attacked because one
of them, a Nassauer Lieutenant, had his hand chopped off by an axe
which was probably wielded by *l'Enfonceur*. It is inconceivable that the
British Guards evacuated Hougoumont on the morning of the 18th,
whatever Slender Billy ordered. No memoir mentions it, and we have
several. So why did Büsgen insist Hougoumont was deserted when he
arrived? It is possible that he led his men into the château itself which,
not being on the perimeter of the buildings, could well have been
empty, but that suggestion is tentative. As for the flight of the Dutch,
there is plenty of evidence that they stayed. Private Leonhard describes
the hornbeam trees of the ornamental walk in the formal garden being
razed and the château walls collapsing from the 'heavy bombardment
or from the severe thunderstorm that raged above us', though no other

participant mentions a severe thunderstorm during the battle. 'The skies,' he wrote:

seemed to have been changed into an ocean of fire, all of the farm buildings were aflame. The soil underneath my feet began to shake and tremble, and large fissures opened before my very eyes.

That, perhaps, is as good a description as any of the sensations of that awful fight. Thousands were to die in and around Hougoumont, and we must forgive the survivors if their accounts are not always coherent.

The struggle for Hougoumont continues. Wellington once remarked that closing the gates was the decisive act of the battle and later, when an eccentric clergyman wanted to arrange an annuity for 'the bravest man at Waterloo' and requested the Duke to make that difficult judgment, Wellington chose Macdonell. Macdonell, in turn, insisted on sharing the money with Sergeant James Graham, an Irishman who had been at his side in those desperate moments. The pair did receive the annuity for two years before the generous clergyman lost his money, but it is significant that Wellington, forced to make a choice, nominated Macdonell and, by association, Graham. Just after Graham helped close the gates he saved the life of a 25-year-old Captain, Henry Wyndham. A Frenchman clambered onto the high wall beside the gate and aimed his musket at Wyndham, but Graham shot first. Wyndham lived till 1860, and the women of his family always complained that his house was excessively cold and draughty because, they claimed, ever since he had helped shut the gates at Hougoumont he had never closed a door again.

The gates at Hougoumont were indeed closed, but the siege was far from over, and the French now start shelling the farm, while off to the west, beyond the main road that bisects the battlefield, the British cavalry are running wild.

* * *

The Duke of Wellington never had much confidence in British cavalry. 'I considered our cavalry', he wrote after the wars:

so inferior to the French from want of order, that although one
squadron was a match for two French, I did not like to see four
British opposed to four French. As numbers increase, order
becomes more necessary. Our men could gallop, but could not
preserve their order.

The Duke prized order above every other military virtue. Order made troops steady under fire, it allowed them to remain firm under horrific artillery bombardment, it sustained men in the close exchange of volley fire. The Duke's infamous remark about his army being 'the scum of the earth' was made when order collapsed. That was after his great victory at Vitoria, when the British troops captured the enemy's baggage train which contained all the French plunder from their occupation of Spain, and discipline went to the wind in an orgy of looting, theft and murder. Order made everything else possible, and the British cavalry famously lacked order. In the Peninsula Wellington trusted the King's German Legion cavalry, but was always wary of his own. It was true that the heavy cavalry had made a battle-winning charge at Salamanca in 1812, but then they had been under the command of Major-General John Le Marchant, probably the best British cavalry leader of the Napoleonic period, who had been killed in that fight.

The Household Brigade, the Inniskillings, the Royal Dragoons and the Royal Scots Greys had done magnificent work in shattering d'Erlon's attack. The French columns, broken into panicked pieces, were retreating fast, leaving behind 3,000 prisoners and about as many others wounded or dead. Cavalrymen were scattered across the long slope, bloodied swords in hand, and the trumpeters were sounding the recall, but almost all the horsemen ignored the summons. 'Our men were out of hand,' a staff officer admitted. Across the valley they could see Napoleon's Grand Battery, the great line of guns which had hammered the British ridge. Those guns were still silent for fear of hitting the survivors of d'Erlon's Corps who were still on the British side of the valley. The Grand Battery was not on the crest of the French ridge, but well forward of it, and the British cavalrymen could not resist. They turned their horses and charged the guns. Corporal Dickson saw Sergeant Ewart carry the Eagle away to the rear and afterwards, he said, 'we spurred on in search of like success'. He and his companions saw another column, almost certainly General Durutte's men on the extreme right of the French attack:

> *Trumpeter Reeves ... who rode by my side sounded a 'rally', and our men came swarming up from all sides, some Enniskillens and Royals being among them. We at once began a furious onslaught ... the [French] battalions seemed to open out for us to pass through, and so it happened that in five minutes we had cut our way through as many thousands of Frenchmen. We had now reached the bottom of the slope. There the ground was slippery with deep mud. Urging each other on we dashed towards the batteries on the ridge above which had worked such havoc in our ranks. The ground was very difficult, and especially where we crossed the edge of a ploughed field, so that our horses sank to their knees as we struggled on. My brave Rattler was becoming quite exhausted, but we dashed ever onwards. At this moment Colonel Hamilton rode up to us crying, 'Charge! Charge the guns!' and went off up the hill like the wind towards the terrible battery that had made such deadly work among the Highlanders ... Then we got among the guns and we had our revenge. Such slaughtering! We sabred the gunners, lamed the horses, and cut their traces and harness. I can hear the Frenchmen yet crying 'Diable!' when I struck at them, and the long-drawn hiss through their teeth as my sword went home ... The artillery drivers sat on their horses weeping aloud as we went among them; they were mere boys, we thought. Rattler lost her temper and bit and tore at everything that came in her way ... The French infantry were rushing past us in disorder on their way to the rear.*

Dickson reckoned that fifteen guns were put out of commission, other cavalrymen suggested the number was higher, but as no one dismounted to use a spike on the vent-holes it is likely that every gun was eventually used again. General Durutte, who had seen his column broken, watched the British cavalry charge on across the valley and decided they 'were either drunk or did not know how to curb their horses'.

Hundreds of British cavalry on blown horses were now on the French side of the battlefield. The French saw their chance and launched lancers and chasseurs against them. The French cavalry came from the east and struck the British hard. 'On no occasion,' General Durutte said, 'did I appreciate as well as in this clash the superiority of the lance over the sabre.' The British tried to regain their own side of the valley, but the French were on fresh horses and cut them down. Colonel Bro de Comères was the commanding officer of the 4th Lancers:

> I took the head of the squadrons and shouted 'En avant, children! We must destroy this rabble!' The soldiers answered, 'En avant! Vive l'Empereur!' Two minutes later the crash happened. Three enemy ranks were thrown over and we struck into the others terribly! The mêlée became dreadful. Our horses trampled on corpses and screams sounded from the wounded.

Colonel de Comères was unlucky to be wounded in the arm, but most of the ill luck was with the British who struggled through the deep mud to escape the lighter French horsemen. Sir William Ponsonby was the brigade commander of the Royals, Scots Greys and Inniskillings, and he had charged with the rest. Now, his tired horse mired in the mud, he gave his aide-de-camp some keepsakes and valuables to hand on to his family, then waited for the inevitable. His body was discovered with seven lance wounds. Lieutenant-Colonel Sir Frederick Ponsonby, second cousin to the doomed Sir William, was wounded in both arms, then knocked senseless from his horse by a sabre cut. He recovered consciousness to see a lancer looming over him. 'Tu n'est pas mort, coquin!' the lancer said, addressing Ponsonby as though he were a child, 'You're not dead, you rascal!' Then the lancer thrust down with his nine-foot lance to pierce Ponsonby's lung. Ponsonby lay there, bleeding. Retreating infantrymen looted him, and later he was used as a musket rest by a French skirmisher before being ridden over by Prussian cavalry, yet somehow he survived. He died, aged fifty-four, in 1837.

The British did not use the lance, but their experience at Waterloo persuaded them to adopt the weapon. John Dickson, on his mare Rattler, made it back safely, but hundreds did not, even though British light cavalry rode to cover the panicky retreat. For a while the valley east of the main road was chaos and Louis Canler was still far down the British slope, having surrendered and been plundered of his knapsack and belongings.

> Suddenly I heard the order, 'At the trot!' French lancers and cuirassiers had arrived to help us. The English dragoons had to abandon us to repulse this charge and I took advantage of the sudden freedom to hide in a nearby wheatfield. The French cavalry attacked the English dragoons furiously, sabering and lancing them so savagely that the English retreated and left a good number of their men on the battlefield. This permitted me to cross the field and rejoin my unit [and] … I found myself close to an English dragoon officer who had been killed in the mêlée. A sabre had split open his head, bursting the brain from his skull. Hanging from his fob was a superb golden chain and in spite of my haste I paused a moment to plunder this chain and a beautiful golden watch.

Canler rejoins the remnants of his battalion, richer than when he left them, and slowly the chaos cleared. The surviving British horsemen go back to their ridge, and by about three o'clock in the afternoon the valley is empty again, except for the dead, the dying and the suffering. The gunners of both armies return to their cannon and start firing. The great attack by d'Erlon's Corps came so close to success, but was shattered by volley fire, by the bayonet and by the British heavy cavalry who, having destroyed the vast columns, destroyed themselves so fool-ishly. Roughly half the men who charged were lost, either killed, wounded or captured; now the rest gathered again behind the ridgeline. For a short while there was little activity in the valley, but the respite would not last long. The Emperor was running short of time.

* * *

'Great battles are won by artillery,' Napoleon once said, though he said so many things that it is difficult to know when he was being serious. He liked making flat, declaratory statements that contained a grain of truth, presumably to provoke an argument that he could win, but he did love his artillery, and now the big guns are firing all along the line, bombard-ing the whole British ridge with roundshot and shell. More guns are shelling Hougoumont, though that battle is out of Napoleon's sight.

Napoleon never went to the left wing of his army to see what happened at Hougoumont, though he must have received reports of the frustrations his men were suffering, because it was the Emperor who ordered howitzers to be used against the fortress. For almost all of the battle Napoleon stayed close to the main high road, either at the Rossomme farm which lies well south of La Belle Alliance, or else close to La Belle Alliance itself. He was wearing a grey greatcoat and many men watched him walking up and down on the patch of high ground from where he could see the smoke-shrouded battlefield. A rush-bottomed chair and a small table had been fetched from the inn and he sat for long periods – some men said he slumped – and gazed at the map spread on the table. He picked his teeth with scraps of straw, or stared through the smoke with his telescope. His brother Jérôme later claimed that Napoleon left the battlefield briefly to have leeches applied to his piles, and it is certain that the Emperor had faith in that remedy, but far from certain that he used it on that fateful day.

In the years after Waterloo the battlefield became a popular tourist spot, and one of the many guides was a man called Decoster, who claimed to have been taken captive on the morning of the battle and forced to be Napoleon's informant on the countryside. It makes sense that a local man would be asked what lay beyond the ridge, and where the lanes went, but Decoster's stories seem to contain a deal of fantasy. The Emperor watched the battle as best he could through the smoke, but he did not mount his horse and visit the various units that were fighting for him. Aides did that on his behalf, their horses dashing across the ridge with news and messages. There was an observation tower on the French ridge, a tall and rickety structure of timber scaffolding which was probably built by surveyors shortly before the battle to help make a map. Undoubtedly some French officers watched from the tower's top, but there is no mention of Napoleon climbing the ladders.

The Duke of Wellington, meanwhile, was never off his horse, Copenhagen. For much of the battle he stayed beside the elm tree at the crossroads, but at moments of great danger he was always with the threatened troops. He had visited Picton shortly before d'Erlon's columns reached the crest, but as the day went on he was more and more out on his right wing. He later claimed that the 'finger of providence' protected him because, though many of his companions were killed or wounded at his side, neither he nor Copenhagen were touched. He was always a 'hands-on' general, giving orders to battalions himself, while Napoleon was content to let Ney run the fight for him. One of the claims made for the Emperor was that he had a sixth sense for the moment when the crisis of a battle had arisen and he would then launch his master-stroke that would cripple the enemy, but if that was true then the sixth sense had abandoned him on 18 June 1815. There were to be many crises, but none elicited the unexpected attack to take advantage of British–Dutch weakness. Wellington reckoned Napoleon's presence on a battlefield to be worth 40,000 men to the French, and undoubtedly the French soldiers worshipped the Emperor, loved him even, and fought for him with a desperate courage, yet Wellington's presence was also worth men. He was neither worshipped nor loved, but he was respected. When he rode along the line, sergeants could be heard ordering their men to 'Look to your front! Silence in the ranks! Here comes Nosey!' They knew he valued order above all else. He also valued his men, and they knew that too, and many accounts pay tribute to the Duke's presence. When the battle was at its fiercest, when canister and roundshot and musket balls were shredding British–Dutch ranks, then Wellington was frequently just paces away. A British officer noticed him in the afternoon, accompanied by a single aide, 'all the rest of the staff being killed or wounded', and Wellington, the officer recorded, 'appeared perfectly composed, but looking very thoughtful and pale'. He looked imperturbable, not because he was, but because he had to look that way. A soldier loading and firing his musket, his face flecked with powder burns, his ears assailed by noise, his view of the battle reduced to a few smoke-shrouded yards, and with his comrades dying or killed, would take a glance at the Duke. If Nosey looked worried then it was time to panic, but if the Duke appeared calm and confident then things were probably all right.

He was neither calm nor confident. He was heard to murmur once 'Let the Prussians come or nightfall!' and he was seen to look at his watch frequently. Later he would often say what a near-run thing that battle was. 'I was never so near being beat.' And all the time he was glancing eastwards. So was Napoleon. They were watching the far hills, watching for troops. The Duke knew the Prussians were coming, he would never have offered battle otherwise, but as his army is worn down, as the fighting goes on, he knows he needs the Prussians desperately. And Napoleon knows he has one chance left now, and that chance is to break Wellington before the Prussians arrive. It is a race now. Except that for Blücher and his Prussian troops it has become an obstacle race.

* * *

The Prussians paused on the eastern side of the Lasne valley. Blücher was in a hurry, but had no choice but to wait as his straggling column caught up with the vanguard. He chivvied them. 'Forwards!' he was quoted as saying. 'I hear you say it's impossible, but it has to be done! I have given my promise to Wellington and you surely don't want me to break it? Push yourselves, my children, and we'll have victory!'

It is impossible not to like Blücher. He was seventy-four years old, still in pain and discomfort from his adventures at Ligny, still stinking of schnapps and of rhubarb liniment, yet he is all enthusiasm and energy. If Napoleon's demeanour that day was one of sullen disdain for an enemy he underestimated, and Wellington's a cold, calculating calmness that hid concern, then Blücher is all passion. He can hear the battle which is being fought just three or four miles to the west, and he knows his troops will make the difference, but for all his impetuosity he also knows he must approach the fight with a certain caution.

There are French troops on the far side of the Lasne defile. They are light cavalry, so they are unlikely to start a troop-killing firefight, but if Blücher throws a few troops over, or sends units piecemeal as they arrive, he is likely to tempt French infantry into the thick woods beyond the Lasne and so suffer his men to be destroyed unit by unit. He has to collect enough troops to cross the small river in force so that they can defend themselves while the rest of his army arrives. So he waits.

The Lasne defile does not appear a major obstacle today, but on 18 June the small river had been swollen by the torrential rains of the previous day and the sides of the valley, steep enough already, were treacherous with mud. There were log steps laid into the tracks to allow carters' horses a chance to rest, and now they served to help the Prussian artillery make the precarious passage, but the guns, far heavier than most carts, needed huge teams of men to control their clumsy weight on the steep, slippery slopes. The cavalry had to lead their horses across, the infantry slid and clambered, but slowly the forces crossed an obstacle that was psychological as well as real. Once across the river's valley Blücher would have small chance of retreating. If his forces were overwhelmed by the French then they would be trapped against the valley and, in all likelihood, annihilated. Yet it is doubtful that Blücher worried about that prospect. He only wanted to get over the river, through the trees, and so burst onto Napoleon's right flank. One proposal was simply to join Wellington's forces, adding the Prussian regiments to the British–Dutch line, but Gneisenau argues for an approach further south, one that will slice behind Napoleon's army and so offer a chance of an encirclement that would inevitably lead to the utter destruction of the French army. Blücher agrees, and so the first target of the Prussians will be the village of Plancenoit.

But first they must cross the Lasne. Prussian light cavalry were the first to cross, and they skirmished with French hussars in the Bois de Paris, the Paris Wood, which lay on the defile's western side. Colonel Marcellin de Marbot commanded the French horsemen:

> *I threw the hussars and lancers that led* [*the Prussian column*] *back twice. I tried to win time by holding the enemy at bay as long as I could. He could only come from the steep muddy tracks with great difficulty.*

The French lost an opportunity. General Lobau had over 6,000 infantry just to the west of the wood, and if those men had been posted on the lip of the Lasne's valley they could have held the Prussians back for hours, but Napoleon had given Lobau specific instructions that he was not to attack the Prussians until he heard Grouchy's guns assailing them from the rear, and so Lobau stayed where he was, listening for a sound that did not arrive, and, unit by unit, the Prussians managed to cross the river. They gathered in the Bois de Paris, cavalry ahead, infantry behind, and artillery on the road. It took time – there was just one narrow bridge across the Lasne – but by mid-afternoon the Prussians were over the river in force. Grouchy, who was supposed to be attacking them, was still advancing on Wavre, where his scouts had discovered the Prussian rearguard left to defend that town. Napoleon might pray for Grouchy's arrival at Waterloo, but the Marshal was about to start a separate battle 12 miles away.

General Baron von Müffling was the Prussian liaison officer with Wellington and he now had messengers going backwards and forwards between himself and Blücher. The allies were in touch, though it would still be some time before the Prussians could engage the enemy in sufficient strength to make a difference. Yet von Müffling was in no doubt that his countrymen's assistance was needed urgently. 'After 3 o'clock,' he wrote in his memoirs, 'the Duke's situation became critical, unless the succour of the Prussian army arrived soon.'

Because it was after three o'clock that the French hurled their most desperate attacks on Wellington's line.

* * *

Hougoumont was on fire. French howitzers were lobbing shells over the high walls. If they could not drive the garrison out, then perhaps they could burn them out. The fire prompted one of Wellington's most famous orders. He kept a supply of ass's skin slips (ass's skin was smooth enough to be wiped clean and re-used) on which he wrote his orders, using the pommel of his saddle as a desk. He had ridden along the crest and stared down at Hougoumont and now wrote to Macdonell, and the order is worth quoting in full, remembering that it was written under fire in a place assailed by noise. The clarity is extraordinary:

> I see that the fire has communicated itself from the haystack to the roof of the Château. You must however still keep your men in the parts to which the fire does not reach. Take care that no Men are lost by the falling in of the Roof or floors. After they will have fallen in, occupy the Ruined Walls inside of the Garden, particularly if it should be possible for the Enemy to pass through the Embers to the Inside of the House.

It might be said that Macdonell hardly needed the order, he would have done precisely as Wellington wished without the careful instructions, but Wellington rarely left anything to chance. Matthew Clay, after his adventure outside the château walls, was now shooting from one of the main house's upper windows which, he noted, were higher than the other buildings and their fire 'annoyed the enemy skirmishers':

> The enemy noticed this and threw their shells amongst us and set the building we were defending on fire. Our officer placed himself at the entrance of the room and would not allow anyone to leave his post until our positions became hopeless and too perilous to remain. We fully expected the floor to sink with us every moment and in our escape several of us were more or less injured.

Flames destroyed the main house, which was never rebuilt. The fire reached the chapel, where many of the injured were lying, but the flames died just as they reached and scorched the crucifix suspended over the small altar. Some took that as a miracle. Other wounded men were in the barn, which was also on fire, but not all the injured could be rescued and their screams could be heard as they burned to death. Some horses were also burned to death there, their suffering adding to the day's cacophony. Yet the garrison still held. Some time in the afternoon a brave driver of the Royal Wagon Train whipped his horses down the lane. Captain Horace Seymour, an aide to Lord Uxbridge, had asked the man to take his wagonload of ammunition to the defenders:

> I merely pointed out to him where he was wanted, when he gallantly started his horses, and drove straight down the hill to the Farm, to the gate of which I saw him arrive. He must have lost his horses, as there was a severe fire kept on him. I feel convinced that to that man's service the Guard owe their ammunition.

That is a reminder of all the heroes at Waterloo. Sous-Lieutenant Legros and his men, Sergeant James Graham, Charles Ewart; so many on both sides. Yet there was also cowardice. Some men offered to help wounded to the rear and never returned. It even happened among the elite units. General Sir Andrew Barnard commanded a brigade of the Light Division that included a battalion of his own 95th Rifles. He wrote after the battle:

> I regret to say that a great number of our men went to the rear without cause after the appearance of the Cuirassiers, there was no less than 100 absentees after the fight and this vexes me very much as it is the first time such a thing has ever happened in the regiment. Kincaid says very few if any quitted the corps after the charge of the cavalry. Many of those that went to the rear were men that I little expected to have heard of in that situation.

Edward Costello, one of Barnard's riflemen, had been wounded at Quatre-Bras. He retreated with the rest of his unit, but on the day of the battle he was ordered to Brussels to have his wound dressed. He walked north through the woods and saw 'droves' of men in the trees:

Belgians, and English also, with fires lighted, busily cooking, having left their comrades in contest with the enemy. There appeared to be nothing the matter with them.

It is worth remembering that far more stayed than went. Some wounded men were ordered to the rear and doubtless they felt relief at the order, but many refused to leave, preferring to stay with their comrades. Others had legitimate reasons to leave the battlefield. Three troops, which was half the survivors, from the Inniskilling Dragoons were given the task of escorting a mass of French prisoners to Brussels. Those prisoners were fortunate because they lived. Wilhelm Schutte was a surgeon with the Brunswick troops. 'Our men', he wrote to his parents, 'were full of a hellish anger,' then provided an example:

At four o'clock in the afternoon some 100 French prisoners were brought in; one of them escaped at a favourable chance. A hussar chased him and shot him through the head with his pistol, others ran towards him and stabbed at him and even wounded men took pieces of wood or whatever else they could find and clubbed him until no single piece of him hung together.

By mid-afternoon there is a constant stream of men retreating northwards from the battlefield. Most had legitimate reasons for going, they were either wounded or helping the wounded reach the surgeons, though not everyone who looked after the injured were doctors. Elizabeth Gale was a five-year-old, the daughter of a rifleman in the 95th, and she and her mother had accompanied the battalion to Mont St Jean. Years later Elizabeth recalled how she helped tear up lint to make bandages for the wounded and even assisted her mother in dressing some wounds. Elizabeth was to live to be 95 years old and to be the last living survivor of the battle, dying in 1904. A journalist interviewed her shortly before she died:

> *She has a vivid recollection of several men dying in the camp and was much frightened when her mother lifted a cloth which covered one of them and she saw the dead man's open eyes apparently staring vacuously towards the battlefield.*

So Marshal Ney, watching from the southern ridge, saw crowds of men making their way north towards Brussels. Most were wounded, some were deserters, many were wagoneers going to fetch ammunition, and thousands were prisoners under escort, and it was that flood of men, horses and wagons that was the direct cause of the next great drama of Waterloo.

CLOCKWISE FROM TOP LEFT | 'Wellington's Orders, Battle of Waterloo, 1815': 'I see that the fire has communicated itself from the haystack to the roof of the Château. You must however still keep your men in the parts to which the fire does not reach. Take care that no Men are lost by the falling in of the roof or floors.' | 'Sir James Macdonell', by William Salter. Macdonell's task that Sunday was to defend Hougoumont with 1,500 guardsmen and 600 Dutch–German allies, against some 9,000 French infantry who eventually massed to evict the defenders. | 'Defence of the Chateau de Hougoumont by the Coldstream Guards', by Denis Dighton. Thousands were to die in and around Hougoumont, and we must forgive the survivors if their accounts are not always coherent.

OVERLEAF | 'Closing the Gates at Hougoumont', by Robert Gibb.

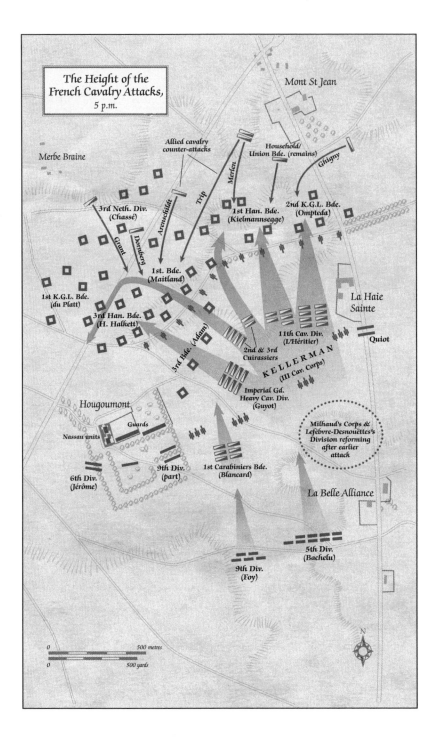

The Height of the
French Cavalry Attacks,
5 p.m.

Mont St Jean

Merbe Braine

Allied cavalry
counter-attacks

Household/
Union Bde. (remains)

Ghigny

Merlen

3rd Neth. Div.
(Chassé)

Arentschildt

Trip

1st Han. Bde.
(Kielmannsegge)

2nd K.G.L. Bde.
(Ompteda)

Grant

Dornberg

1st. Bde.
(Maitland)

La Haie
Sainte

1st K.G.L. Bde.
(du Platt)

3rd Han. Bde.
(H. Halkett)

11th Cav. Div.
(L'Héritier)

Quiot

3rd Bde. (Adam)

2nd & 3rd
Cuirassiers

KELLERMAN
(III Cav. Corps)

Imperial Gd.
Heavy Cav. Div.
(Guyot)

Hougoumont

Guards

Milhaud's Corps &
Lefebvre-Desnouëttes's
Division reforming
after earlier
attack

Nassau units

9th Div.
(part)

1st Carabiniers Bde.
(Blancard)

La Belle Alliance

6th Div.
(Jérôme)

5th Div.
(Bachelu)

9th Div.
(Foy)

0 ————— 500 metres

0 ————— 500 yards

N

228

CHAPTER TEN

The most beautiful troops
in the world

THE REVEREND WILLIAM LEEKE, a graduate of Cambridge, was the Perpetual Curate in the parish of Holbrook in Derbyshire and the author of several earnest works which strove to improve the Anglican Church. Yet before he studied theology and before he became a priest, he had been a soldier, and in 1815 he was a seventeen-year-old Ensign in the 52nd Foot. 'The standing to be cannonaded,' he wrote in the memoirs of his military service:

> and having nothing else to do, is about the most unpleasant thing that can happen to soldiers in an engagement. I frequently tried to follow, with my eye, the course of the balls from our own guns, which were firing over us. It is much more easy to see a round-shot passing away from you over your head, than to catch sight of one coming through the air towards you, though this occurs occasionally. I speak of shot fired from six, eight, nine or twelve pounder guns.

Leeke was holding one of the regiment's colours, though the two flags, having been carried through the battles of Vimeiro, Corunna,

Bussaco, Fuentes d'Onoro, Ciudad Rodrigo, Badajoz, Salamanca, Vitoria, Nivelle, Orthez and Toulouse, were now little more than tattered rags on bare poles. The 52nd was the largest infantry battalion at Waterloo, with over a thousand men in its ranks, about half of them Peninsular veterans. It would soon have a chance of glory, but for now it must endure the 'most unpleasant thing that can happen to soldiers'. The Reverend Leeke continues his tale:

> After we had been stationed for more than an hour so far down in front of the British position, a gleam of sunshine, falling on them, particularly attracted my attention to some brass guns in our front which appeared to be placed lower down the French slope, and nearer to us, than the others. I distinctly saw the French artillerymen go through the whole motion of sponging out one of the guns and reloading it … and when it was discharged I caught sight of the ball, which appeared to be in a direct line for me. I thought, Shall I move? No! I gathered myself up, and stood firm, with the colour in my right hand. I do not exactly know the rapidity with which cannon-balls fly, but I think that two seconds elapsed from the time I saw this shot leave the gun until it struck the front face of the square. It did not strike the four men in rear of whom I was standing, but the four fellows on their right. It was fired at some elevation, and struck the front man about the knees, and coming to the ground under the feet of the rear man of the four, whom it most severely wounded, it rose and, passing within an inch or two of the colour pole, went over the rear face of the square without doing further injury. The two men in the first and second rank fell outward, I fear they did not survive long; the two others fell within the square. The rear man made a considerable outcry on being wounded, but on one of the officers saying kindly to him, 'O man, don't make a noise,' he instantly recollected himself, and was quiet.

Leeke's battalion was in square. They had been in reserve, but Wellington had brought them forward to the right of his line which, so far, had not been attacked. Some men reported that the battle went 'quiet' after the repulse of d'Erlon's Corps and after the waste of the British cavalry that followed d'Erlon's defeat, but 'quiet' was relative. The noise still hammered the eardrums, Hougoumont was ablaze and under siege, but for a while the French made no attempt to cross the valley. The survivors of d'Erlon's Corps were being re-formed on the right of Napoleon's line, making ready to fight again, but Marshal Ney, who had operational command of the French forces, was now on the French left opposite the 52nd. He was on horseback, which gave him added height, and he was also on a rise of ground on the French ridge which let him stare through his telescope at the smoke-wreathed British line.

And what he saw elated him. He saw the salvation of France. He saw victory.

What he really saw was a scattering of British–Dutch guns along the crest with some infantry just beyond. He would have seen the smoke of the exploding French howitzer shells that were being dropped on that infantry, but what caught his attention was what happened beyond that slaughter and, because he was just high enough to see the ground behind Wellington's line, he saw hundreds, maybe thousands, of retreating men. He saw wagons going north, he saw wounded men being carried by comrades, he saw prisoners being escorted, and he jumped to the conclusion that Wellington was disengaging his army and attempting to retreat. In short, he saw the British running away. He also knew that the last thing a good soldier did was allow an enemy to withdraw unmolested. He had made that mistake himself just two days before when he had allowed Wellington to slip away from Quatre-Bras unmolested. Napoleon had savaged Ney for that mistake, and Ney was not going to risk another reprimand. He could see Wellington's men strung along the road as they hurried north towards Brussels, which meant that the troops left behind on the ridge must be few and becoming fewer every minute, so this was the moment to redeem himself and to give France victory!

He ordered the cavalry to charge.

Initially he wanted one brigade of cuirassiers to make the attack, and so he gave the order for almost 900 heavy horsemen with their distinctive breastplates to charge the British ridge between Hougoumont and La Haie Sainte, but the brigade commander, Lieutenant-General Delort, stopped the advance. Delort protested to a fellow general:

> *that I only received orders from the general who commanded the corps to which my division belonged. During this dispute, which stopped the movement of the brigade, Marshal Ney himself arrived, seething with impatience. Not only did he insist on his first order being obeyed, but, in the name of the Emperor, he demanded two other divisions as well! I still hesitated, pointing out that heavy cavalry should not attack infantry that was well posted on high ground, that had not been weakened and was well positioned to defend itself. The Marshal yelled, 'Forwards! The salvation of France is at stake!' I obeyed reluctantly.*

General Edouard Milhaud was the Corps commander who should have given orders to Delort, but Milhaud was himself now caught up in the excitement of the moment. He told Delort to charge, then shook hands with the commander of the Imperial Guard Light Cavalry and urged him, 'We're going to charge! Join us!', which he did and so still more horsemen joined the assault. Colonel Michel Ordener commanded the 1st Cuirassiers and wondered whether military history contained 'other examples of such a mass of horsemen charging simultaneously'. In fact the famous French charge through the snows of Eylau in 1807 was almost twice as large, but Ordener (who had been present at Eylau, but could probably see little through the blinding snowstorm) nevertheless reckoned he had never seen such a mass of cavalry. The 900 had grown to almost 5,000.

*Marshal Ney placed himself at our head, it was 4.00 pm. At first
our impact was irresistible. In spite of a hail of iron which beat
on our helmets and breastplates, in spite of a sunken lane above
which were sited the English batteries, we reached the crest of the
heights and went like lightning through the guns.*

The key words there are 'at first'. Because what was beginning was
perhaps the most extraordinary passage of fighting on that extraordinary day. At first Ordener probably thought Ney was doing the right
thing because, as his horse breasted the British–Dutch ridge, he saw
'the enemy baggage and massed fugitives hurrying along the road to
Brussels', and he saw abandoned artillery through which the horsemen
had passed 'like lightning', but then he saw something else.

British squares. The British were not running away. Wellington was
not disengaging and trying to withdraw his forces. Yes, there were men
and wagons on the road, but most of the British–Dutch army was still
on the ridge and they were ready to fight. The allied guns were indeed
abandoned, but that was temporary because the gunners had taken
refuge inside the squares. Those guns had already taken a toll of the
horsemen, sending roundshot through their ranks to leave crippled
and dying horses in the valley, then they had fired canister at deadly
short range before the gunners ran to the shelter of the nearest infantry
square.

So now it was horsemen against infantry, and every cavalryman
must have known what Captain Duthilt had written, that 'it is difficult,
if not impossible, for the best cavalry to break infantry who are formed
in squares', so while at first the cavalrymen seemed to have pierced the
British–Dutch line, instead they were faced with the worst obstacle a
horseman could encounter. The wide plateau of the ridge top was
packed with squares, at least twenty of them, in a rough chequer pattern
so that if a horseman rode safely past one square he was immediately
faced with another, and then encountered more beyond. And each
square bristled with bayonets and spat musket fire. At that moment the
sensible thing for Marshal Ney to have done was to recognize his

mistake and withdraw the cavalry from danger, but Michel Ney was rarely sensible in battle. He believed courage and passion could drive men through any hardship, and so it might, but it would not drive horses onto the face of a square.

What followed was murderous for both sides. Johnny Kincaid said of Waterloo that he had never 'heard of a battle in which everybody was killed, but this seemed likely to be an exception'. The allies, of course, had warning that the cavalry was coming; they had seen the horsemen massing across the valley and had time to make preparations, which was why young Ensign Leeke's battalion had formed square. The artillery readied themselves too. Sir Augustus Frazer commanded the horse artillery and he galloped to Captain Mercer. 'Left limber up, and as fast as you can! At the gallop, march!' Mercer goes on:

> *I rode with Frazer, whose face was as black as a chimney-sweep's from the smoke, and the jacket-sleeve of his right arm torn open by a musket-ball or case-shot, which had merely grazed his flesh. As we went along he told me that the enemy had assembled an enormous mass of heavy cavalry in front of the point to which he was leading us (about one-third of the distance between Hougoumont and the Charleroi road), and that in all probability we should immediately be charged on gaining our position. 'The Duke's orders, however, are positive,' he added, 'that in the event of their persevering and charging home, you do not expose your men, but retire with them into the adjacent squares of infantry.' As he spoke we were ascending the reverse slope of the main position. We breathed a new atmosphere – the air was suffocatingly hot, resembling that issuing from an oven. We were enveloped in thick smoke … cannon-shot, too, ploughed the ground in all directions, and so thick was the hail of balls and bullets that it seemed dangerous to extend the arm lest it should be torn off.*

The British and Dutch guns were deployed on the flat crest of the ridge and the approaching French cavalry made an unmissable target.

The French talked of 'charging', and going like 'like lightning', but few men could gallop. The charge was restricted by those great bulwarks forward of Wellington's line, La Haie Sainte and Hougoumont. Fire from those two fortresses forced the cavalrymen inwards and the resultant pressure was so great that some horses were lifted off the ground by the animals on either side. They were advancing, too, across wet ground, uphill and through high, obstinate crops, none of which had yet been trampled flat. Mercer said that the leading cavalry came at a 'brisk trot'. When his battery was deployed he estimated the enemy was already within a hundred yards. He ordered case-shot. 'The very first round, I saw, brought down several men and horses.' His five other guns came into action:

> *making terrible slaughter, and in an instant covering the ground with men and horses. Still they persevered in approaching us – the first round had brought them to a walk – though slowly, and it did seem they would ride over us. We were a little below the level of the ground on which they moved, having in front of us a bank of about a foot and a half or two feet high – and this gave more effect to our case-shot ... for the carnage was dreadful.*

It is interesting that Mercer reckons his guns 'were a little below the level of the ground on which they moved'. He was certainly on the ridge's summit, but here the ridge is flat-topped, making a fairly wide plateau, and the British squares are set well back from the forward lip of that flatter land which is about to become a killing ground. Mercer's battery shoot at point-blank range into the horsemen and then Mercer quotes a French account which, he was certain, referred to his guns. 'Through the smoke,' the French cavalryman wrote,

> *I saw the English gunners abandon their pieces, all but six guns stationed under the road, and almost immediately our cuirassiers were upon the squares, whose fire was drawn in zig-zags. Now, I*

*thought, those gunners would be cut to pieces; but no, the devils
kept firing with grape; which mowed us down like grass.*

Thousands of horsemen were now struggling to attack the squares,
but the arithmetic was fatal to them. Assume that a British battalion
had 500 men and made a square of equal sides, then each face of the
square would present four ranks of about thirty men each. That makes
480 men in the four sides of the square, the rest are officers or sergeants
who are in the square's centre. Now take one side of the square. Thirty
men are kneeling and holding their muskets braced and pointing
outwards with fixed bayonets. Thirty more men are crouching in the
second rank with their bayonets also bristling outwards, and behind
them stand sixty men firing muskets. Thirty men take up about fifty
-two feet, which is the width of our notional square, but a horseman
needs much more space, well over three feet and closer to four, so only
about fourteen or fifteen horsemen can charge at the square's face. They
can come in ranks, but the front rank cannot hold more than fifteen
men, and those fifteen are faced by 120 men, half of whom are firing
muskets. That is notional. Squares were usually oblongs, but the arithmetic still holds. If cavalry charged the square, they would be shot
down. Men and horses would fall in agony, and the following horsemen
would be baulked by thrashing hoofs and fallen bodies. The charge is
reduced to chaos with one volley. Lieutenant Eeles, a Rifleman,
describes it well enough. The cuirassiers had charged to within 'thirty
or forty yards' of his square:

> *when I fired a volley from my Company which had the effect,
> added to the fire of the 71st, of bringing so many horses to the
> ground, that it became quite impossible for the Enemy to
> continue their charge. I certainly believe that half of the Enemy
> were at that instant on the ground; some few men and horses
> were killed, more wounded, but by far the greater part were
> thrown down over the dying and wounded.*

So most of the fallen enemy had simply stumbled over the casualties in the front ranks of the charge, and even if the volley had missed, and that often happened with inexperienced troops who tended to fire high, the cavalry still cannot charge into the face of the square because their horses will swerve away from such an obstacle. When the King's German Legion broke the squares at Garcia Hernandez it was because the French volley killed both a horse and its rider and the deadweight of the two corpses acted like a battering ram that drove open a gap in the square's face through which other horsemen galloped, but that battle had been on dry, hard ground, while at Waterloo the horsemen were struggling through mud and matted crops and had already been shaken by roundshot and blasts of canister tearing through their ranks. A Royal Engineer officer took shelter in a square of the 79th and reckoned that too many men fired high with their opening volley, because the musket balls had little effect on the cavalry, but still the horsemen swerved aside to spur along the flanks of the square where, of course, they were greeted with more musket fire. And behind the first row of squares were more squares and more bayonets and more muskets. Ney had led his cavalry into a maze of death.

Cavalry could break squares. It might happen by accident, as it did at Garcia Hernandez, but most likely it would be fear that broke the infantry. A cavalry charge was a fearsome spectacle, big men on big horses, men in breastplates and helmets and plumes, a thunder of hoofs, the sight of swords and sabres raised to strike. Raw troops could panic, or squares could be ripped apart by cannon fire and musketry, offering a chance for horsemen to finish the bloody business. At the battle of Wagram in 1809 the French Chasseurs broke an Austrian square with an oblique attack that slanted into the face which had just fired a volley at another cavalry unit, but the feat was so rare that the Colonel commanding the victorious Chasseurs was immediately rewarded with a promotion.

Even experienced troops could feel overawed by the sight of attacking cavalry. Sergeant Tom Morris, whose officer's pregnant wife had walked all the way from Quatre-Bras to Brussels, was in square and saw the cuirassiers come over the crest.

> *Their appearance, as an enemy, was certainly enough to inspire a feeling of dread, none of them under six feet, defended by steel helmets and breast plates ... The appearance was of such a formidable nature that I thought we could not have the slightest chance with them.*

Rees Howell Gronow was an Ensign in the 1st Foot Guards. His battalion had been left in London to perform ceremonial duties, but young Gronow, just three years out of Eton College and desperate to accompany the army to Flanders, had borrowed £200 and gambled that into £600, which was enough to buy him horses, and without requesting leave he embarked for Belgium. Now, instead of standing guard at St James's Palace, he was on the ridge and no man, he said, could have forgotten 'the awful grandeur of that charge'.

> *You perceived at a distance what appeared to be an overwhelming, long moving line, which, ever advancing, glittered like a stormy wave of the sea when it catches the sunlight. On came the mounted host until they got near enough, whilst the very earth seemed to vibrate beneath their thundering tramp. One might suppose that nothing could have resisted the shock of this terrible moving mass. They were the famous cuirassiers ... who had distinguished themselves on most of the battle-fields of Europe. In an incredibly short period they were within twenty yards of us, shouting 'Vive l'Empereur!' The word of command, 'Prepare to receive cavalry', had been given, every man in the front ranks knelt, and a wall bristling with steel, held together by steady hands, presented itself to the infuriated cuirassiers ... The charge of the French cavalry was gallantly executed; but our well-directed fire brought men and horses down, and ere long the utmost confusion arose in their ranks ... Again and again*

various cavalry regiments, heavy dragoons, lancers, hussars,
carabineers of the Guard, endeavoured to break our walls of steel.

Some of the French cavalry carried carbines, short-barrelled smoothbore muskets, which they fired at the squares, but Gronow reckoned such shots 'produced little effect' and the riders had small chance to reload in the mêlée, while the redcoats were reloading with practised skill. 'Our men', Gronow recorded, 'had orders not to fire unless they could do so on a near mass.' Even the most inaccurate musket could not miss a regiment of cavalry at twenty paces, and the men had orders to shoot at the horses because a fallen and wounded horse was a real obstacle to other riders. 'It was pitiable to witness the agony of the poor horses,' Gronow said. And the musketry worked. Steady, relentless, pitiless volleys reduced the cavalry charge to impotence. The musket fire, he said:

Brought down a large number of horses, and created
indescribable confusion. The horses of the first rank of cuirassiers,
in spite of all the efforts of their riders, came to a stand-still,
shaking and covered with foam, at about twenty yards distance
from our squares, and generally resisted all attempts to force
them to charge the line of serried steel.

Green-jacketed Riflemen formed square too. The rifle was a shorter weapon than a musket, so it carried a longer bayonet, 23 inches of steel. Rifleman John Lewis saw the cuirassiers coming 'all clothed in armour'. Gronow might have thought the carbine fire was ineffective, but Lewis would not have agreed:

We all closed in and formed a square just as they came within
ten yards of us, and they found they could do no good with us;
they fired with their carbines on us, and came to the right-about
directly, and at that moment the man on my right hand was shot
through the body, and the blood ran out at his belly and back like

a pig stuck in the throat; he dropt on his side; I spoke to him; he just said, 'Lewis, I'm done!' and died directly. All this time we kept up a constant fire at the Imperial Guards as they retreated, but they often came to the right-about and fired; and as I was loading my rifle, one of their shots came and struck my rifle, not two inches above my left hand, as I was ramming down the ball with my right hand, and broke the stock, and bent the barrel in such a manner that I could not get the ball down; just at that time ... a nine-pound shot came and cut the serjeant of our company right in two; he was not above three file from me, so I threw down my rifle and went and took his.

Gronow had compared the oncoming cavalry to a 'wave of the sea', and like a wave breaking on a beach the cavalry came, were baulked and retreated. As soon as the horsemen had retreated from the ridge's summit the allied gunners ran from the squares and opened fire again. Captain Mercer double-shotted his cannons, loading a canister on top of a roundshot. The cavalry were re-forming just fifty or sixty yards away, then they charged again and he gave the word 'Fire!'

The effect was terrible, nearly the whole leading rank fell at once; and the round-shot, penetrating the column, carried confusion throughout its extent ... Our guns were served with an astonishing activity ... Those who pushed forward over the heaps of carcasses of men and horses gained but a few paces in advance, there to fall in their turn and add to the difficulties of those succeeding them. The discharge of every gun was followed by a fall of men and horses like that of grass before the mower's scythe.

Yet still the French pushed on, penetrating the gaps between the squares where they were cut down by musket fire. The allied squares were safe enough when the horsemen charged because, with the squares surrounded by cavalry, the French artillery stopped firing, but as soon as the cavalry withdrew the enemy guns started again and, because the horsemen only withdrew a short distance beyond the ridge's crest, the infantry could not lie down. So the squares were pounded with roundshot and shell. The French had also brought horse artillery forward and placed them on the forward lip of the plateau, and those guns joined the bombardment. John Lewis again:

> *The man that stood next to me on my left hand had his left arm shot off by a nine-pound shot, just above his elbow, and he turned round and caught hold of me with his right hand and his blood run all over my trousers.*

Sergeant Tom Morris reckoned that some French gunners advanced with the horsemen and turned a British cannon around and fired what he called 'grape-shot', which was almost certainly canister. 'Our situation', he wrote, 'was truly awful':

> *our men were falling by dozens from the enemy fire. About this time also a large shell fell just in front of us, and while the fuze was burning out we were wondering how many of us it would destroy. When it burst, about seventeen men were killed or wounded.*

Ensign Gronow was appalled at the sights inside the square. 'It was impossible to move a yard,' he wrote:

> *without treading upon a wounded comrade, or upon the bodies of the dead; and the loud groans of the wounded and dying was most appalling … Our square was a perfect hospital, being full of dead, dying and mutilated soldiers. The charges of the cavalry were in appearance very formidable, but in reality a great relief, as the artillery could no longer fire on us.*

Astonishingly, Ney persisted with the cavalry attacks. Not one square had been broken, but still he led the horsemen back up the hill and into the tangled crossfire of disciplined musketry. And he insisted on more men joining the charge until it was almost as large as the charge at Eylau; perhaps 9,000 cavalry were now being hurled at 20,000 infantry. Ney saw a brigade of carabiniers, men with steel breastplates, waiting in a patch of low ground near Hougoumont. Their commander, General Blanchard, had been ordered by General Kellerman not to join the madness, but, as Kellerman recalled, Marshal Ney:

> *galloped over to [the brigade] and lost his temper over its inactivity. He ordered it to throw itself on seven or eight English squares … flanked by numerous artillery batteries. The carabiniers were forced to obey, but their charge met with no success and half the brigade was left lying on the ground.*

'The best of all that France possesses,' General Foy said, watching in amazement as the cavalry rode again and again to its doom. 'I saw their golden breastplates,' a French infantry officer said of the cuirassiers, 'they passed me by and I saw them no more.'

At times the cavalry paused between the squares. They were daring the British infantry to fire because all horsemen knew that their best chance of breaking a square was just after a volley had been fired and when the rear two ranks were reloading; that was how the square at Wagram had been broken, but British infantry was trained to fire by platoon or company so that there were always some loaded muskets. The French cavalry stood no chance. They rode on past the squares, taking fire, and were met by British light cavalry who waited at the rear of the infantry formations. Some Frenchmen tried to escape the return trip through the musket-spitting squares by riding clean round the back of Hougoumont and thus back to their own side of the valley. They were cuirassiers, their horses were tired and many were wounded, but the horsemen found a sunken lane that seemed to offer a safe way back to the French lines, except it was not safe. The lane was blocked with an abatis and the 51st, a Yorkshire battalion, and a regiment of

Brunswickers were waiting close by. Sergeant William Wheeler of the
51st tells what happened in a letter written to his parents five days later:

> *We saw them coming and was prepared, we opened our fire, the
> work was done in an instant. By the time we had loaded and the
> smoke had cleared away, one and only one, solitary individual
> was seen running over the brow in our front. One other was
> saved by Capt. Jno. Ross from being put to death by some of the
> Brunswickers. I went to see what effect our fire had, and never
> before beheld such a sight in as short a space, as about an
> hundred men and horses could be huddled together, there they
> lay. Those who were shot dead were fortunate for the wounded
> horses in their struggles by plunging and kicking soon finished
> what we had begun.*

Wheeler saw just the one survivor, but in truth there were a few
more, and a French infantry major saw them return to his side of the
valley:

> *We saw smoke rising, like that from a burning hay stack … We
> ran to the place and saw fifteen to eighteen cuirassiers … Men
> and horses were distorted, covered in blood and black with mud
> … One sous-lieutenant had gathered these men from that
> terrible, lethal passage through half an army! The horses were
> smothered in sweat and the smoke we had seen was nothing
> more than the steam from their bodies … What a dreadful
> charge!*

And still the horsemen returned and still they were repulsed. The
14th Foot was a Bedfordshire regiment and, alone of all the British
battalions at Waterloo, was not a veteran of Wellington's Peninsular
campaigns. The commanding officer was Lieutenant-Colonel Tidy,
'Old Frank' to his men, and his daughter wrote down her father's advice

to his inexperienced soldiers as they watched the fearsome cavalry come towards them:

> 'Now, my young tinkers,' said he, 'stand firm! While you remain in your present position, old Harry himself can't touch you, but if one of you give way, he will have every mother's son of you, as sure as you are born!'

And that was the key. To stand firm, because as long as the square kept its cohesion then the French cavalry was impotent. Sergeant Wheeler admired:

> the cool intrepid courage of our squares, exposed as they often were to a destructive fire from the French Artillery and at the same time or in less than a minute surrounded on all sides by the enemy's Heavy Cavalry, who would ride up to the very muzzles of our men's firelocks and cut at them in the squares. But this was of no use, not a single square could they break.

Yet the French cavalry was just as brave, riding again and again through the hell of artillery fire into the murderous musket barrages. Lieutenant John Black, of the Royal Scots, almost pitied the enemy, 'it was the grandest sight you can imagine', he wrote to his father:

> to see the men coming at full gallop all in shining armour and shouting 'Vive l'Empereur' with all their souls and our men shouting too as loud as they could bawl. We gave them such a volley their two front ranks fell to a man and away they scampered, our men pricking them down in the most horrid manner until they rode round the outside of the hill and came down on the opposite face, here they met the same reception and faced about … to our rear where they made their third charge with the lancers in front. The cuirassiers were nearly all destroyed, the few remaining were in rear of the lancers, they

*pushed the charge within ten yards of us but our fire was so hot
they could not stand it and they broke in the centre and a part
ran round one side of our square and some on the other, so they
had the whole fire of these two sides and also our front and some
of the men ran to the top of the hill and snapped them going
down and out of 500 or 600 [of] the most beautiful troops in the
world 5 men and 4 horses escaped, can you believe it, but it is
true on my honour.*

But if the most beautiful troops in the world were dying, so were
the redcoats. They hardly suffered from the cavalry, but in between the
charges the French gunners kept firing and 'Close ranks!' was the
repeated command. Some squares shrank into triangles. The roundshot
skimmed the crest, slamming into squares. Sergeant Wheeler saw
General 'Daddy' Hill, who commanded the right flank of Wellington's
army, come into the 51st's square and ask for a drink because he was
parched, and while he was drinking from a private's wooden canteen, a
roundshot killed four men close by. The cavalry charges were failing, at
least as far as Marshal Ney was concerned. He was so frustrated after
having yet another horse shot from beneath him that he was seen beating his sword against a British cannon barrel, but inadvertently he was
abrading the British–Dutch forces because, so long as they must stay in
square to resist the threat of cavalry, so long were they a choice target
for the skilled French gunners.

The Dutch and British cannon were abandoned between charges,
then re-manned as soon as the horsemen withdrew. Those horsemen
did not retreat far. Several eyewitnesses say that the cavalry went back
across the ridge, but their caps and helmets stayed visible just beyond
the crest as they re-formed their ranks for yet another fruitless assault.
How many charges? No one knows. Some say seven or eight, others
twelve or even more, and it is doubtful that the French themselves
knew. They just kept coming until they could stand the losses no longer,
and in between, as they prepared for yet another charge, the French
guns bit at the Dutch–British line. One battalion officer recorded:

We had three companies almost shot to pieces, one shot killed or wounded twenty-five of the 4th Company, another of the same kind killed poor Fisher, my captain, and eighteen of our company … I was speaking to [Fisher] and I got all his brains, his head was blown to atoms.

Private John Smith of the 71st was more graphic: 'Limbs, arms, heads was flying in all directions, nothing ever touched me.' He reckoned the French cavalry 'was the boldest we ever seed, charged us many times but we stood like a rock … they fell to the ground in fifties and sixties, horses and men tumbling in heaps.' So many horses died. Earlier in the battle, before the great cavalry charge, Captain Mercer had watched the gunners of a neighbouring battery try to drive a wounded horse away from their guns and limbers, but the poor beast kept returning, wanting to be with the other horses. They finally drove the animal away and he took refuge with Mercer's team-horses. 'A sickening sensation came over me,' Mercer recalled, 'mixed with a deep feeling of pity.'

A cannon shot had completely carried away the lower part of the animal's head, immediately below the eyes. Still he lived, and seemed fully conscious of all around, whilst his full, clear eye seemed to implore us not to chase him from his companions. I ordered the farrier to put him out of his misery, which, in a few minutes he reported having accomplished, by running his sabre into the animal's heart. Even he evinced feeling.

Some French infantry skirmishers had followed the cavalry and they proved a nuisance, sniping from the lip of the plateau at the gunners while the cavalry re-formed on the lower slope. Mercer's men wanted to use canister on the skirmishers, but he had been ordered to conserve his ammunition and, besides, using canister on a scattered skirmish line was wasteful and probably ineffective. So Mercer decided he must set an example by riding his horse up and down in front of his guns' muzzles:

This quieted my men; but the tall blue gentlemen, seeing me thus dare them, immediately made a target of me, and commenced a very deliberate practice, to show me what bad shots they were, and verify the old artillery proverb, 'The nearer the target, the safer you are.' One fellow certainly made me flinch, but it was a miss; so I shook my finger at him and called him coquin, etc. The rogue grinned as he reloaded, and again took aim ... As if to prolong my torment, he was a terrible time about it. To me it seemed an age. Whenever I turned, the muzzle of his infernal carbine still followed me. At length bang it went, and whiz came the ball close to the back of my neck.

The cavalry charges lasted around two hours. It was a waste, destroying much of Napoleon's cavalry for small purpose and, more importantly, using up precious time. Marshal Ney persevered with a tactic that was not working, and Napoleon, watching from close to La Belle Alliance, did not interfere. Wellington, in contrast, was in the thick of it, riding from battalion to battalion, sometimes taking shelter inside a square and sometimes using his horse's speed to escape an onrush of enemy cavalry. His presence was important. Men watched him, saw his apparent calm and took confidence from it. He spoke to officers, making sure men could hear him above the appalling din: 'Damn the fellow, he's a mere pounder after all!' He encouraged men to endure, promising them a period of peace if the battle was won. He was also heard to mutter that nightfall or the Prussians had better come soon. Yet, so close to the longest day of the year, nightfall was still at least four hours away.

But sometime during the massacre of the French horsemen guns sounded far off to the east. Probably no one in the British–Dutch squares or in the charging squadrons noticed the sound. It would have been drowned out by the blast of allied cannon, by the rattle of musketry, by the distinct sound of musket balls striking breastplates like 'the noise of a violent hail-storm beating on panes of glass', Gronow said, and by the thunder of hoofs, but it was an ominous sound, at least to the French, because it was the thunder of the first Prussian guns. The battle of Waterloo had just become the battle of three armies.

* * *

The Prussians had endured a long, gruelling march on bad roads, and all the while they could hear the guns of Mont St Jean getting nearer and louder. Once past the treacherous defile of the River Lasne they were in the deep, thick Bois de Paris, through which a single muddy track led westwards, and all their guns and ammunition limbers had to be dragged by tired horses along the rutted road. It all took time. There was no point in leaking men onto the battlefield, battalion by battalion, where they would be easy meat for the French; they had to arrive together, ready to fight, and so Blücher arrayed his men in the wood.

He had a choice. He could have tended northwards so that his army joined Wellington's men on their ridge, or he could be bold and strike southwards in an attempt to encircle the French. He chose the latter course. General von Bülow's Corps, which had not fought at Ligny, would attack towards the village of Plancenoit, which lay behind Napoleon's position. Thirty-one thousand men would make the initial attack, and when they came from the wood and spread into their battalion columns on the fields beyond they would see the spire of Plancenoit's church as a landmark.

The 1st Corps, under General von Zieten, which had suffered terribly at Ligny, followed von Bülow's men towards the battlefield. They were taking a more northerly route because their task was to link up with the British–Dutch on their ridge. Messengers had been riding back and forth all day, but now Blücher sent two cavalry officers to announce his arrival to the Duke of Wellington. The two men, in their distinctive Prussian uniforms, galloped along the face of the Duke's left wing which was still littered with the corpses of d'Erlon's infantry. They were cheered all along the line.

It was around 4:30 p.m. when the Prussians made their dramatic appearance from the woods, and so the flanking tactic, which had failed at Ligny and at Quatre-Bras, had at last worked. Napoleon had hoped d'Erlon would make a flank attack at Ligny, while Blücher had the same hopes of Wellington. Now, two days later, a flank attack was happening. Napoleon had prayed it would be Grouchy making the assault, but Grouchy was still at Wavre, where he had found the Prussian rearguard and was attacking it. Grouchy was fighting the wrong battle in the wrong place and the men he had been sent to fight were now fighting Napoleon. 'Our men were exhausted,' Franz Lieber wrote, 'but old Blücher allowed us no rest.'

> As we passed the Marshal ... our soldiers began to hurrah, for it was always a delight to them to see the 'Old One' as he was called. 'Be quiet, my lads,' said he, 'hold your tongues; time enough after the victory is gained.' He issued his famous order ... which concluded with the words, 'We shall conquer because we must conquer.'

Lieber's Colberg Regiment was in reserve, and they watched as von Bülow's men advanced across the open fields towards the distant church spire. Cavalry, infantry and artillery advanced together, an 'all-arms' attack, which was precisely what Marshal Ney had failed to do when he sent the French cavalry up their slope of death. The French artillery began a duel with the heavy Prussian guns, which needed to be moved every few minutes to keep up with the advance. It was a classic attack: guns and infantry together with cavalry supporting them, and with skirmishers out in front. French cavalry constantly threatened the Prussian skirmish line, but only charged them once. Major von Colomb, of the Prussian hussars, chased them away. A little later von Colomb was ordered to attack a French square and he asked for volunteers from his regiment. 'Volunteers, advance!' called von Colomb, and his whole regiment spurred their horses a few paces forward.

There was no cover on those open fields, no reverse slopes to shelter men, and the gunners of both sides had easy targets. Colonel Auguste Pétiet watched as a single roundshot:

> beheaded one squadron commander, took two legs from the horse of another and killed the horse of Colonel Jacquinot, the

*commanding officer of the 1st Lancers and brother to the
Division's general. At a stroke the three senior officers of the 1st
Lancers were down.*

General Lobau was outnumbered and being pushed back, but
behind him was Plancenoit, the biggest village in the district. The
French and Prussians had learned in the narrow alleys of Ligny and
St-Amand just how vicious a fight in a village could be; now they faced
the same ordeal at Plancenoit. The cottages were stone-walled, as was
the churchyard, and Lobau made the village into a fortress. It had to be
held, or else the Prussian army could march behind Napoleon's forces
and cut the Brussels road. Lobau did not disappoint Napoleon, his men
offered a superb defence, but Prussian numbers mounted and soon
Blücher's battalions threatened to surround the village. Lobau appealed
for help.

Lieutenant-General Johann von Thielmann also pleaded for help. He
was the commander of the Prussian rearguard, left at Wavre to stave off
any attack by Grouchy's Corps. Grouchy had 33,000 men, von Thielmann
just half that number, but the Prussians had the River Dyle as a defence
line. The fighting was fierce, especially about the Bridge of Christ in
Wavre, but French numbers allowed Grouchy to outflank von Thielmann,
who sent messengers to Blücher appealing for reinforcements.

'Not a horse's tail shall he get,' was Blücher's response. Blücher knew
that the fight at Wavre was a sideshow. As Gneisenau said, 'it doesn't
matter if he's beaten, so long as we gain the victory here.'

It was a summer evening. Smoke lay thick across the valley and
now spread from the guns at Plancenoit. The fight for that village had
begun, but meanwhile, to the north, where Wellington's line was bloodied and thinned, the French attacked again.

* * *

Marshal Ney's cavalry assault had been brave and hopeless, hurling
horses and men against immovable squares.

Those squares could have been broken by artillery if Ney had
managed to bring more guns close to the line, or he could have

destroyed them with infantry. That was the scissors, paper and stone reality of Napoleonic warfare. If you could force an enemy to form square then you could bring a line of infantry against it and overwhelm it with musket fire, and very late in the afternoon Marshal Ney at last tried that tactic, ordering 8,000 infantry to attack the British squares. One historian has suggested that Napoleon allowed the cavalry charges to continue because the presence of the horsemen forced the British–Dutch forces to stand in square and so become vulnerable to his artillery, and doubtless the artillery had made a terrible slaughter in Wellington's ranks, but was it enough to weaken them and so let a further infantry attack break through the line?

The 8,000 were the infantry from General Reille's Corps who had not been sucked into the fight for Hougoumont. That battle still raged, but the French were no nearer taking the château. Musket balls still hammered the walls, shells exploded in the smouldering wreckage of the main house, and the dead were piled in the orchard and kitchen garden, but Hougoumont was holding.

The château's defenders would have seen the French columns climbing the slope to their east. Eight thousand men marched, their drums beating and Eagles flying. Waterloo was such a vast battle, so overwhelming in its intensity and drama, that this attack by Reille's 8,000 infantry is often overlooked, as if it was a minor skirmish, yet it deserves notice. The largest French infantry assault in the whole Peninsular War was the same size, when 8,000 Frenchmen marched into the horrors of Albuera, and now Marshal Ney sent General Bachelu's division and General Foy's division up the long slope. Their task was to deploy into line and then smother the British squares with musketry, but the British would only be in square if the cavalry threatened and the French cavalry was exhausted. They had charged again and again, they had shown extraordinary courage and too many of them were now dead on the hillside. There was no charge left in them, so the infantry climbed the hill without cavalry support, which meant the British could receive them in line. It was a four-deep line, which restricted British firepower, but the battalion commanders knew that the cavalry might return and a four-deep line was a compromise which allowed a square to be formed more swiftly.

The French infantry had formed up in the bullet-shattered wood below Hougoumont, then marched to the attack. They sent skirmishers ahead, and those men fought against British skirmishers, both sides using the numerous dead and dying horses for shelter. And behind the French *tirailleurs* came the attack columns. 'No sooner had we left the wood', Colonel Trefçon, an aide to General Bachelu, said:

> *than musket balls and canister rained on us. I was next to*
> *General Bachelu when he was hit and had his horse killed …*
> *Just as we reached the English with our bayonets we were met by*
> *a fire of unbelievable violence. Our soldiers fell in hundreds and*
> *the rest had to retreat hurriedly or not one of them would have*
> *come back.*

'Retreat hurriedly' is one way of describing it. General Foy, who led his brigade to the left of Bachelu's division, was blunter:

> *When we were on the point of meeting the English we received a*
> *very lively fire of canister and musketry. It was a hail of death.*
> *The enemy … had their front rank kneeling and presented a*
> *hedge of bayonets. The columns of [General] Bachelu's division*
> *fled first and their flight caused my columns to flee. At that*
> *moment I was wounded. A ball passed through the top of my*
> *right arm, though the bone was not touched. I thought I only had*
> *a bruise and stayed on the battlefield. Everyone was fleeing. I*
> *rallied the remnants of my brigade in the valley next to the wood*
> *of Hougoumont. We were not pursued.*

British infantry firepower had again shown its effectiveness and again the line had overcome the column. Eight thousand men had been defeated in seconds, blasted off the ridge by concentrated musket volleys and shredded by canister. The survivors fled down that terrible slope that was slick with blood, thick with dead and dying horses, and with dead and wounded men. It was littered with breastplates discarded by unhorsed cuirassiers running for their lives, and with scabbards because many of the French cavalry had pointedly thrown away their sword scabbards to show that they would not sheathe their blades until they had victory.

It had been foolish to send unsupported infantry to attack British troops who, though wounded, were unbroken, as foolish as it had been to send cavalry unsupported by infantry or adequate close artillery support. If the Emperor had really thought that sacrificing his cavalry would mean the destruction of Wellington's infantry then he had been proved horribly wrong by 'a hail of death' and 'a fire of unbelievable violence'. If the French were going to break through Wellington's line then they would have to play the lethal game of scissors, paper and stone with far more skill, because Generals Foy and Bachelu had just discovered that the British battalions, battered though they might be, could still deliver overwhelming volleys of musket fire.

The long-range cannonade continued. The redcoats moved further back from the crest and the howitzer shells fell among them and the roundshot skimmed the flat-topped ridge, but this battle was not going to be won by artillery. The French had to attack the British–Dutch line again, and so far every attempt to break through had failed. But then, at last, came the success the French needed.

It was the great crisis at the centre of Wellington's line.

FROM TOP | *'Battle of Mont-Saint-Jean': this view was painted and annotated during the action by Major Kunts of the Hanoverian unit. Hougoumont can be seen burning fiercely at the right.* | *'Attack on the British Squares by French Cavalry at the Battle of Waterloo', by Denis Dighton. Fire from La Haie Sainte and Hougoumont forced the cavalrymen inwards and the resultant pressure was so great that some horses were lifted off the ground by the animals on either side.*

FROM TOP | *'Cuirassiers charging the Highlanders' (detail), by Felix Philippoteaux. The cavalry charges were a waste, destroying much of Napoleon's cavalry for small purpose and, more importantly, using up precious time.* | *'The Duke of Wellington Rallying the Infantry on the Battlefield', by Robert Alexander Hillingford. Wellington was in the thick of it, riding from battalion to battalion, sometimes taking shelter inside a square and sometimes using his horse's speed to escape an onrush of enemy cavalry. His presence was important.*

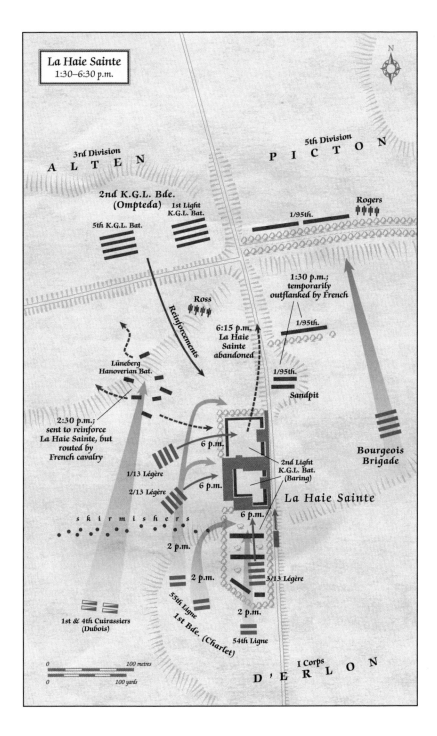

La Haie Sainte
1:30–6:30 p.m.

N

3rd Division
ALTEN

5th Division
PICTON

2nd K.G.L. Bde.
(Ompteda)

1st Light
K.G.L. Bat.

5th K.G.L. Bat.

Rogers

1/95th.

Reinforcements

Ross

1:30 p.m.;
temporarily
outflanked by French

1/95th.

6:15 p.m.,
La Haie
Sainte
abandoned

Lüneberg
Hanoverian Bat.

1/95th.

Sandpit

2:30 p.m.;
sent to reinforce
La Haie Sainte, but
routed by
French cavalry

6 p.m.

1/13 Légère

2nd Light
K.G.L. Bat.
(Baring)

Bourgeois
Brigade

2/13 Légère

6 p.m.

La Haie Sainte

s k i r m i s h e r s

6 p.m.

2 p.m.

3/13 Légère

2 p.m.

55th Ligne

1st Bde. (Charlet)

2 p.m.

1st & 4th Cuirassiers
(Dubois)

54th Ligne

I Corps
D'ERLON

0   100 metres

0   100 yards

256

CHAPTER ELEVEN

Defend yourselves! Defend yourselves! They are coming in everywhere!

'HARD POUNDING THIS, GENTLEMEN,' the Duke of Wellington said as the French guns kept up their bombardment of his line, 'let's see who will pound longest.'

The Duke's strategy was simple enough. He had decided to fight on the ridge and hope to hold Napoleon at bay until Blücher arrived. Now Blücher was at the battlefield, but the Prussian advance seemed frustratingly slow. Wellington gave the appearance of calm, but men noticed how often he consulted his watch and the Duke later remarked that the hands seemed to have slowed to an imperceptible crawl. The Prussian attack on Plancenoit was drawing French troops away from the battle being fought between the two ridges, but that was not yet apparent to Wellington or to his men. They were still being bombarded by the massed artillery, and infantry was being assembled on the French ridge in preparation for another assault on the Duke's position.

Napoleon's beautiful daughters were pounding Wellington's ridge, but artillery alone would not shift the British–Dutch. There would have to be another assault. So far the French had unwittingly helped Wellington. They delayed the start of the fighting to let the ground dry and, on a day when every minute counted, that was a godsend to the Duke. Then d'Erlon had attacked in a cumbersome formation that made it almost impossible for his men to form square, and so they had been broken by cavalry, while Ney, in a fit of optimistic hubris, had thrown the Emperor's cavalry onto British firepower. But now, as the sound of gunfire hammered from around Plancenoit, the French got it right.

La Haie Sainte (the name, mysteriously, means the Holy Hedge) was the central bastion of the Duke's position, a fortress that lay ahead of the ridge beside the main Brussels-to-Charleroi highway. It was a substantial farm, though nowhere near as large as Hougoumont, and built entirely of stone. Nearest the French was an orchard, beyond that lay the farmyard, while closest to the British ridge, and about two hundred yards from the crossroads, was the kitchen garden. The farmyard had buildings on three sides, while the fourth side, flanking the road, was protected by a long and high stone wall pierced by two gates. A large barn formed the southern side of the farmyard, and the barn had big doors that opened onto the fields where the French cavalry had charged, but in their desperation for fires during the wet night the garrison had pulled down, broken up and burned the two doors. The western side of the farmyard was a row of stables and cowsheds, while the northern flank was the farmhouse itself, which was pierced by a narrow passage running from the yard out to the kitchen garden.

The farm had been under siege throughout the battle, but unlike Hougoumont it had not been properly prepared for defence. Those huge barn doors were gone, offering the French an easy entranceway, while the walls had not been loopholed. The pioneers, the men who performed engineering work on the battlefield, had all been sent to prepare Hougoumont for its ordeal and La Haie Sainte had been ignored. A British staff officer was bitter about this failure:

The garrison was insufficient, the workmen were taken away, the place was declared to be sufficiently strong for all that was wanted of it, and nothing whatever was done during the night

towards its defence; in place of which, the works of scaffolding,
loopholing, building up gates and doors, partial unroofing,
throwing out the hay and securing a supply of ammunition,
should have been in progress all the night.

Nevertheless the German defenders staved off every French assault. The French had captured the orchard and kitchen garden, but they were baulked by the stone-built quadrangle of stout buildings and by the riflemen of the King's German Legion. The kitchen garden was recaptured by the garrison when d'Erlon's Corps was broken and retreated, but French skirmishers remained in the orchard. They tried to set fire to the barn roof, but a small pond in the yard provided the garrison with water that they hurled up to extinguish the flames. Major George Baring, an experienced and talented officer, led the defenders. He had started the battle with 400 men, but now, with the reinforcements who had been fed into the farm through the afternoon, he commanded some 800 men.

Their existence was a huge nuisance to the French. Any attack on Wellington's ridge came under flanking fire from the KGL rifles and from the British riflemen in the sandpit just behind the farm and across the road. La Haie Sainte denied the French a chance to attack straight up the centre of Wellington's ridge, forcing them to channel their assaults between the farm and Hougoumont, or between the farm and the buildings on the left of the British–Dutch line.

So La Haie Sainte, despite being underprepared for its ordeal, was proving a major obstacle to French attacks, and they had been attempting to capture it all afternoon. The enemy, Baring wrote, 'fought with a degree of courage which I had never before witnessed in Frenchmen'. The wide-open barn door had been barricaded and it was now partially blocked by enemy corpses, while crude loopholes had been hacked in the exterior walls, some by enemy cannon fire, through which both sides fired. Now, late in the afternoon, after the failure to break through the British left, Marshal Ney was ordered to get rid of the nuisance. He mustered the battalions from d'Erlon's Corps and led them north along the high road, and this time he brought cavalry and mobile artillery too.

The outcome, though Ney was not to know it, was inevitable because the garrison was running perilously short of ammunition. Baring had sent messenger after messenger, desperately appealing for cartridges, but none arrived. The ammunition was behind the ridge, ready to be distributed, but for some reason none of Baring's messages reached the right person and so the garrison's supply dwindled. 'What must have been my feelings,' Baring asked, 'when, on counting the cartridges, I found that on average there was not more than three to four each!'

So, under the sinking sun and the thinning clouds, and beneath the thick pall of sulphurous smoke, the French attacked again. They surrounded the farm and the story of what happened next is best told by one of the German survivors, Rifleman Frederik Lindau. He was singled out as a hero by Baring because earlier in the afternoon he had been twice wounded in the head and, ordered to make his way back to the ridge to find medical help, he had refused to abandon his comrades. He fought on with an inadequate rum-soaked bandage round his scalp so that blood continually trickled down his face. He was in the barn when the big assault came:

> As the loopholes behind us were not fully manned the French fired vigorously at us through these. I and some comrades posted ourselves at these loopholes whereupon the enemies' fire became weaker. Just as I had fired a shot a Frenchman seized my rifle to pull it away. I said to my neighbour; 'Look, that dog is pulling at my rifle.' 'Wait,' he said, 'I have a shot loaded,' and the Frenchman fell away. Just then another grabbed at my rifle, but my neighbour to the right stabbed him in his face. Now as I was about to pull my rifle back to reload a mass of balls flew by me … one of them ripped off my woollen shoulder roll and another smashed my rifle's cock. To obtain another I went to the pond where Sergeant Reese was about to die, he could not even talk

anymore, but when I tried to take his rifle, I knew it was a good one, he made a grim face at me. I took another one, there were plenty lying about, and went back to my loophole. But I had soon fired off all my cartridges and before I could keep on firing I searched the pouches of my fallen comrades, most of which were already empty … Soon after I heard an [officer] shouting all through the farm; 'Defend yourselves! Defend yourselves! They are coming in everywhere!' I observed several Frenchmen on top of the wall. One of them jumped down … but at that same moment I drove my sword bayonet into his chest. He fell down on me and I flung him aside, but my sword bayonet had been bent and I had to throw it away. I saw my Captain in a hand to hand fight with the French at the door of the house. One of them was about to shoot Ensign Frank, but Captain Graeme pierced him with his sword and struck another in the face. I tried to run there to help, but suddenly I was surrounded by the French. I now made good use of the butt of my rifle. I flailed about until only the barrel of my rifle was left, but freed myself. Behind me I heard curses … and noticed two Frenchmen driving Captain Holtzermann into the barn. I was going to help him when a Frenchman gripped me by the chest … then another stabbed at me with his bayonet. I threw the Frenchman sideways so that he became the one to be stabbed; he let go of me and shouting 'Mon Dieu, mon Dieu,' fell to the ground. Now I hurried to the barn where I hoped to escape, but when I found the entrance blocked by a crowd I leaped over a partition to where Captain Holtzermann and some of my comrades were standing. Soon a great crowd of Frenchmen moved in on us …

Lindau was taken prisoner. He was fortunate. He was looted of a great deal of plunder that he, in turn, had looted, but he was not killed by his captors who, in their battle-anger, slaughtered many of the garrison who were trying to surrender. Of the 400 men who had formed the original garrison, just 42 escaped by the narrow passageway that led through the farmhouse. One of those was Lieutenant George Graeme:

> *We all had to pass through a narrow passage. We wanted to stop there and make a charge but it was impossible; the fellows were firing down the passage. [One Frenchman] was about five paces away and levelling his piece at me when [an officer of my company] stabbed him in the mouth and out through his neck; he fell immediately. But now they crowded in.*

Major Baring takes up the tale. Not all the men trying to escape through the passage could reach the garden, presumably because the narrow corridor became blocked by dead or dying men:

> *Among the sufferers here was Ensign Frank, who had already been wounded; the first man that attacked him he ran through with his sabre, but at the same moment his arm was broken by a ball from another; nevertheless he reached a bedroom and succeeded in concealing himself behind a bed. Two of the men also took refuge in the same place, but the French followed close at their heels, crying 'No pardon for you bastard greens!' and shot them before his face.*

Ensign Frank stayed hidden and was never discovered. Lieutenant Graeme also managed to evade capture and made a dash through the kitchen garden and so back to the ridge top. While this struggle was going on the Prince of Orange, Slender Billy, ordered a battalion of the King's German Legion to advance on the farm in an attempt to relieve the garrison. The commander of the battalion, Colonel Ompteda, protested that the French had cavalry in support of their infantry and that his battalion could not cope with both, but the callow Prince of Orange knew better and insisted that Ompteda, a vastly experienced soldier, obey his orders. Ompteda obeyed and died, and his battalion was virtually destroyed by cuirassiers, who captured another colour. Slender Billy had struck again.

La Haie Sainte was lost because its garrison had run out of ammunition, so that men were forced to fight against an outnumbering enemy with bayonets, swords and rifle butts. Wellington took responsibility for the loss. Many years later the 5th Earl Stanhope recorded a conversation with the Duke, who:

> *lamented the loss of La Haie Sainte from the fault of the officer commanding there 'who was the Prince of Orange'; but immediately correcting himself – 'No – in fact it was my fault, for I ought to have looked into it myself.'*

The French had lost a large number of men in the assault, but their capture of the farm meant they were able to bring horse artillery to the compound. They garrisoned the buildings and sent skirmishers up the slope to harass the British–Dutch line. The cannons, especially, made horrific slaughter among Wellington's men because they were now close enough to fire canister. Ensign the Honourable George Keppel, just sixteen years old, was in the 14th Regiment that was marched to reinforce the centre of Wellington's threatened line. The battalion was forced to form square because of the proximity of enemy cavalry and a bugler of the 51st Regiment, who had been out with the skirmishers and now retreated, mistook the 14th's square for his own, but took refuge anyway. 'Here I am again,' Keppel remembers the bugler saying, 'safe enough.'

> *The words were scarcely out of his mouth, when a round shot took off his head and spattered the whole battalion with his brains, the colours and the ensigns in charge of them coming in for an extra share. One of them, Charles Fraser, a fine gentleman in speech and manner, raised a laugh by drawling out, 'How extremely disgusting!'*

The 14th was the young regiment that had not served with Wellington in the Peninsula. About half its men and half its officers were below the age of twenty, and now it suffered grievously because the French gunners, Keppel said, had 'brought us completely within range'. The regiment was ordered to lie down and Keppel instead took a seat on a drum where he petted the muzzle of the Colonel's horse.

> *Suddenly my drum capsized and I was thrown prostrate, with the feeling of a blow on my right cheek. I put my hand to my head, thinking half my face was shot away, but the skin was not even abraded. A piece of shell had struck the horse on the nose exactly between my hand and my head, and killed him instantly. The blow I received was from the embossed crown on the horse's bit.*

Shells, canister and roundshot hammered at the 14th. 'If we had continued much longer in this exposed situation I should probably not have lived to tell the tale,' Keppel wrote, but then the regiment was ordered further back from the crest, which had become too dangerous for any troops.

Ney saw the backward movement and he saw too that the centre of Wellington's line was perilously undermanned. The troops in Wellington's centre had been hurt by artillery fire and the Prince of Orange had managed to destroy a whole battalion of the King's German Legion, but the French were also weakened. The troops who had captured La Haie Sainte had suffered enormous losses and they were not sufficient to mount a new attack on the ridge top, so Ney sent an urgent message to Napoleon asking for reinforcements. Those reinforcements could march straight up the main road and, supported by the guns at La Haie Sainte and by the French cavalry which had already captured one KGL colour, they could smash their way through the centre of the British–Dutch position. It was a real opportunity and Ney saw it; he just needed the troops.

Napoleon refused to send them. 'Where does he think I'll find the troops?' he asked sarcastically. 'Does he think I'll make them?'

Yet he did have the troops. The Emperor's reserve, the Imperial Guard, was still intact and unblooded, but Napoleon held most of them back. Some were being sent to Plancenoit where the Prussians were pushing hard, so hard that roundshot from their cannon was now falling on the Brussels-to-Charleroi high road behind the Emperor, but most of the Guard, the Immortals, were still in reserve and could have gone to Ney. The Emperor waited instead.

And now, as the evening set in, came the hard time on the British ridge. It was as if the French sensed their weakness and redoubled their efforts with their cannon, some of which were now posted between La Haie Sainte and the elm tree at the crossroads. 'We would happily have charged those guns,' Ensign Edward Macready of the 30th Foot recalled:

> but, had we deployed, the cavalry that flanked them would
> have made an example of us … It was now to be seen which
> side had most bottom, and would stand killing longest. The
> Duke visited us frequently at this momentous period; he was
> coolness personified. As he crossed the rear face of our square a
> shell fell amongst our grenadiers, and he checked his horse to
> see its effect. Some men were blown to pieces by the explosion,
> and he merely stirred the rein of his charger … No leader ever
> possessed so fully the confidence of his soldiery, 'but none did
> love him'; wherever he appeared, a murmur of 'Silence – stand
> to your front – here's the Duke!' was heard … and then all was
> steady as on a parade. His aides-de-camp, Colonels Canning
> and Gordon, fell near our square, and the former died within it.
> As [Wellington] came near us late in the evening, Halkett rode
> out to him and represented our weak state, begging His Grace
> to afford us a little support.

Wellington's answer was grim. General Halkett's request for relief was, the Duke said, impossible. 'Every Englishman on the field must die on the spot we now occupy.' One measure of just how dire the outlook appeared was an order to take the 30th's regimental colours to the rear. 'This measure has been reprobated by many,' Macready said, 'but I know I never in my life felt such joy, or looked on danger with so light a heart, as when I saw our dear old rags in safety.'

Colours were only sent to the rear at moments of supreme danger so that, if defeat ensued, at least the enemy would not have the satisfaction of taking the trophies. Other battalions thought about retiring their colours. Ensign James Howard was with the 33rd, the Duke's old regiment, and 18 June was young Howard's birthday. He wrote to his brother that 'we had our share of bloody work. I shall never forget the scene and the carnage.' After the fall of La Haie Sainte Howard looked around:

> *Our brigade and a brigade of guards were the only soldiers that we could see, and we were so [isolated] ... that I thought that things were going badly, and we made up our minds to send all our colours to the rear, still determined to stay while we had a man left. There we were, we could just maintain our ground, when to our delight came up lots of reinforcements.*

Wellington himself brought the reinforcements, and they were his last reserve. For the moment all he could do was keep his men on the ridge and shelter them from the enemy cannon as best he could, but when battalions retreated onto the reverse slope to escape the round-shot and shells, they left the crest open to enemy skirmishers and the French had sent thousands of men in open order to harass the British–Dutch line. The fall of La Haie Sainte had allowed the French to occupy most of the forward slope of the British ridge and the voltigeurs were thick there, while behind them cavalry lurked in the dense powder smoke. 'The regiment', Ensign Leeke of the 52nd wrote:

> *Stood about forty paces below the crest of the position, so that it was nearly or quite out of fire. The roar of round-shot still*

*continued, many only just clearing our heads, others
striking the top of our position and bounding over us, others
again, almost spent and rolling down gently towards us. One
of these, when we were standing in line, came rolling down like
a cricket ball, so slowly that I was putting out my foot to stop
it, when my colour-sergeant quickly begged me not to do so,
and told me that it might seriously have injured my foot.
Exactly in front of me, when standing in line, lay, at the
distance of two yards, a dead tortoise-shell kitten. It had
probably been frightened out of Hougoumont, which was the
nearest house to us.*

Shells were lobbed over the ridge and did more damage, though one seventeen-year-old private in the 23rd picked up a smoking shell, its fuse fizzing and smoking as it burned towards the central charge, and the boy hurled it far away as if he were throwing a ball. It exploded harmlessly. The roundshot, because their trajectory was flatter, were less dangerous to those men protected by the reverse slope, but even so many soldiers ducked as the balls flew low overhead. Sir John Colborne, the charismatic commanding officer of the 52nd, told them to stop ducking, else it would be thought they were the second battalion. It was customary, at least in two battalion regiments, for the first to see active service and for the second to stay at home and train recruits. The reprimand worked and the men stayed upright. The 52nd might have been relatively safe from roundshot, but they were suffering badly from the French skirmishers on the ridge's crest. Captain Patrick Campbell, a company officer who had been on leave and had returned to the regiment that same afternoon, said the fire was particularly thick when the Duke rode by.

Next to the 52nd was a battalion of the 1st Foot Guards which, like the 52nd, was in square for fear that French cavalry might surge over the ridge top again. Being in square made them an easy target for the skirmishers who infested the ridge's crest, but the Duke, seeing what was happening, took command of the Guards battalion and ordered it into line, a four-deep line, and took the line forward himself. They drove the skirmishers off the ridge top with volleys of musket fire. Ensign Leeke watched from one of the 52nd's two squares:

> *A body of cavalry was now seen approaching, but the [Guards] battalion reformed square with rapidity and regularity. The cavalry refused the square, but receiving its fire, and then dashing along the face of the 52nd regiment, it exposed itself to another vigorous fire by which it was nearly destroyed. The third battalion of the 1st Guards retired in perfect order to its original position.*

Other battalions followed the example of the Guards and formed line to drive the voltigeurs away, yet all the discipline in the world, and Leeke's dry account is witness to the superb drill and discipline of the redcoats in that murderous environment, could not prevent losses mounting as shells exploded, roundshot slashed through ranks and the enemy skirmishers swarmed back. But the French skirmishers did at least one favour for the allies when a sharpshooter put a musket ball into the Prince of Orange's left shoulder. Slender Billy left the field to get medical attention, which meant he could do no more damage. The French hardly needed his help. Mercer described 'a cloud of skirmishers' who had closed up to the British ridge and were galling it with cannon fire while the big guns roared on, their missiles screaming across the smoke-filled valley where the shadows lengthened. Poor Major Baring, who had been evicted from La Haie Sainte, joined his few survivors to another KGL battalion. He had found an abandoned French cavalry horse which he mounted, but five bullets hit the saddle and another knocked off his hat. 'Nothing', he wrote:

> *seemed likely to terminate the slaughter but the entire destruction of one army or the other. My horse, the third which I had had in the course of the day, received a ball in his head; he sprung up, and in coming down again, fell on my right leg, and pressed me*

*so hard into the deep loamy soil, that, despite of all exertion, I
could not extricate myself.*

He was finally rescued, but he noted that the centre of Wellington's
line 'was only weakly and irregularly occupied'. He was just to the
right of the 27th Foot, which was among the worst-hit of all the
British–Dutch units. They were an Irish regiment, brought up from the
reserves to strengthen Wellington's centre, and they were close to the
French guns emplaced at La Haie Sainte. The Irishmen stood their
ground, and died there too: 16 of their 19 officers were killed or
wounded, while out of around 700 other ranks no fewer than 463 were
casualties. When the battle was over the 27th was still in square, but a
square made largely of dead men. In the square of the 73rd Highlanders
who had fought so hard at Quatre-Bras, the ranks were reluctant to
close up, fearing perhaps that the next enemy roundshot would follow
the same path as the ball that had just slaughtered their comrades.
Lieutenant-Colonel Harris, their commanding officer, rode his horse
into the gap and said, 'Well, my lads, if you won't, I must,' and that
persuaded them to their duty. At some point during their ordeal the
Duke approached the square of the 73rd and asked who commanded
it. 'I replied "Colonel Harris",' Captain John Garland recalled, and the
Duke 'then desired me to tell Colonel Harris to form line, but should
we be attacked by the cuirassiers to reform square'. A line, even one of
four ranks, was far less vulnerable to cannon fire than a square.

Poor Garland was to be badly wounded and spent months in a
Brussels hospital before returning to his native Dorset, where he
named his home Quatre-Bras Cottage. His encounter with Wellington
is a reminder of how the Duke was ever at the point of most danger
and ready to offer advice or orders. Napoleon watched the battle from
afar, but Wellington needed to see and hear what was happening. He
had briefly taken command of the Guards battalion, then moved on
down the ridge, encouraging men and, above all, being seen. Shaw
Kennedy, a British staff officer, talked of the Duke's 'coolness', his
'precision and energy', his 'complete self-possession'.

He left the impression that he was perfectly calm during every phase, however serious, of the action. He felt confident of his own powers of being able to guide the storm which raged around him; and from the determined manner in which he then spoke, it was evident that he had resolved to defend to the last extremity every inch of the position which he then held.

The Duke must have known that Napoleon would make a last effort to break his line and all he could do was preserve that line in readiness for the assault, and so the allied troops had to endure the cannonade. Mark Adkin, who has done more than anyone to study the grim statistics of the battle, estimates that two-thirds of the Duke's casualties were caused by artillery, and it was during this period that most of those casualties were made. All along the ridge there was death and mutilation. Marshal Ney was probably right. One sharp attack, well conducted by a combination of guns, cavalry and infantry, would surely have shattered Wellington's attenuated line, but Napoleon's refusal to send the reinforcements had given the Duke time. He was using it to rally his troops and, because the leading Prussian troops of von Zieten's Corps were now reaching the eastern end of the ridge, he could bring men from the extreme left of his line to thicken the centre. He sent orders for Major-General Sir Hussey Vivian to bring his light cavalry brigade to the centre of the ridge, but Vivian, an intelligent and experienced cavalry commander, had anticipated the order and was already on his way. He led his men to where the redcoats were suffering:

Never did I witness anything so terrific; the ground actually covered in dead and dying, cannon shots and shells flying thicker than I ever heard even musketry before, and our troops, some of them, giving way.

The troops giving way were some raw young Brunswickers who retreated in panic from the carnage at the ridge top. Vivian's cavalry checked their flight, but it was the Duke himself who rallied them and led them back to the ridge. He did the same with a strong battalion of Dutch–Belgians, the very last of his reserves. Henry Duperier who, despite his French name, was an officer in the 18th Hussars serving under General Vivian, was posted behind these raw troops and watched their officers:

> *leathering away (as the drover did the cattle in Spain) to make them smell the gunpowder ... I done like the Belgian officers, every one that faced about I laid my sword across his shoulders, and told him that if he did not go back I would run him through, and that had the desired effect, for they all stood it.*

By advancing his battalions in strong four-deep lines the Duke managed to clear most of the skirmishers from the ridge's crest, and that enabled riflemen from the 95th to snipe at the French artillerymen who had established their batteries so close to the crossroads. Yet the lines could not stay on the crest, for fear of the larger French guns further back, and so the skirmishers would swarm back as soon as the allied infantry retired. For many of the allied army these were the worst moments of the battle. The French occupied the forward slope of the Duke's position and their guns were causing terrible damage to the defenders. Yet it was not the Duke who was in trouble, it was the Emperor, because the Prussians were on the battlefield now and it was Napoleon who was running out of time.

* * *

Marshal von Bülow's troops drove the French out of Plancenoit. It was gutter fighting, close-quarters carnage with bayonets and musket butts in alleys and cottage gardens. Cannon blasted roundshot and canister down narrow streets fogged by powder smoke and puddled with blood. A few French troops hung on to some houses on the village's western edge, but they were in danger of being surrounded by Prussian troops advancing in the fields either side of the village.

Napoleon could not afford to lose Plancenoit. It lay behind his line and would make a base from which Blücher's troops could advance on the Brussels highway. If that highway was cut, then the French would have no road on which to retreat. They would be effectively surrounded, and so the Emperor sent his Young Guard to retake the village.

The Young Guard was part of the Imperial Guard, those elite troops so beloved of the Emperor. To join the Guard a soldier had to have taken part in three campaigns and be of proven character, a requirement less moral than disciplinary, and the successful applicants were rewarded with better equipment, higher pay and a distinctive uniform. Traditionally the Guard, which had its own infantry, cavalry and artillery and so formed an army within the army, was held back from battle so that it was available to make the killing stroke when it was needed. There was, naturally enough, some resentment within the wider French army of the privileges accorded to the Guard, but never-theless most soldiers held the ambition of being chosen to join its ranks. Their nickname, 'the Immortals', was partly sarcastic, referring to the many battles when the Guard had not been called into action (the Guard called themselves *grognards*, grumblers, because they found it frustrating to be held in reserve when other men were fight-ing). But if there was resentment there was also admiration. The Guard was intensely loyal to Napoleon, they were proven to be brave men, they fought like tigers, and their boast was that they had never been defeated. No enemy would ever underestimate their fighting ability or their effectiveness.

The Young Guard were skirmishers, though they could fight in line or square like any other battalion, and there were just over 4,700 of them at Waterloo. When it became apparent that Lobau's outnumbered men were being driven from Plancenoit the Emperor despatched all eight battalions of the Young Guard to retake the village. They were led by General Guillaume Philibert Duhesme, a thoroughly nasty character who was a child of the French Revolution. A labourer's son, he had risen to high rank because he was competent, but he was also corrupt, venal, cruel and sadistic. He had trained as a lawyer, then become a soldier, and regarded Napoleon with some suspicion, believing, rightly, that the Emperor had betrayed many of the principles of the French Revolution, but Duhesme was too good a soldier to be ignored and

Napoleon trusted him with the Young Guard. Duhesme was an expert on light infantry tactics, indeed his slim textbook *Essai Historique de l'Infanterie Légère* became the standard work on the subject for much of the nineteenth century.

Light infantry, trained to think and act independently, were perfectly suited to the counter-attack on Plancenoit. The Young Guard advanced and took musket fire from houses on the village edge, but Duhesme refused to let them answer that fire, instead leading them straight into the streets and alleys that would be cleared by their bayonets. It worked, and the Prussians were tumbled back out of the village and even pursued for some distance beyond. General Duhesme was badly wounded in the head during the vicious fighting and was to die two days later.

The Young Guard had done everything asked of it and upheld the traditions of the Imperial Guard, but von Bülow's men were being reinforced minute by minute as more troops crossed the Lasne valley and made their way through the woods to the battlefield. The Prussians counter-attacked, driving the French out of the houses on the western side of the village and besieging the stone-walled churchyard. Colonel Johann von Hiller led one of two Prussian columns that:

> *succeeded in capturing a howitzer, two cannon, several ammunition wagons and two staff officers along with several hundred men. The open square around the churchyard was surrounded by houses from which the enemy could not be dislodged ... a firefight developed at fifteen to thirty paces range which ultimately decimated the Prussian battalions.*

The Young Guard was fighting desperately, but Blücher could feed still more men into the turmoil and slowly, inevitably, the Young Guard was forced back. The Prussians recaptured the church and its graveyard, then went house by house, garden by garden, fighting through alleys edged by burning houses, and the Young Guard, now hopelessly outnumbered, retreated grudgingly.

Napoleon had thirteen battalions of the Imperial Guard left in his reserve. He had arrayed them north and south to form a defensive line in case the Prussians broke through at Plancenoit, but to prevent that he now sent two battalions of the Old Guard to reinforce the hard-pressed French troops in the village. The two battalions went into the smoke and chaos with fixed bayonets, their arrival heartened the French survivors and the fight for Plancenoit swung again, this time in favour of the French. The newly arrived veterans of the Old Guard fought their way back to the high churchyard, captured it and garrisoned themselves inside its stone wall. Even they were hard-pressed and at one moment their General, Baron Pelet, seized the precious Eagle and shouted, 'A moi, Chasseurs! Sauvons l'Aigle ou mourons autour d'elle!' To me, Chasseurs! Save the Eagle or die around her! The Guard rallied. Pelet, later in the fight, discovered Guardsmen cutting the throats of Prussian prisoners and, disgusted, stopped the murders. For the moment, at least, Pelet had stiffened the French defence and Plancenoit belonged to the Emperor, and so the threat to Napoleon's rear had been averted.

Yet von Bülow's men were not the only Prussians arriving at the battlefield. Lieutenant-General Hans von Zieten's 1st Corps had left Wavre early in the afternoon and taken a more northerly route than von Bülow's men. They had been delayed because General Pirch's 2nd Corps was following von Bülow's southern route and von Zieten's and Pirch's Corps, each of several thousand men with guns and ammunition wagons, met at a crossroads and there was inevitable confusion as the two columns tried to cross each other's line of march. Von Bülow and Pirch had been sent to attack Napoleon's right wing at Plancenoit, while von Zieten's men took the more northerly roads so that they could link up with Wellington's men on the ridge.

General von Zieten's men had been heavily engaged in the fighting at Ligny, where they had lost almost half their strength. Now, in the slanting sun of the evening, von Zieten led around five thousand men towards Wellington's position. They would have heard the battle long before they saw it, though the pall of powder smoke, lit by the sheet-lightning of gun-flashes, would have been visible above the trees. The first contact came when the leading troops reached the château of Frichermont, a substantial building on the extreme left of Wellington's position. It had been garrisoned by Bernhard of Saxe-Weimar's Nassauer troops, the same men who had saved Quatre-Bras with their gallant defence two days before. Saxe-Weimar had been fighting all afternoon, staving off French attacks on Papelotte and La Haie; now suddenly he was attacked from the rear. One of his officers, Captain von Rettburg, recalled how his infantry was driven back 'by numerous skirmishers followed by infantry columns':

> *Skirmishers even attacked me from the hedges in my rear. When I drove them off I became aware that we were faced by Prussians! They in turn recognised their error which had lasted less than ten minutes but had caused several dead and wounded on both sides.*

What von Rettburg does not say is that it was his bravery that ended the unfortunate clash of allies. He made his way through the musket fire to tell the Prussians their mistake. The Nassauers wore a dark green uniform, which could be mistaken for the dark blue of French coats, and their headgear was French in shape.

More chaos was to follow. General von Zieten's men were needed desperately on the ridge. Wellington knew another French assault was likely, and if the Prussians reinforced his left wing he could bring troops from there to strengthen his centre. General von Zieten sent scouts ahead and one of them, a young officer, returned to say that all was lost. He had seen Wellington's army in full retreat. Just like Marshal Ney he had mistaken the chaos behind Wellington's line for defeat, thinking it was a panicked attempt to escape when in fact it was just wounded men being taken to the rear, ammunition wagons, servants and stray horses. Shells exploded among them and roundshot, skimming the ridge, threw up gouts of earth where they landed. It looked as if the French were cannonading the panicked mass, adding to the impression of a rout. The Prussian officer could probably see little that happened on the ridge itself, it was so fogged by powder smoke, but through that smoke he would have seen the red flash of French cannons firing and the smaller flicker of muskets, their sudden flames lighting the smoke and fading instantly. Every now and then there was a larger explosion as a shell found an artillery caisson, and the 'cloud' of French skirmishers was close to the ridge's crest, and so were some of the cannon, and behind the skirmishers were prowling cavalry, dimly visible through the smoke. No wonder the young officer believed that the French had captured Wellington's ridge and that the Duke's forces were in full retreat. He galloped back to von Zieten and told him it was hopeless, that there was no point in joining Wellington because the Duke was defeated.

And at that same moment a staff officer arrived from Blücher with new orders. The newcomer, Captain von Scharnhorst, could not find von Zieten, so he galloped to the head of the column and gave them their orders directly: they were to turn round and march south to help Blücher with his stalled attack on Plancenoit. Wellington, it seemed, would not be reinforced; instead the Prussians would fight their separate battle south of Napoleon's ridge.

General von Müffling, the liaison officer with Wellington, had been waiting for von Zieten's arrival. He had expected it much earlier, but now, at last, von Zieten's Corps was in sight at the extreme left wing of Wellington's position. Then, to von Müffling's astonishment, those troops turned and marched away. 'By this retrograde movement,' he wrote, 'the battle might have been lost.' So von Müffling put spurs to his horse and galloped after the retreating Prussians.

Meanwhile a furious argument was raging between Lieutenant-Colonel von Reiche, one of von Zieten's staff officers, and Captain von Scharnhorst. Von Reiche wanted to obey the original orders and go to Wellington's assistance, despite the report of the Duke's defeat, but von Scharnhorst insisted that Blücher's new orders must be obeyed. 'I pointed out to him', von Reiche said:

> *that everything had been arranged with von Müffling, that Wellington counted on our arrival close to him, but von*

Scharnhorst did not want to listen to anything. He declared that I
would be held responsible if I disobeyed Blücher's orders. Never
had I found myself in such a predicament. On one hand our
troops were endangered at Plancenoit, on the other Wellington
was relying on our help. I was in despair. General von Ziethen
was nowhere to be found.

The troops had paused while this argument raged, but then General
Steinmetz, who commanded the advance guard of von Zieten's column,
came galloping up, angry at the delay, and brusquely told von Reiche
that Blücher's new orders would be obeyed. The column dutifully
continued marching eastwards, looking for a smaller lane that led south
towards Plancenoit, but just then von Zieten himself appeared and the
argument started all over again. Von Zieten listened and then took a
brave decision. He would ignore Blücher's new orders and, believing
von Müffling's assurance that the Duke was not in full retreat, he
ordered his troops onto the British–Dutch ridge. The Prussian 1st
Corps would join Wellington after all.

The 1st Corps had its own guns, 6-pounder cannons and 7-pounder
howitzers, and they were the first of von Zieten's weapons to be
unleashed on the French. They were presumably firing along the face
of the ridge, probably aiming at the gun-flashes lighting the smoke
around La Haie Sainte, and fairly soon after opening fire the Prussian
guns found themselves being answered with counter-battery fire.
Captain Mercer, of the Royal Horse Artillery, tells the story best:

We had scarcely fired many rounds at the enfilading battery,
when a tall man in the black Brunswick uniform came galloping
up to me from the rear, exclaiming 'Ah! Mine Gott! Mine Gott!
Vat is it you done, sare? Dat is your friends de Proosiens; ans you
kills dem!'

The Prussian guns had been aiming at Mercer's battery and caused
casualties, and Mercer, despite the Duke's orders that forbade counter-

battery fire, had responded. That mistake too was eventually corrected. Such errors were probably unavoidable: there were too many unfamiliar uniforms in the allied armies and the smoke was casting a gloom over a battlefield lit by the glare of flames. It was past seven in the evening now and the fortunes of war had swung sharply against the Emperor, yet all was not lost.

Napoleon's Imperial Guard was working its magic again. Ten battalions had been sufficient to stall the Prussian attack on Plancenoit, and eleven battalions remained in reserve. The French were pushing hard at Wellington's line, they were close to the ridge top now, especially at the centre above La Haie Sainte. Ney had pleaded for more troops so he could launch a killer blow at Wellington's centre and Napoleon had refused him, but now, with Prussian numbers increasing, it was time to throw the best troops of France, if not of all Europe, at the Duke's wounded line.

John Cross was a Captain in the 52nd, the largest of Wellington's battalions, so large that it formed two squares instead of one. Cross, a Peninsular veteran, had been badly bruised earlier in the day, but had stayed with his company. The battalion had repeatedly advanced over the crest to push French skirmishers down the forward slope, and as they did it again, firing volleys to drive the voltigeurs back, Cross saw enemy cuirassiers riding through the smoke towards Hougoumont. There was nothing very unusual about that, cavalry had been prowling in the valley ever since their charges had failed to break the allied squares, but now Cross saw one of the cuirassier officers suddenly break away from the rest of the horsemen. The Frenchman galloped full speed 'towards the 52nd', Cross remembered, 'hallooing lustily, "*Vive le Roi!*" as he approached.' He held his sword high over his head, but the sword was in its scabbard as a signal that he did not come to fight. He was a Royalist and he came with a warning, that 'the Imperial Guards were on the march to make a grand attack'.

The Imperial Guards were the undefeated, they were the Immortals. And they would finish the battle.

ABOVE | 'Wellington at Waterloo', by Ernest Crofts. Wellington gave the appearance of calm, but men noticed how often he consulted his timepiece and the Duke later remarked that the watch's hands seemed to have slowed to an imperceptible crawl.

OVERLEAF | 'Attacking the Prussians in Plancenoit in the Battle of Waterloo', by Adolf Northen. Eventually, von Bülow's troops drove the French out of Plancenoit. It was gutter fighting, close-quarters carnage with bayonets and musket butts in alleys and cottage gardens. Cannon blasted roundshot and canister down narrow streets fogged by powder smoke and puddled with blood.

ABOVE | 'The Kings German Legion defending La Haie Sainte', by Adolf Northen. The presence of the KGL was a huge nuisance to the French. Any attack on Wellington's ridge came under flanking fire from their rifles and from the British riflemen in the sandpit just behind the farm and across the road. La Haie Sainte denied the French a chance to attack straight up the centre of Wellington's ridge.

BELOW | 'The Battle of Waterloo', by Sir William Allan. Depicting the so-called 'crisis of the battle' at around 7:30 p.m. as Napoleon and his staff in the foreground prepare for their final attack, while the battle rages in the background. The painting was purchased from the artist by Wellington and now hangs in Apsley House in London.

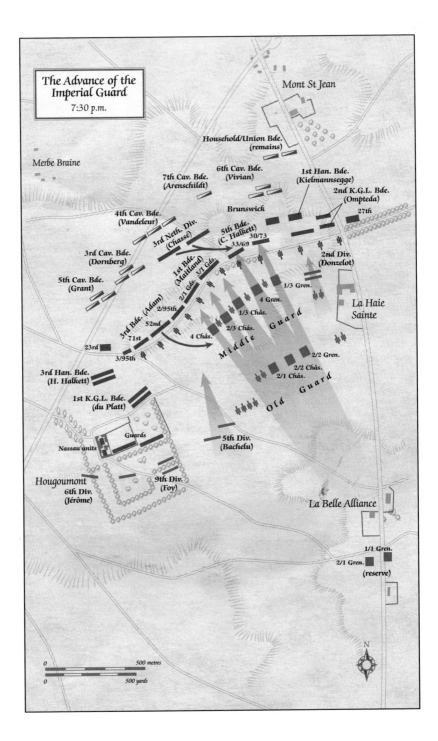

The Advance of the
Imperial Guard
7:30 p.m.

Mont St Jean

Merbe Braine

Household/Union Bde.
(remains)

6th Cav. Bde.
(Vivian)

7th Cav. Bde.
(Arenschildt)

1st Han. Bde.
(Kielmannsegge)

2nd K.G.L. Bde.
(Ompteda)

27th

Brunswick

4th Cav. Bde.
(Vandeleur)

3rd Neth. Div.
(Chassé)

5th Bde.
(C. Halkett)
33/69

30/73

2nd Div.
(Donzelot)

3rd Cav. Bde.
(Dornberg)

1st Bde.
(Maitland)
2/1 Gds. 3/1 Gds.

La Haie
Sainte

5th Cav. Bde.
(Grant)

1/3 Gren.

4 Gren.

2/95th

3rd Bde. (Adam)

1/3 Châs.

52nd

2/3 Châs.

Middle Guard

71st

23rd

4 Châs.

2/2 Gren.

2/2 Châs.

3/95th

Old Guard

2/1 Châs.

3rd Han. Bde.
(H. Halkett)

1st K.G.L. Bde.
(du Platt)

Guards

Nassau units

5th Div.
(Bachelu)

Hougoumont
6th Div.
(Jérôme)

9th Div.
(Foy)

La Belle Alliance

1/1 Gren.

2/1 Gren.

(reserve)

N

0   500 metres
0   500 yards

CHAPTER TWELVE

Next to a battle lost, the greatest misery is a battle gained

I T IS NOW ABOUT seven in the evening, still light though the shadows are lengthening. The weather has cleared, the last showers travelling eastwards to where Marshal Grouchy was fighting the Prussian rearguard at Wavre. The sky over Mont St Jean is ragged with cloud, the sun slanting through the gaps to light the sullen pall of smoke that hangs above the rye, barley and wheat which has been trampled, one British officer said, to the consistency of an Indian rush mat. Thousands of corpses lie in the valley and on the ridge which Wellington's men have held through eight hours of fighting. It is still not over, but Napoleon knows he has only one chance of victory left. And the Emperor is a gambler, so he rolls the dice. They come up five and three.

Five battalions of the Middle Guard and three battalions of the Old Guard would march towards the bloodied slope in a last attack on the allied line. Eight battalions. Napoleon had started the day with twenty-one battalions of the Imperial Guard, but he had been forced to send ten of those to hold off the Prussians at Plancenoit. Of the eleven who remained (there was another battalion at Rossomme, guarding the

Emperor's baggage and too far away to be summoned for this last assault) he kept three in reserve. Napoleon gave the order to General Drouot, the commander of the Guard, *'La Garde au feu!'*

At most the eight battalions contained around 5,000 men, probably slightly fewer. The first infantry attack on Wellington's line had consisted of 18,000 troops, the second, the assault by Bachelu and Foy, around 8,000. Count d'Erlon's 18,000 men had come close to success, but the intervention of the British Heavy Cavalry had shattered them. Bachelu and Foy had been defeated with almost contemptuous ease, blasted off the slope by redcoat musketry, so at first sight the attack by the Imperial Guard looks hopeless before it begins, especially as the three battalions of the Old Guard, the *grognards*, were held in reserve. Those three battalions marched down into the valley and stayed there, ready to follow up the success of the five attack battalions of the Middle Guard. Those five numbered around 3,500 men, perilously few to assault a position defended by the Duke of Wellington, but those 3,500 were all veterans and all fanatical supporters of the Emperor. They had a reputation to keep and they were imbued with enormous confidence. They knew they were only sent into battle when things were desperate and their boast was that they were undefeated, and there were few men who would have denied that Napoleon's Imperial Guard were perhaps the finest troops in Europe.

Nor would the Middle Guard attack alone. The remnants of all Napoleon's infantry were sent forward to press on the allied ridge. True, they were not marched in columns, but sent as a thick skirmish line, and behind them were the survivors of the Emperor's cavalry. Two batteries of Imperial Guard horse artillery accompanied the eight battalions, and the Grand Battery was firing at the ridge until their own men obscured their targets.

Napoleon himself led the Guard forward. He rode at their head down from the French ridge to the valley floor where he handed them over to Marshal Ney, who would lead them to the British–Dutch ridge. And off to Napoleon's right, somewhere beyond the skeins of smoke lying over the corpses of d'Erlon's men, there were new troops visible on the allied ridge, new troops and new guns, and the Emperor, knowing that the arrival of the Prussians would damage the morale of his men, lied to them. He sent officers to spread the untruth that the newcomers were Grouchy's men come to assault Wellington's left wing while the Immortals broke through his centre. One of the officers who was ordered to spread the lie was Colonel Octave Le Vavasseur, an artillery officer and an aide to Marshal Ney. Le Vavasseur wrote in his memoirs:

> I set off at a gallop with my hat raised on the tip of my sabre and rode down the line shouting 'Vive l'Empereur! Soldats, voilà Grouchy!' The shout was echoed by a thousand voices. The excitement of the troops reached feverish levels and they were all shouting, 'En avant! En avant! Vive l'Empereur!'

The line that Le Vavasseur galloped was virtually the width of the battlefield. Every man who could advance was being urged forward. The infantry who had captured La Haie Sainte went up the ridge, as did the rest of d'Erlon's Corps. The survivors from General Bachelu's brigade were attacking close to Hougoumont and there was renewed fighting at the château itself as Foy's men assaulted the walls. General Reille's men advanced behind the Guard, and all of them knew this was the supreme effort to win the day. Ney had harangued the troops. Captain Pierre Robinaux, one of the infantrymen besieging Hougoumont, heard the red-haired Marshal yell, 'Courage! The French army is victorious! The enemy is beaten everywhere!' and shortly after a staff officer arrived with the Emperor's announcement that Grouchy's troops had come to the battlefield. Napoleon was deceiving his men in an effort to raise their morale, and most soldiers believed the report, but a General who encountered Le Vavasseur knew better. 'Look,' he said disgustedly, gesturing towards the left wing of Wellington's ridge, 'it's the Prussians.'

Throwing in the Guard was a gamble, of course, yet Napoleon faced a grim choice. 'Space', he once said, 'I can recover, but time never.'

Blücher's attack on Plancenoit was being stalled by Lobau's men and by the ten battalions of the Guard who had gone to Lobau's help, but Napoleon knew that Prussian numbers would only increase. He knew too that Prussian reinforcements had reached the eastern end of Wellington's line and it was only a matter of time before those newcomers spread along the width of the ridge. In short, he would soon face two armies that together outnumbered him hugely. But there were still two hours of daylight left, and that was time enough to destroy one of the armies. If the Guard could break through Wellington's line, if the French could swarm over the ridge and send the British–Dutch reeling back in chaotic defeat, then he could turn on the Prussians, and they, seeing their ally so comprehensively defeated, might retreat. Or just stay where they were till nightfall. Then 19 June could bring a new battle, only this time Grouchy really would return to take part. It was a gamble, but victory on the British-held ridge would tip the odds back in France's favour. 'On s'engage,' Napoleon had once said in one of those statements that made war seem so simple, 'et alors on voit.' You engage, then you see what happens! So he would engage and the world would see what happened.

What was his alternative? If he did not attack then he would be attacked. He was already being assaulted in Plancenoit and if he withdrew his soldiers to the ridge where they had started the day then he could expect a combined assault from the British–Dutch and the Prussians. The sensible course was to retreat, to take what was left of his army and withdraw across the River Sambre and so live to fight another day, but retreat would be difficult if not impossible. He would have to send thousands of men south along the Charleroi road and hope to hold off the enemy as his troops withdrew, and a few miles along that road was the narrow bridge at Genappe, a bridge just eight feet wide, the only place where all his cannon and ammunition and baggage wagons could cross the smaller River Dyle. Retreat would probably lead to chaos, to confusion and defeat. So attack. Send the Immortals to do what they were so good at doing: winning the Emperor's battles. 'Fortune', the Emperor once said, 'is a woman, she will change!' But fortune needed help, and that was why the Imperial Guard existed, to make certain fortune gave the Emperor victory.

La Garde au feu! En avant! Vive l'Empereur! The drums were beating the *pas de charge* as the Guard, the unbeaten Guard, marched north along the highway led by 150 bandsmen playing patriotic tunes. The band stopped well short of La Haie Sainte and the Emperor stayed with the musicians as the eight battalions swerved left off the road. They were in the flat valley bed now where five battalions of the Middle Guard formed their attack columns. Roundshot and shell screamed overhead, hammering the British–Dutch ridge. The Guard sent no skirmishers ahead, there were already skirmishers enough on the slope. The Guard would march to the attack and spread into line when they reached the enemy and blast him off the ridge's top with musketry. Some historians have wondered why Ney led them leftwards instead of marching straight up the highway, but it would have been almost impossible to keep the columns in formation if the Guard had to negotiate the sunken road beside La Haie Sainte, let alone the farm itself and the sandpit beyond and the shattered gun carriages and the hundreds of corpses that lay on the crushed rye. So Ney led them towards the slope where he had charged with the cavalry, and that slope was thick with the dead too, but it was less obstructed, more inviting ground. The Guards wore tall bearskin hats that made them seem huge. They wore blue greatcoats with red epaulettes and those tall bearskin hats were plumed in red. They did not always wear the plumes, which could be stored in a cardboard tube, but they had been told they would parade in full dress uniform in the *Grand Place* of Brussels, and it seems they wore the plumes to battle that summer evening. The road to Brussels was the open ground that rose to the ridge's crest, a slope of dead horses and dying men, a road to victory.

Officers led the columns. They could see the ridge ahead through the smoke, and they saw no enemy there except for the gunners who opened fire almost as soon as the Guard columns formed. Shrapnel cracked overhead, roundshot slashed through the ranks that closed up and kept closing up as they marched. The drums beat, pausing to let the Guardsmen shout, 'Vive l'Empereur!'

They were assaulting Wellington's right, his strongest flank, the same flank that had seen off Bachelu and Foy. Beyond the crest, unseen on the reverse slope, Wellington had three of his strongest units. To the west, nearest Hougoumont, was General Adam's brigade, every battalion a veteran of the Peninsular War. They included the 52nd, the large Oxfordshire battalion. To their left was Maitland's Brigade of Guards. The British Guards would defend against the Imperial Guard, and closest to the crossroads was a division of Hanoverian troops reinforced by King's German Legion battalions and General Halkett's British redcoats. They were on the reverse slope, so the French, marching up the slope, saw no enemy infantry. They saw the flash of gunfire from blackened cannon muzzles, saw the smoke billow thick, saw their own ranks fall as the roundshot slashed through, and as they got closer the gunners switched to double-shot, loading canister over roundshot, and the carnage got worse, but it was never enough to stop the Guard. They were the Immortals and they were marching to destiny.

Napoleon watched from the valley's far side. He saw the Imperial Guard divide into two columns; no one is sure why that happened, but the two climbed up the far slope and did Napoleon remember his conversation at breakfast? He had asked his generals for their opinion of Wellington and of British troops and he had not liked their answers. It was General Reille who had said that British infantry, well posted, was impregnable. Well, that remained to be seen. *On s'engage, et alors on voit.* The Immortals were about to engage the Impregnable. The unbeaten would fight the unbeatable.

* * *

It is strange that this climactic clash between the Imperial Guard and Wellington's infantry is still wrapped in mystery. There is disagreement about what formation the Imperial Guard used. Was it in column or did they advance in square? And why did the original formation divide into two? We do not know. The fight that ensued is one of history's most famous passages of arms, we have eyewitness accounts, thousands of men took part and many retold their experiences, yet still we do not know exactly what happened. There is even disagreement about who should take the victor's honours, yet perhaps none of that is surprising. No one on either side was taking notes. The survivors disagreed about what time the clash occurred, though probably the Guard was ordered to advance soon after 7:30 p.m. and it was all over by 8:30 p.m. And the men who were there, the men who made history, could only see a few yards around them, and what they saw was obscured by thick smoke, and their ears were assailed by the buzz of musket balls, the crash of cannons firing, the cries of the wounded, the clamour of officers and sergeants shouting, the explosions of shells, the incessant hammering of musket volleys, the pounding of more distant guns, the drums beating and trumpets screaming. It was noise without relief, deafening. One British officer recalled that he shouted orders and even the man standing next to him could not hear his words. How was a man to make sense of what happened when all he could see was smoke, blood and flame, and he was deafened, and life itself depended on doing your duty despite the fear that clawed at the heart? That was the purpose of training and discipline, that at the moment when destiny hangs in the balance, when chaos rules, when death is leering close, then a man does his duty. The instinct is to flee such horror, but discipline offers another way through.

The Old Guard's horse artillery was the first of the Guard into action. They had divided into four sections and the batteries unlimbered where the steepest part of the slope ended, so they were firing from the edge of the crest's fairly flat summit. The ridge curved so that the Imperial Guard was attacking into the belly of the arc and the allied guns were converging their fire into the tight-packed ranks that kept advancing. Now, as the Guard's own artillery came into action, the French could hit back. 'The rapidity and precision of this fire was appalling,' Captain Mercer wrote:

> Every shot almost took effect, and I certainly expected we should all be annihilated. Our horses and limbers being a little retired down the [reverse] slope, had hitherto been somewhat under

cover from the direct fire in front; but this plunged right amongst
them, knocking them down by pairs and creating horrible
confusion. The drivers could hardly extricate themselves from
one dead horse ere another fell ... One shell I saw explode under
the two finest wheel-horses in the troop, down they dropped.

Not every allied cannon could fire. Some had lost their crews, or a wheel of their carriage had been smashed and not yet replaced, but sufficient guns remained to do terrible damage to the advancing Guard, yet not enough to stop them. Smoke thickened with every discharge, men remembered seeing the passage of roundshot through the Guard's ranks marked by flying muskets, but the Guard closed ranks and the drummers drove them up the slope towards the flat crest where the allied infantry waited. Ensign Macready, who we last met as he watched his battalion's colours being carried to the rear, was in position to receive the easternmost column of the Guard, the one advancing closest to the ridge's centre. Macready was just seventeen, and facing the Emperor's veterans. They were seen 'ascending our position,' he said:

in as correct order as at a review. As they rose step by step before
us, and crossed the ridge, their red epaulettes and cross-belts put
on over their blue great-coats, gave them a gigantic appearance,
which was increased by their high hairy caps and long red
feathers, which waved with the nod of their heads as they kept
time to a drum in the centre of their column. 'Now for a clawing,'
I muttered, and I confess, when I saw the imposing advance of
these men, and thought of the character they had gained, I
looked for nothing but a bayonet in my body, and I half breathed
a confident sort of wish that it might not touch my vitals.

Macready and his battalion, the 30th, would be attacked by two battalions of the Middle Guard, both Grenadiers of the Guard. The name Grenadiers was obsolete; the troops no longer carried grenades, but traditionally the Grenadiers were the heavy infantry, the assault troops. In a British battalion there was a Light Company, who were the skirmishers, and a Grenadier Company, who were expected to do the heavy, close-quarters work. These two battalions of the Middle Guard were marching directly at Major-General Sir Colin Halkett's brigade. Halkett was a Peninsular veteran who had served most of his career in the King's German Legion, though at Waterloo he commanded four British battalions. All four had suffered severely at Quatre-Bras thanks to Slender Billy's stupidity, so the four battalions were reorganized as two. Macready's 30th was in square with the 73rd, while to their left was a square of the 33rd and the unfortunate 69th, who had lost their colour at Quatre-Bras. They were not alone, of course. To their right were the British Guards and to their left were battalions of German and Dutch troops. But nor were the two attacking battalions alone either. They were supported by the heav   arms of men from General Reille's Corps who climbed the ridge ' ehind the Guard, they were being assisted by close-quarters a *illery fire, and the remaining French cavalry were ready to take advantage of any breakthrough. Historian Mark Adkin says: 'In effect this attack was as near a general advance, spearheaded by the Guard, that the French achieved at Waterloo.'

The Guard's spearhead was on the flat ridge top. Were they in column? Or square? Mark Adkin demonstrates very persuasively that, though many of the eyewitnesses on th   allied side saw columns, the French were in square, presumably because they feared a repetition of the disaster that had struck d'Erlon's attack. A compact square, its sides shrinking as the ranks closed up after artillery strikes, would look very much like a column, and neither formation, column or square, would be fully coherent on that evening. Not only were the ranks and files being struck by roundshot and canister, but their route was littered with the bodies of dead or wounded horses. Only the best infantry could hope to keep their formations tight under such circumstances and the Imperial Guard were the best and so, despite the obstacles and despite the cannon fire '   eached the ridge's wide crest where they had to deploy into line. .   al Halkett's four British battalions had also been in square because of the French cavalry that had threatened all evening, but as the French Guard reached the ridge top the General ordered the redcoats into a four-deep line. 'My boys,' he shouted, 'you have done everything I could have wished and more than I could expect, but much remains to be done. At this moment we have nothing for it but a charge!'

Macready takes up the story:

The enemy halted, carried arms about forty paces from us, and fired a volley. We returned it, and giving our 'Hurrah!' brought down the bayonets. Our surprise was inexpressible, when, pushing through the clearing smoke, we saw the back of the Imperial Grenadiers; we halted and stared at each other as if mistrusting our eyesight. Some 9-pounders from the rear of our right poured in the grape amongst them, and the slaughter was dreadful. In no part of the field did I see carcasses so heaped upon each other.

Macready wrote to his father some three weeks after the battle. 'When they came within twenty paces,' he says in that letter:

we gave them a volley and a huzza, and prepared for a charge, but they spared us the trouble, away they went ... But I am endeavouring to do an impossibility, to describe a battle; so little did we know of it ... Our General of Brigade Halkett ... made an elegant speech to us in the middle of the action, which was answered, by the reiterated shouts of our brave fellows, 'Let's charge your honour, we'll stick it to them.'

Macready makes it sound easy, which it was not. A Hanoverian brigade to the left of the redcoats was forced back by what a Hanoverian officer described as 'such a powerful attack'. The Hanoverians had run out of ammunition, and their commanding officer was killed as they retreated. Meanwhile Halkett's brigade had driven the French Guards back by volley fire and by the threat of bayonets, but then something strange happened. The Imperial Guard gunners were close to Halkett's brigade and firing at the redcoats who had advanced across the road running along the ridge's top. For the moment it seemed the Guard infantry was defeated, but the gunners were raking the redcoat four-deep line and so the brigade was ordered to turn about and take shelter behind the hedge and bank that lined the road behind them. Macready again:

> *We faced about by word of command, and stepped off in perfect order. As we descended the [reverse slope] the fire thickened tremendously, and the cries from men struck down, as well as from the numerous wounded on all sides of us, who thought themselves abandoned, were terrible. An extraordinary number of men and officers of both regiments went down almost in no time. Prendergast of ours was shattered by a shell, McNab killed by grape-shot, and James and Bullen lost all their legs by round-shot during this retreat, or in the cannonade immediately preceding it. As I recovered my feet from a tumble, a friend knocked against me, screaming, half maddened by his five wounds and the sad scene going on, 'Is it deep, Mac, is it deep?' At this instant we found ourselves commingled with the 33rd and 69th Regiments; all order was lost.*

The brigade had panicked. They had turned the Grenadiers of the Imperial Guard back, then frightened themselves into retreat and the panic was spreading fast. Officers and sergeants tried to halt them, to no effect. 'Fifty cuirassier would have annihilated our brigade,' Macready reckoned, and for a moment it seemed the brigade's discipline had gone entirely. Men were fighting, jostling their way to the rear, but then, Macready says, one man cheered and the cheer reversed the panic as other men joined in. General Halkett is said to have seized a colour of the 33rd, just as General Pelet had seized an Eagle in Plancenoit, and stood with it till men formed on him, and Wellington was there and he was ever a steadying influence. Besides, he had once commanded the 33rd, and God help them if they disgraced him now. And a Dutch gun battery opened fire on the French at close range, decimating the Guard's wounded ranks, and a Dutch–Belgian brigade was firing volleys at the Frenchmen, and somehow the panic was stilled. 'The officers did wonders,' Macready said, 'but the shout alone saved us. I never could learn who raised it.' And so, after the momentary terror, the four battalions turned, formed line again and stood their ground. To Henry Duperier, the paymaster of the British 18th Hussars, the sudden reappearance of Halkett's brigade was a surprise. He was stationed with the rest of the cavalry behind the infantry on Wellington's ridge and watching the Dutch infantry fire when 'Lord Wellington brought some little red-coated fellows from where I do not know, I could just see them through the cloud of smoke.'

'I am endeavouring to do an impossibility,' Macready had written to his father, 'to describe a battle.' So what did happen at the ridge top when the first column, or square, of Imperial Guardsmen attacked? There was confusion on both sides. The Hanoverians retreated in some disorder, but so did the redcoats. The Dutch–Belgians had fought well, and their gunners did sterling work. The French also retreated, blasted by that immense opening volley from General Halkett's line. The French gunners were causing havoc, and it was their fire more than anything else that provoked the panic in General Halkett's brigade. It is to the brigade's credit that the panic was momentary, but they were fortunate that no French troops were able to take advantage of the brief disorder. The French themselves were probably close to panic. They had retreated from the terrible opening volley, the Dutch guns were crashing canister and roundshot into them, the ridge was shrouded in smoke and their leading ranks were dead or wounded. All that can be said with certainty is that the westernmost column of the Imperial Guard failed, that they were thrown back from Wellington's line and stayed back. General Halkett was wounded in the fight, but had the satisfaction of knowing his men had rallied and were holding their ground.

Meanwhile the second French attack, the larger attack, struck the ridge's crest to Halkett's right where the British Brigade of Guards and

General Adam's fine brigade of light infantry waited for them. Harry Powell was a Captain in the 1st Foot Guards and, like the rest of that battalion, had been lying flat on the reverse slope:

There ran along this part of the position a cart road, on one side of which was a ditch and a bank, in and under which the Brigade sheltered themselves during the cannonade, which might have lasted three-quarters of an hour. Without the protection of this bank, every creature must have perished. The Emperor probably calculated on [that] effect, for suddenly the firing ceased, and as the smoke cleared away a most superb sight opened on us. A close Column of Grenadiers (about seventies in front) of la Moyenne Guard, about 6,000 strong, led, as we have since heard, by Marshal Ney, were seen ascending the rise au pas de charge shouting 'Vive l'Empereur'. They continued to advance till within fifty or sixty paces of our front, when the Brigade were ordered to stand up. Whether it was from the sudden and unexpected appearance of a Corps so near them, which must have seemed as starting out of the ground, or the tremendously heavy fire we threw into them, La Garde, who had never before failed in an attack, suddenly stopped.

Captain Powell believed, as did the whole Brigade of Guards, that they faced the Grenadiers of the Middle Guard, when in truth they were facing the Chasseurs of the Guard, and that mistake is why to this day we have a regiment called the Grenadier Guards. The 1st Foot Guards were honoured with the name of their enemy, though in truth it was Halkett's men who had confronted the French Grenadiers. Powell also reckons their numbers at 6,000, a pardonable error in that evening of noise and chaos, but in truth the larger French column could not have had more than 2,000 men.

The Duke was there, of course. He was sitting on Copenhagen, his trusted horse, and watching the French Guard approach. He waited till they were close, Captain Powell reckoned fifty or sixty paces, and once again the Duke took command. 'Now, Maitland!' he called to the brigade commander, 'Now's your time! Up Guards!' They stood, shook themselves into line, 'Make ready!' a pause while those big heavy muskets were raised to bruised shoulders, 'Fire!'

And the slaughter began. This was what British infantry did best. Harry Powell called it 'tremendously heavy fire', the shock of disciplined musket volleys fired at close range. 'In less than a minute,' Powell said:

above 300 were down. They now wavered, and several of the rear divisions began to draw out as if to deploy, whilst some men in their rear beginning to fire over the heads of those in front was so evident a proof of their confusion.

The Imperial Guard was trying to deploy into line, but once again, as had happened so many times in the Peninsula, they had left it too late. The Brigade of Guards outnumbered them and overlapped them, the musket balls were coming from in front and from the sides, and when they tried to spread into a line they were beaten back by those steady, relentless volleys. To the Imperial Guards in the leading ranks it must have come as a dreadful surprise. They had climbed the ridge and taken their punishment from the artillery and, just as it seemed they had reached the crest and could surge across the road running along its summit, an enemy appears from behind the low bank. An enemy that outnumbers them and an enemy that is already far too close to allow the French Guard to deploy into line, an enemy that fires with a terrible efficiency. Raw, badly trained troops often opened fire at far too long a range and then had a tendency to shoot high, but not the Brigade of Guards. They were shooting at a range where a musket could hardly miss, and their enemy, if he wanted to reload, had to halt, and then the ranks behind pushed him on, and so the Chasseurs fell into confusion and still those relentless volleys struck them and more men died. They were obstructed now by their own dead and wounded, and the Brigade of Guards was still firing until Lieutenant-Colonel Alexander, Lord Saltoun, shouted them forward. Saltoun had taken a company to reinforce Macdonell in Hougoumont, but had brought them back to the ridge for these closing moments of the fight, or rather he brought back the survivors, just one-third of the number that had gone down to the château. 'Now's the time, my boys!' he shouted, and the Guards levelled bayonets and charged. 'At that moment,' Captain Reeve, another Peninsular veteran recalled, 'we charged them, they went to the right about and fled in all directions.'

The British Guards advanced down the slope, herding the panicked Imperial Guard, and presumably at that moment the Grenadiers of the Guard, who had assaulted Halkett's Brigade, also retreated. Marshal Ney had his last horse shot from under him, but the French Guard had not finished with their assault. Some eyewitnesses claim that the second, larger attack was composed of two columns, not one (or two formations in square). What they saw was the 4th Chasseurs of the Guard who had lagged behind the others, probably because they had to march the farthest, and who were now climbing the ridge to make their own attack. They were the closest Imperial Guard to Hougoumont, out on the British right, and their disciplined fire checked the British Guards, and at the same moment French cavalry was seen in the smoke of the valley and an order was shouted for the British Guards to form square. There was a moment's confusion as, apparently, other officers tried to keep the men in line to take on the 4th Chasseurs, and the confusion was only resolved by taking the Guards back to the ridge's crest where, once again, they formed in four-deep line.

There is a natural tendency to make order out of disorder, to describe a battle in the simplest terms to make chaos comprehensible. In most accounts of Waterloo the charge of the Imperial Guard is the climactic moment, an isolated event that decides the day, but though it was decisive, it was not isolated. Virtually every man who remained on the battlefield was engaged in fighting. All the surviving guns were firing. To the east of the main highway d'Erlon's men were pushing up the ridge's slope, fighting against British, Dutch and now Prussian troops. The noise is deafening, so intense that men cannot hear orders shouted by an officer or by a sergeant next to them. The Imperial Guard who have reached the ridge top and been pushed back by Dutch and British musketry have not retreated into the valley, they are still on the forward slope, supported there by General Reille's infantry, ready to advance again into that terrible musketry. They are in some disorder, but they are not yet beaten, and their enemies are in disorder too. And the whole curving ridge of Wellington's line is shrouded in smoke so that men cannot see what happened just a few paces away. We know that four of the five attacking battalions of the Imperial Guard have been checked and pushed backwards, but to the men in General Adam's brigade, only some two or three hundred yards eastwards, that was all hidden. They just saw smoke lit by gunfire, they heard the unending percussion of the guns, the crackling noise of muskets, the screams. And they heard the *pas de charge*, the drum-driven chant of France's warriors marching to glory. It came from the 4th Chasseurs, the last of the Imperial Guard's attacking battalions, coming up the slope. Ensign Leeke of the 52nd could not see them yet because they were still on the forward slope, but he could hear them:

> *The drummers were beating the pas de charge, which sounded, as*
> *well as I recollect, very much like this, 'the rum dum, the rum*
> *dum, the rummadum dummadum, dum, dum', then 'Vive*
> *l'Empereur'. This was repeated again and again.*

The 4th Chasseurs were the last of the brave trying to break Wellington's line, but on their left, at the ridge's crest, was General Adam's brigade, which contained the 52nd, the big Oxfordshire battalion that was under the command of Sir John Colborne. Sir John was thirty-seven years old and an immensely experienced soldier who had fought through the Peninsular War. At a time when most officers gained their promotion by purchase, buying their way up the hierarchy, Colborne had gained every step by merit. He had been a protégé of the great Sir John Moore, who had promoted him to Major, and it had been Moore's dying wish at the battle of Corunna that Colborne should get his Lieutenant-Colonelcy, which was granted. He was as efficient as he was popular, and now, as the 4th Chasseurs of the Guard reached the ridge-top plateau and tried to deploy into line, he made himself famous.

He took the 52nd out of line. Half Colborne's men were Peninsular veterans, they knew their business. Sir John marched his battalion forward, then wheeled it round so that his men faced the left flank of the Guard Chasseurs. His brigade commander, Sir Frederick Adam, galloped to discover what he was doing and Colborne later thought he answered that he was going 'to make that Column feel our fire'. General Adam, just thirty-four years old, had the sense to let Colborne continue; indeed he rode to the 71st and ordered them to follow the 52nd, who were now on the forward slope, their own flank exposed to whatever enemy lurked in the valley's smoke, but they were in position to slaughter the Guard and they did. They began firing volleys into the French flank so that the Imperial Guardsmen were being attacked from their front and from their left. It was merciless. The Unbeaten were being killed by the Unbeatable. Colborne's men took heavy casualties from the French Guard, but his own volleys were tearing the 4th Chasseurs apart and the frontal fire of the British Guards was hammering into their leading ranks and, like the other battalions of the Imperial Guard, they broke. They did not just retreat, they broke. They had been beaten by British volleys and they fled that terrible musketry and when they fled so did the rest of the Guard.

And when they broke, so did the hopes of France. 'Fortune is a woman,' Napoleon had said, and now she spat in his face. When the 4th Chasseurs broke, so did his army. The morale of the French troops collapsed, panic set in, men saw the undefeated Guard fleeing in defeat and they fled too. Even Napoleon admitted it:

Several regiments ... seeing part of the Guard in flight thought it was the Old Guard and were shaken; shouts of 'All is lost! The Guard is beaten!' were raised. The soldiers even declare that at some points ill-disposed men shouted, 'Every man for himself!' ... a panic spread over the whole battlefield; a disorderly rush was made towards our line of retreat; soldiers, gunners, wagons all crowded to reach it.

It was so sudden. All afternoon and evening the battle had raged, the French pushing hard and bravely against Wellington's line, and suddenly, in an instant, there was no French army, just a rabble of panicked fugitives.

Wellington rode back towards the centre of his line. Leeke had seen him just before the 52nd marched out of line to destroy an Emperor's dreams. The Duke's clothes, Leeke said, 'consisted of a blue surtout coat, white kerseymere pantaloons, and Hessian boots. He wore a sword with a waist belt, but no sash.' The plain blue coat and black cocked hat made Wellington instantly recognizable to his men, and now, as the French began to flee, he watched from the ridge's centre for a few moments. He saw an enemy in panic, a retreating enemy that was dissolving into chaos. He watched them, then was heard to mutter, 'In for a penny, in for a pound.' He took off his cocked hat and men say that just then a slanting ray of evening sunlight came through the clouds to illuminate him on the ridge he had defended all day. He waved the hat towards the enemy. He waved it three times, and it was a signal for the whole allied line to advance.

Not every man saw the signal. Just as it took time for the panic to infect the whole French army, so it took a time for the relief of victory to become apparent to the allies. Captain John Kincaid had been fighting French skirmishers with his riflemen when:

> presently a cheer, which we knew to be British, commenced far to the right, and made everyone prick up his ears; it was Lord Wellington's long-wished-for orders to advance; it gradually approached, growing louder as it drew near, we took it up by instinct, charged through the hedge … sending our adversaries flying at the point of the bayonet. Lord Wellington galloped up to us at the instant, and our men began to cheer him; but he called out, 'No cheering, my lads, but forward, and complete your victory.'

Moments earlier the 52nd, who had advanced across the face of the forward slope before turning right to march up the highway towards La

Belle Alliance, had mistaken some British light cavalry for French horse-men and emptied some saddles with their musket fire. Wellington had been there. 'Never mind!' he had shouted at Colborne. 'Go on! Go on!' Some 95th Riflemen advanced with Colborne's battalion, 'such a carnage I never before beheld,' wrote Captain Joseph Logan of the Greenjackets:

> *That noble fellow Lord Wellington moved on with the 95th and frequently cried out 'Move on my brave fellows.' I feared for his safety; myself I did not care about. My god! Had he fallen what a bitter day it would have been for England.*

So the whole allied line advanced into the valley, except it was no longer a line because the casualties had been too great. Baron von Müffling, the Prussian liaison officer, recalled:

> *When the line of infantry moved forward, small masses of only some hundred men, at great intervals, were seen everywhere advancing. The position in which the infantry had fought was marked, as far as the eye could see, by a red line caused by the red uniforms of the numerous killed and wounded who lay there.*

A red line of dead, dying and suffering men. It is a terrible image. And in front of them, in the valley, were more casualties, and thousands of wounded and dying horses. Leeke said some horses were:

> *lying, some standing, but some of both were eating the trodden down wheat or rye, notwithstanding that their legs were shot off ... there was a peculiar smell at this time, arising from a mingling of the smell of the wheat trodden flat down with the smell of gunpowder.*

And it was over that trodden-down wheat and rye, and past the dying horses, and through the litter of battle that the allied infantry advanced. 'I have seen nothing like that moment,' Sir Augustus Frazer, commander of the Royal Horse Artillery, remembered, 'the sky literally darkened with smoke, the sun just going down.' And in that lurid, unearthly light the allied army advanced into the valley. 'No language can express how the British army felt at this time,' Sergeant Robertson of the 92nd Highlanders remembered:

> *their joy was truly ecstatic ... We did not take time to load, nothing was used now but the bayonet ... all was now destruction and confusion. The French at length ran off throwing away knapsacks, firelocks, and everything that was cumbersome, or that could impede their flight.*

The British cavalry joined in the rout, cutting ruthlessly into the panicked French units. Captain Henry Duperier, of the 18th Hussars, remembered charging, and 'in an instant we fell on the cavalry, who resisted but feebly; and in running, tumbled over their own infantry'. Duperier's men, many of them Irish, then massacred some gunners before turning on a disorganized battalion of infantry. The French infantry tried to surrender. It was 'nothing but "*Vive le Roi*",' Duperier said, 'but it was too late, besides our men do not understand French, so they cut away.'

Captain Pierre Robinaux had spent the day in fruitless attacks on Hougoumont, and now the panic spread to the soldiers still besieging the château. They retreated fast. 'We were being fired on from behind,' Robinaux wrote:

> *and our soldiers, already frightened, caught sight of our Polish lancers and mistook them for British cavalry, shouted 'We're lost!' The cry was echoed everywhere and soon we were in total disorder. Each man thought only of his own safety. Frightened men are impossible to control. The cavalry followed the example of the infantry; I saw Dragoons fleeing at the gallop, riding over unlucky infantrymen and trampling their bodies with their horses. I was knocked over once.*

Robinaux might have thought 'frightened men are impossible to control,' but he managed to control some. He threatened some dragoons with a musket and succeeded in stopping their flight. He collected some sixty or seventy soldiers and led them south, but was sensible enough to avoid the main road where the pursuit was in full cry. He escaped, but in the valley, beneath the long rays of the setting sun, the killing was still not done. Not yet.

* * *

The French army died, but it was not an instantaneous death. It took time for the news to reach the men defending Plancenoit and they continued to fight till around 9 p.m. Some gunners in the Grand Battery kept on firing while the army disintegrated around them. It was one of those final shots that seared past Wellington, missing him by inches, and took off his second in command's leg. 'By God, Sir,' Uxbridge is supposed to have said, 'I've lost my leg!' 'By God, Sir,' the Duke responded, 'so you have.'

Then there were those three battalions of the Old Guard who had stayed in the valley's floor. They were still there, still in square and still under discipline. They retreated slowly, pressed by allied infantry. A squadron of the 10th Hussars charged one of the Old Guard squares and was blasted away; their commanding officer, Major the Honourable Frederick Howard, son of the Earl of Carlisle, was among the last British officers killed that day. He fell unconscious from his horse in front of the Old Guard square and a guardsman was seen stepping out of the ranks to beat in Howard's head with his musket butt. Some panicked French infantry tried to take refuge in the squares, but the *grognards* were too experienced to allow that to happen; men clawing their way into a square could open a passage for enemy horsemen and so the Guards shot indiscriminately at friend and foe.

General Pierre Cambronne commanded a brigade of the Guard and was in one of the squares. Their position was hopeless. British and Hanoverian infantry had caught up with them and officers were calling on the Guard to surrender. And so was born one of Waterloo's most persistent legends, that Cambronne replied, '*La Garde meurt, mais ne se rend pas!'* The Guard dies, it does not surrender! They were fine words, and almost certainly invented by a French journalist some years after the battle. The other version has Cambronne shouting the one word *'Merde!'* as his answer, Shit! Both responses have become famous, a fine defiance in the face of inevitable defeat. Cambronne himself claimed that he said, 'Buggers like us don't surrender,' but surrender he did. He was struck from his horse by a musket ball that grazed his head and knocked him unconscious. Colonel Hugh Halkett, a British officer in Hanoverian service, took Cambronne prisoner, and the squares he had commanded shrank under the flail of musketry and canister, they became triangles and then, somewhere close to La Belle Alliance, they finally dissolved and the French guardsmen joined the panicked flight.

An officer of the 71st Foot claimed to have fired the last gun at Waterloo. The 71st, what was left of it, advanced with Sir John Colborne's 52nd and, somewhere near the last defiant squares of the Old Guard, the Grenadier company of the 71st found an abandoned French cannon with a burning portfire nearby. A firing-tube, which carried the fire to the gunpowder in the barrel, was jutting from the cannon's vent, suggesting the weapon was loaded. Lieutenant Torriano and some of his men turned the gun till it faced the Old Guard, touched the portfire to the firing-tube, and shot into the ranks of the Old Guard.

It was almost night. The sun had set, the smoke hung thick across the valley, but it was no longer lit by those lurid flashes of gunfire. Blücher rode through the wreckage of Plancenoit to the Brussels high road where, somewhere south of La Belle Alliance, he met Wellington. It was about half past nine when the two commanders shook hands. Some say they leaned from their saddles to embrace. *'Mein lieber Kamerad,'* Blücher said, *'quelle affaire!'* My dear comrade, what an affair!

'I hope to God that I have fought my last battle,' the Duke said to Frances, Lady Shelley, just one month after the battle. Wellington was always more forthcoming with women than men, and especially with young, beautiful and clever women, and the young, beautiful, clever

Lady Shelley became a lifelong friend to the Duke. 'It is a bad thing to be always fighting,' he told her:

While in the thick of it, I am much too occupied to feel anything; but it is wretched just after. It is quite impossible to think of glory. Both mind and feelings are exhausted. I am wretched even at the moment of victory, and I always say that next to a battle lost, the greatest misery is a battle gained. Not only do you lose those dear friends with whom you have been living, but you are forced to leave the wounded behind you. To be sure one tries to do the best for them, but how little that is! At such moments every feeling in your breast is deadened. I am now just beginning to retain my natural spirits, but I never wish for any more fighting.

It really was over.

THIS PAGE FROM TOP | *Defiant to the last: General Cambronne's last stand – 'The Guard dies, it does not surrender!' But surrender, he did.* | *'The Total Defeat and Flight of the French Army at the Battle of Waterloo commanded by Napoleon Bonaparte, June 18th 1815', English School , 1816.*

FACING PAGE | *'The Battle of Waterloo, 18th June 1815', (detail) by Nicolas Toussaint Charlet. The last square of the Imperial Guard.*

OVERLEAF | *'The Meeting of Wellington and Blücher after Waterloo', detail of wall painting by Daniel Maclise. Wellington, exhausted, later wept and remarked: 'Well, thank God, I don't know what it is to lose a battle, but certainly nothing can be more painful than to gain one with the loss of so many of one's friends.'*

'After the Battle of Waterloo', (detail) by William Heath.

AFTERMATH

A thousand shall fall beside thee, and ten thousand at thy right hand, but it shall not come nigh thee

ELLINGTON RODE THROUGH THE darkness to Waterloo. He dismounted from Copenhagen and gave the horse a friendly pat, whereupon Copenhagen lashed out with a hoof. The Duke was tired. 'Both mind and feelings are exhausted,' he was to tell Lady Shelley. There must have been a huge sense of relief too, 'thank God I have met him!' he was to exclaim later, and not only met him, but to have survived such a meeting. 'It has been a damned nice thing,' he told Creevey in Brussels the next day, 'the nearest thing you ever saw in your life!' He used the word 'nice' in its old sense of a narrow escape, a sliver. He also told Creevey, surely rightly, 'By God! I don't think it would have been done if I had not been there!' He was to write to his brother, William:

> You'll see the account of our Desperate Battle and victory
> over Boney!! It was the most desperate business I was ever in.
> I never took so much trouble about any battle, and was never
> so near being beat. Our loss is immense, particularly in that

best of all Instruments, British Infantry. I never saw the
Infantry behave so well.

He ate a lonely supper in Waterloo. He could not use his own bed because an aide was dying in it so he slept on a pallet. He was woken early by Doctor John Hume, who had a list of casualties. Hume recounted:

He was much affected. I felt the tears dropping fast upon my
hand. And looking towards him, saw them chasing one another
in furrows over his dusty cheeks. He brushed them away
suddenly with his left hand, and said to me in a voice tremulous
with emotion, 'Well, thank God, I don't know what it is to lose a
battle, but certainly nothing can be more painful than to gain
one with the loss of so many of one's friends.'

He had been so exhausted that he had gone to sleep without washing, and the Duke was a most fastidious man. Now, in the dawn of Monday 19 June, he began composing the despatch which was his official report to the British government, then he returned to his quarters in Brussels where he finished the despatch and wrote letters. One of the first was to Lady Frances Webster:

My dear Lady Frances … I yesterday, after a most severe and
bloody contest, gained a complete victory, and pursued the
French till after dark. They are in complete confusion; and I have,
I believe, 150 pieces of cannon; and Blücher, who continued the
pursuit all night, my soldiers being tired to death, sent me word
this morning that he had got 60 more. My loss is immense. Lord
Uxbridge, Lord FitzRoy Somerset, General Cooke, General
Barnes, and Colonel Berkeley are wounded. Colonel de Lancey,
Canning, Gordon, General Picton killed. The finger of Providence
was upon me, and I escaped unhurt.

The Duke was wrong about Colonel de Lancey, who still lived, though he was badly wounded. Towards the end of the battle a cannonball had struck a glancing blow on his back, leaving his skin unbroken, but separating his ribs. He was Wellington's Deputy Quartermaster-General and undoubtedly one of the friends whose loss Wellington felt so keenly. William de Lancey had been born in New York to a Loyalist family who lost their property at American independence. The family moved to England and William had a distinguished military career, fighting in the Peninsula and earning Wellington's trust. In April 1815, de Lancey, by now Sir William, married Magdalene Hall, a Scottish girl, and she accompanied her husband to Flanders when the Duke insisted that de Lancey serve as his Deputy Quartermaster-General. Lady de Lancey had gone to Antwerp before the battle, but returned immediately after to discover her husband in a cottage bedroom at Mont St Jean. She nursed him, and it seemed he would make a miraculous recovery, but on Monday 26 June, eight days after his injury, Sir William died. Magdalene was distraught. They had been married less than three months. She later wrote an account of her tragically doomed romance that was published as *A Week at Waterloo in 1815*.

The Prussians had undertaken the night-time pursuit of the French army. That made sense. There had already been more than enough accidental clashes between the British–Dutch troops and Blücher's men, and in the moonlit night such mistakes would have been even more likely. Gneisenau organized the pursuit, cleverly mounting drummers on cavalry horses so that the French would think Prussian infantry was close on their heels. The Prussians pursued till past midnight, feeding the panic, scattering Napoleon's survivors and slaughtering fugitives. Blücher spent the night at Genappe, the small town on the road to Quatre-Bras, from where next morning he wrote to his wife:

The enemy's superiority in numbers obliged me to retreat on the 17th, but on the 18th, together with my friend Wellington, I put an end once and for all to Buonaparte's dancing. His army is

completely routed, and the whole of his artillery, baggage,
caissons and equipment are in my hands; the insignia of all the
various orders he had worn are just brought to me, having been
discovered in a casket in his carriage. I had two horses killed
under me yesterday.

'My friend Wellington' shows a generosity of spirit that was utterly lacking in Gneisenau and, indeed, in Wellington himself. Gneisenau did acknowledge that the British fought with 'superb bravery', but he never reconciled his opinion of Wellington.

The narrow bridge at Genappe proved a huge obstacle to the retreating French. Baggage wagons made a traffic jam which completely blocked the street so that fleeing soldiers had to crawl beneath the wagons to reach the bridge. Napoleon had managed to find his coach, but the coachman could not get through the village, so the Emperor had to abandon the carriage just moments before Prussian cavalry captured it. He abandoned a fortune in jewels too. The army's treasury, stored on wagons, had managed to reach Charleroi and there became stalled by another traffic jam, whereupon it was looted by fugitives who slit open the sacks of gold coins with sword and bayonet.

Napoleon was given a horse and, escorted by a handful of Imperial Guardsmen, went on southwards. At Quatre-Bras, in the moonlight, the Emperor saw thousands of naked bodies on the battlefield, all of them stripped and plundered by the local peasantry. He avoided the crush at Charleroi and by 9 a.m. on Monday was across the French border, where he stopped. He dictated a letter to his brother Joseph, who was his deputy in Paris. 'All is not lost', the Emperor wrote:

I estimate that collecting all my forces I shall have 150,000 men
left. The National Guard and a few brave battalions will give me
100,000 men; the depot battalions 50,000. I therefore have
300,000 men to face the enemy immediately. I can drag my
artillery with carriage horses; I can raise 100,000 conscripts ... I
am starting for Laon, I shall doubtless find troops there. I have

*not heard from Grouchy, unless he is captured, which I fear he is,
I shall have 50,000 troops in three days.*

He was building castles in the air. Grouchy had been horrified by
the news of Waterloo, then conducted a skilful retreat from his fruitless
victory at Wavre and brought 25,000 men safely across the border, but
whatever Napoleon thought, all was lost. The Emperor reached Paris
on 21 June, a Wednesday, and found the city already unsettled by
rumours of a disastrous defeat. Émile Labretonnière, who had been so
excited at Sunday's false news of victory which had been heralded by
the cannon at Les Invalides, heard the rumours and went to the Élysée
Palace, which was Napoleon's summer residence:

*The palace courtyard was full of horses covered in dust and
sweat; aides-de-camp kept arriving and looked to be utterly
exhausted. Several cavalrymen of the Imperial Guard were
sitting gloomily on a bench while their tethered horses waited in
the yard. One of the horsemen had his face bandaged with a
black scarf. The whole scene spoke of shame and grief.*

France had given Napoleon a last chance, and that chance had died
in the valley at Mont St Jean. The Chamber of Deputies would not
support the Emperor any more. Blücher and Wellington were leading
their armies south towards Paris, the Austrians had crossed the eastern
frontier and the Russians were not far behind. Napoleon raged against
his fate, then accepted it. Paris surrendered to the allies on 4 July,
though their forces did not enter the city till the 7th. By then Napoleon
had abdicated. He was at Malmaison, Josephine's house, and he flirted
with the idea of emigrating to the United States. He ordered books on
America, then travelled to Rochefort, where he hoped to find ships that
would carry him to the New World, but instead found a British naval
blockade. He gave himself up to Captain Maitland of HMS *Bellerophon*,
the Billy Ruffian of Trafalgar fame, and so began his journey to Saint
Helena.

At Genappe, far to the north, thousands of copies of a proclamation were still lying in the mud. The proclamation had been printed in Paris, though at its top the sheet of paper announced it had been issued from 'The Imperial Palace of Laeken in Bruxelles'. It was addressed to the people of Belgium:

> *The brief success of my enemies detached you for a short time from my Empire, but in my exile on a sea-bound rock I heard your grief. The God of battles has decided the destiny of your beautiful provinces: Napoleon is among you! You are worthy to be Frenchmen! Rise en masse, join my invincible forces to exterminate the rest of the barbarians who are your enemies and mine; they will flee with rage and despair in their hearts.*

But it was the Emperor who had fled with rage and despair, and now the Prussians were determined to execute him. Gneisenau wrote to von Müffling, still the liaison officer with Wellington, and demanded that the Duke must agree to the Emperor's execution. 'That is what eternal justice demands, and what the declaration of March 13th requires, and so the blood of our soldiers … will be avenged.'

Müffling delivered the demand, which was reinforced by a Prussian ultimatum to the interim government in Paris that Blücher would only accept a cessation of hostilities if Napoleon was handed over 'alive or dead'. The Duke of Wellington, Müffling recorded:

> *stared at me in astonishment, and in the first place disputed the correctness of this interpretation of the [March 13th] Viennese Declaration of Outlawry, which was never meant to incite to the assassination of Napoleon … Such an act would hand down our names to history stained by a crime, and posterity would say of us that we did not deserve to be the conquerors of Napoleon.*

'If the Sovereigns wished to put him to death,' Wellington wrote tartly, 'they should appoint an executioner, which should not be me.'

Gneisenau, ever ready to accuse Wellington of ulterior and sly motives, called this 'theatrical magnanimity', but the Prussians ceded the point, however reluctantly. This was not the only disagreement between the allies. On a minor point Blücher wished to call the events of 18 June the battle of La Belle Alliance, under which name it is still known in Germany, but Wellington preferred Waterloo. The French usually term it the battle of Mont St Jean. And when the allies occupied Paris the Prussians decided to blow up the Pont d'Iéna, the bridge across the Seine which celebrated Napoleon's great victory over the Prussians at Jena in 1806. To Wellington this was a nonsense. A bridge was useful! What point was there in destroying it? Lady Shelley tells us that the Duke saved the bridge:

> by the simple device of posting an English sentry upon it ... the Prussians tried hard to get rid of the sentry, for they were determined to blow up the bridge. But the sentry would not leave his post. 'You may blow up the bridge if you like,' said he, 'but I don't stir from here.' He kept his word and the bridge was saved!

Napoleon reached Paris on 21 June, and on the same day Major the Honourable Henry Percy of the 14th Light Dragoons reached London. He arrived late in the evening, a hot evening, and went to No. 10 Downing Street to deliver Wellington's despatch to Earl Bathurst, the Secretary of War, and was redirected to Grosvenor Square where the Earl was at dinner. From there Percy was despatched to St James's Square to give the news to the Prince Regent, who was attending a ball. Percy had been at the Duchess of Richmond's ball just six days before and had been given no opportunity to change out of his silk stockings and dancing shoes, which were now covered in mud. The ball was being given by Mrs Boehm, a merchant's wife and rich enough to attract aristocratic society to her dances and dinner parties. Many years later she described the events of the evening to the Reverend Julian Young, who recorded her words. It was about 10 p.m. when Mrs Boehm:

walked up to the Prince, and asked if it was his Royal Highness's pleasure that the ball should open. The first quadrille was in the act of forming, and the Prince was walking up to the dais on which his seat was placed, when I saw everyone without the slightest sense of decorum rushing to the windows, which had been left wide open because of the excessive sultriness of the weather. The music ceased and the dance was stopped; for we heard nothing but the vociferous shouts of an enormous mob, who had just entered the Square, and were running by the side of a post-chaise and four, out of whose windows were hanging three nasty French eagles. In a second the door of the carriage was flung open, and, without waiting for the steps to be let down, out sprang Henry Percy – such a dusty figure! with a flag in each hand, pushing aside every one who happened to be in his way, darting up stairs, into the ball-room, stepping hastily up to the Regent, dropping on one knee, laying the flags at his feet, and pronouncing the words 'Victory, Sir! Victory!'

Three Eagles? The account says so, and Wellington's official despatch also mentions three Eagles, though Mrs Boehm says that Major Percy had a flag in each hand, which suggests just two. The third flag might have been a cavalry pennant. Mrs Boehm should have been delighted at the news, instead she saw only the ruin of her social aspirations as the Reverend Young reports with, one suspects, more than a little acid in his inkwell:

The splendid supper which had been provided for our guests stood in the dining-room untouched … all our trouble, anxiety and expense were utterly thrown away in consequence of, what shall I say? Well, I must say it! The unseasonable declaration of the Waterloo victory! Of course, one was very glad to think one had beaten those horrid French, and all that sort of thing; but still, I always shall think it would have been far better if Henry

Percy had waited quietly till the morning, instead of bursting in upon us, as he did, in such indecent haste.

Or perhaps, she suggested, Henry Percy might have had the decency to whisper the news to the Prince Regent who, she was sure, 'would have shown consideration enough for my feelings not to have published the news till next morning'. In that hope she would almost certainly have been disappointed, because a guest at the ball recorded the Prince's reaction on hearing of the victory; she wrote to her husband that the Prince 'fell into a sort of womanish hysteric. Water was flung in his face. No, that would never do. Wine was tried with better success, and he drowned his feelings in an ocean of claret'.

The news reached Edinburgh the following day, preceded by rumours of a great defeat which claimed that the Prussians had been annihilated and that Wellington had been trounced at Quatre-Bras. Not everyone believed the rumours and bets were taken on their veracity. Then the official news came from London. James Taylor, a lawyer, heard it in court:

The bearer of the glad tidings was soon in the Court where the judges were sitting; the cheers of the Outer Hall were suspended only to be renewed in the Inner. Further law proceedings were out of the question; adjournment was ruled; and judges, advocates, agents and officers were speedily in the street, already crowded by their excited and exultant townsmen. Nobody could stay at home. The schools were let loose. Business was suspended, and a holiday voted by acclamation.

Edinburgh Castle's 24-pounder cannons fired a nineteen-gun salute. The mail-coach that brought the London newspapers arrived garlanded with laurels and bright with flags. The losers paid the winners their wagers which, Taylor said, were speedily handed over to the fund that had been started for the wounded and for the widows and orphans made by Waterloo.

And they were far too many.

* * *

The news reached London on the Wednesday, and that night, a full three days after the battle had ended, there were still wounded men lying untended on the battlefield. The last would not be rescued till the Thursday. Many who might have been saved had died in the meantime. The dead lay in heaps. Major Harry Smith, the Rifleman-hero of the Peninsular War, rode over the battlefield the day after the fight:

> *I had been over many a field of battle, but with the exception of one spot at New Orleans and the breach of Badajos, I had never seen anything to compare with what I saw. At Waterloo the whole field from right to left was a mass of dead bodies. In one spot, to the right of La Haie Sainte, the French Cuirassiers were literally piled on each other; many soldiers not wounded lying under their horses; others, fearfully wounded, occasionally with their horses struggling on their wounded bodies. The sight was sickening ... All over the field you saw officers, and as many soldiers as were permitted to leave the ranks, leaning and weeping over some dead or dying brother or comrade. The battle was fought on a Sunday, the 18th June, and I repeated to myself a verse from the Psalms of that day – 91st Psalm, 7th verse; 'A thousand shall fall beside thee, and ten thousand at thy right hand, but it shall not come nigh thee.'*

At night the scavengers moved onto the field to plunder the dead and wounded, and if the wounded resisted they were killed. Men and women used pliers to pull teeth from the dead and, for years after, false teeth were known as Waterloo Teeth.

Some of the wounded had been taken back to Waterloo. Sergeant Johann Doring, a Nassauer infantryman, marched through the small town on the day after the battle:

*as we passed the last buildings of Waterloo, a place in front of a
barn was full of amputated arms and legs, some still with parts
of uniforms, and the surgeons, with rolled-up sleeves like
butchers, were still busy at work. The scene looked like a
slaughterhouse.*

Other casualties were carried all the way to Brussels where, for lack
of any other accommodation, they were laid on straw in the city's
squares. Edward Costello, the Rifleman, was astonished at the sight:

*The scene surpassed all imagination, and baffles description:
thousands of wounded French, Belgians, Prussians and English;
carts, waggons and every other available vehicle, were
continually arriving heaped with sufferers. The wounded were
laid, friends and foes indiscriminately, on straw, with avenues
between them, in every part of the city, and nearly destitute of
surgical attendance. The humane and indefatigable exertions of
the fair ladies of Brussels however, greatly made up for this
deficiency; numbers were busily employed – some strapping and
bandaging wounds, others serving out tea, coffee, soups, and
other soothing nourishments.*

Charles Bell, a surgeon, heard the news of Waterloo in England and
travelled at his own expense to Brussels where, to his horror, he discovered wounded men still being fetched from the battlefield. The worst
cases were in a hospital where badly wounded Frenchmen were taken
and where no surgeons were working. Bell began operating at six in the
morning and worked till seven at night, three days in a row:

*All the decencies of performing surgical operations were soon
neglected. While I amputated one man's thigh, there lay at one
time thirteen, all beseeching to be taken next; one full of
entreaty, one calling upon me to remember my promise to take
him, another execrating. It was a strange thing to feel my clothes*

stiff with blood, and my arms powerless with the exertion of using the knife.

We shall probably never know exactly how many men died or were wounded at Waterloo. The various regiments kept records, of course, but in the chaos that followed the battle thousands of men were unaccounted for, and when at last musters could be taken there was no telling whether such men had simply deserted, were prisoners or were among the casualties. That was especially true of the French army. We know that Napoleon began the battle with about 77,000 men and that a week or so later the musters showed that over 46,000 were missing. Mark Adkin, who has done so much careful work on the statistics of the battle, provides the best estimates. The British–Dutch forces under Wellington were missing 17,000 men after the battle, of whom 3,500 were killed, 10,200 were wounded, and the rest deserted. Most of those deserters were Dutch–Belgians, close to home, and the Cumberland Hussars who, despite their English name, were a regiment of Hanoverian cavalry who simply ran away. The Prussians suffered badly over the three days of Ligny, the retreat to Wavre and Waterloo, in all losing over 31,000 men. Ten thousand of those deserted during the retreat, the rest were battle casualties. The fighting in Plancenoit was especially vicious, and some 7,000 Prussians were casualties there. The French lost far more. Probably over 30,000 Frenchmen were killed or wounded at Waterloo, but the figures are at best an estimate. We do know that 840 British infantry officers fought at Quatre-Bras and at Waterloo, and that very nearly half were casualties. A third of the British cavalry was killed or injured. The Royal Scots Guards lost thirty-one of their thirty-seven officers, the 27th Foot sixteen out of nineteen. As night fell on 18 June there were probably around 12,000 corpses on the battlefield and between thirty and forty thousand wounded men, all within three square miles. Many of the wounded were to die in the subsequent days. The 32nd, a British regiment, had 28 men killed during the fight and 146 wounded, but 44 of those wounded died in the next month.

Local men were hired to clean up the battlefield. Trenches were dug for the allied dead, though never deep enough and one tourist noted how faces and limbs showed above the soil. The French corpses were burned. A visitor to the battlefield ten days after the fight saw the funeral pyres at Hougoumont:

The pyres had been burning for eight days and by then the fire was being fed solely by human fat. There were thighs, arms and legs piled up in a heap and some fifty workmen, with handkerchiefs over their noses, were raking the fire and the bones with long forks.

A year later there were still visible human remains, some of them dug up by people hoping to find a souvenir. In the end a contract was given to a company to collect the visible bones and grind them up for fertilizer.

* * *

The battle was over, but controversy does not die.

Who won the battle? That might seem a ridiculous question, but it has generated much hot air and anger over the years and still does. But at least one theory can be dismissed. Victor Hugo, in his great novel *Les Misérables*, wrote passionately about Waterloo, but in the process he established various myths that are still believed in France. 'The cuirassiers', he claimed, 'annihilated seven squares out of thirteen, took or spiked sixty pieces of ordnance, and captured from the English regiments six flags, which three cuirassiers and three chasseurs of the Guard bore to the Emperor.' No, they did not. Not one square was broken, not one cannon was spiked by the French, nor was any British colour lost. The defenders of Hougoumont, he declared, tossed living prisoners down the château's well:

This well was deep, and it was turned into a sepulchre. Three hundred dead bodies were cast into it. With too much haste perhaps. Were they all dead? Legend says they were not. It seems that on the night succeeding the interment, feeble voices were heard calling from the well.

The well has been explored by archaeologists and not one trace of human remains was discovered; the legend of the living dying slowly in its depths was spread by Victor Hugo himself. 'Was it possible', he asked, 'that Napoleon should have won that battle? We answer No. Why? Because of Wellington? Because of Blücher? No. Because of God.' That blurs the victor's identity somewhat, which was Hugo's purpose. Waterloo, he declared, was not a battle, but 'a change of front on the part of the Universe'. Such legends and lyricism moved the battle onto a mythic plane where the French are not beaten fairly and squarely, but are victims of a cosmic fate.

Slender Billy reckoned he had won the battle. He wrote to his parents: 'We had a magnificent affair against Napoleon today … it was my corps which principally gave battle and to which we owe the victory.' It is fairer to say that the allied victory owed a great deal more to the French skirmisher who managed to put a musket ball into the Prince of Orange's shoulder.

A more convincing argument was advanced by the Reverend William Leeke when, in 1866, he published his book, *The History of Lord Seaton's Regiment (The 52nd Light Infantry) at the Battle of Waterloo*. 'It is beginning to be more and more widely understood', the preface to the book begins, 'that very great injustice has been done to Lord Seaton and the 52nd Light Infantry.' Lord Seaton was Sir John Colborne; he was ennobled in 1839 after a successful spell as Lieutenant-Governor of Upper Canada. Leeke's complaint is that Colborne and the 52nd were not given the credit for defeating the Imperial Guard. The advertisement for the book, printed in bold letters on the title page, reads:

The author claims for Lord Seaton and the 52nd the honour of having defeated, single-handed, without the assistance of the 1st British Guards or any other troops, that portion of the Imperial

Guard of France, about 10,000 in number, which advanced to make the last attack on the British position.

Leeke claims that the 52nd:

had moved down 300 or 400 yards from the British position by itself, and had, single-handed, attacked and routed two heavy columns of the French Imperial Guard, consisting of about 10,000 men, and further we saw with our own eyes that this defeat was followed by the flight of the whole French army …

Leeke was a muscular Christian, much exercised by Sabbath Observance, a cause to which he devoted many years, as he did to the scandal that Protestant officers and men of the British army were 'forced' to attend 'the idolatrous ceremonies of the Roman Catholic and Greek Churches'. This 'forced' attendance was an irrelevant, temporary and quite harmless effect of Britain's participation in the Crimean War. The Reverend Leeke, it seems, could become very hot under his dog-collar, and his book caused a considerable stir.

Undoubtedly Sir John Colborne's action at Waterloo was brave and effective. On his own initiative he took the 52nd out of line, placed them on the flank of the 4th Chasseurs of the Imperial Guard, and poured a devastating fire into their ranks. One question is whether this last attack by the Imperial Guard even reached the crest of the ridge. Patrick Campbell, an officer of the 52nd who had fought through some of the hardest battles of the Peninsular War, wrote that the French Guards were 'retreating and in confusion' when the 52nd made their flank attack, which suggests that the British Guards had already begun the defeat of the enemy before the 52nd made it complete. Then, to complicate matters, Captain John Cross, another experienced soldier in the 52nd, reckons it was the fire of Colborne's battalion which halted the French column: 'The instant that the French columns felt the fire of [the 52nd's] skirmishers they halted, appeared to be in some confusion and opened a heavy fire on the 52nd.' The British Guards, Cross claims, were 'stationary and not firing', which would suggest that this last French battalion had not advanced into musket range of the British Guards. So, if Cross and Leeke are right, then the 52nd did defeat the last assault of the Imperial Guard, but Leeke is surely wrong in saying that the 52nd routed the Guard 'single-handed' because the British Guards had already defeated a larger attack, as had the Dutch and British further along the ridge.

Leeke may not even have been aware of those previous attacks. There was so much smoke, noise and confusion that it is very unlikely that Leeke, a seventeen-year-old in his first battle and carrying one of the regiment's colours at the centre of the 52nd's line, was aware of what happened uphill beyond the battalion's left flank or what had occurred farther eastwards along the slope. The battalion had formed two lines of half-companies with ten paces between them, and Leeke was almost certainly in the rearmost of those lines where the regimental colour would be most protected, which, if true, would have restricted his view even more. Nor did the 52nd defeat two columns as Leeke maintains. They attacked the final battalion of the Guard, but the other four battalions had already been driven down the slope. And 10,000 men? No doubt in the horror of the firefight, in which so many of Colborne's men died, it felt that way, but the French Guard numbered far fewer than 10,000.

Sir John Colborne's own account shares the credit with the British Guards and 'the appearance of a general attack on its flank from Sir F. Adam's Brigade and Sir Henry Clinton's Division'. None of this should detract from Sir John Colborne's initiative and achievement. What he did was courageous and magnificent, and Leeke and some others of the 52nd's officers felt ill-used that their regiment was not singled out for praise in the Duke's despatch. They have a point. The Duke did mention the British Guards, saying they 'set an example which was followed by all', and that rankled with Leeke, who felt his own battalion deserved equal billing. The survivors of other regiments could feel the same. The 92nd, hugely outnumbered, checked one of d'Erlon's columns with the bayonet and drove it backwards. The 27th held the most vulnerable place in the Duke's line and died there, almost to a man. They all contributed to the victory. When the Duke was asked, late in life, what he regretted most, he answered that he should have given more praise, and that surely lies at the heart of Leeke's complaint. He felt aggrieved that the Guards received the laurels of victory in the Duke's despatch and he wrote a powerful book of rebuttal, but the 52nd did not cause the French collapse 'single-handed', any more than the British Guards did.

Yet the bitterest controversy is between the school of Gneisenau and the school of Wellington. Somehow Gneisenau's unforgiving and vituperative attitude towards the Duke has persisted down to the present. Broadly speaking, the accusation is that the Duke failed to give the Prussians their due and claimed the victory as all his own, but there are more specific charges too. It is contended that he deliberately deceived his allies before the battles of Ligny and Quatre-Bras, that he failed to fulfil his promise to reinforce Blücher at Ligny, and that after the campaign, for the rest of his life, he used his fame and eminence to suppress any suggestion that the Prussians saved the day.

The first accusation is the most serious. It maintains that Wellington had news of the French concentration much earlier on 15 June, the eve of the battles of Ligny and Quatre-Bras, but for his own nefarious reasons pretended not to know till the evening. To believe this we must also believe that a Prussian officer, bringing the news to Wellington, told no one else in Brussels about the imminent French attack. And we must also ask what possible advantage could accrue to the Duke by concealing the news. The usual answer is that it left Blücher exposed, thus giving Wellington time to retreat. It makes no sense. If the Duke was so frightened of confronting the French, then why not begin the retreat as soon as he hears the news? To ask the question is to realize its stupidity. And what does the Duke gain if Blücher is defeated? The whole campaign was predicated on an alliance, on the knowledge that neither Wellington nor Blücher could defeat the Emperor alone, and that they must therefore combine their armies. By exposing Blücher to defeat the Duke ensures the defeat of his own army. In the event Blücher was defeated, but the campaign survived by the skin of its teeth because the Prussians were not routed and so lived to fight another day. Victory came because Blücher made the brave decision to retreat to Wavre instead of Liège, which he would only have done if he was convinced Wellington was prepared to fight, and because Wellington made a desperate defence of the ridge at Mont St Jean, which he would only have done if he was convinced Blücher was coming to his aid. In brief the campaign was successful because Blücher and Wellington trusted each other, and to suggest that Wellington would have risked that trust by deceiving his ally is to fly in the face of probability and everything we know about Wellington's character.

So did he promise to come to Blücher's aid at Ligny? The answer is simple, yes, but only if he was not attacked himself. He was attacked and so there was no possible chance to help the Prussians. The promise, qualified as it was, was made at the meeting between Blücher and Wellington at the windmill in Brye. Prussian accounts of the meeting make no mention of the qualifying 'providing I am not attacked myself', while von Müffling does record those words. General von Dornberg, Prussian-born but serving in the British army, recalled something similar; he claimed Wellington said, 'I will see what is opposing me and how much of my army has arrived and then act accordingly.' Yet three Prussian accounts claim that not only did the Duke promise to come, but that he even offered Blücher the exact time he expected to arrive, though as one account says the expected arrival time was 2 p.m., the second 3 p.m. and the third, von Clausewitz, who was not even present, 4 p.m., those claims are dubious at best. So the accounts differ, but Wellington had already seen for himself the French presence at Quatre-Bras and he would hardly have given a promise that he knew was most unlikely to be kept. He expected a fight at Quatre-Bras and must have warned his Prussian allies of that strong possibility. Gneisenau always blamed Wellington for the outcome of Ligny, describing it as 'the defeat we had suffered because of him', but that tells us more about Gneisenau's small-mindedness than about Wellington's truthfulness.

One other question is whether the two commanders spoke to each other directly, or through interpreters. Wellington spoke fluent French, but no German. Blücher had no English and very little French. When he met Wellington after Waterloo Blücher said '*Quelle affaire!*' and the Duke joked that those two words were all the French Blücher knew, but his Chief of Staff, Gneisenau, spoke both French and English. The suspicion is that Gneisenau did most of the talking at Brye. We do know that when Wellington suggested that the Prussians would do better by posting their infantry on Ligny's reverse slopes it was Gneisenau and not Blücher who answered him and the answer was fatuous: 'the Prussians like to see their enemy'. Gneisenau was no fool, and that answer is almost insolent in its dismissiveness, which suggests that Gneisenau, even at that moment, could not overcome his distaste for the British and his mistrust of Wellington. There may have been a conference at the Brye windmill, but surviving accounts suggest there was not much communication. The discussions were riven by suspicion and misunderstanding. Blücher appears to have held no grudge against his 'friend' Wellington, which he surely would have done if he thought himself betrayed.

And Gneisenau himself could be accused of bad faith. When, on the 18th, he sent the Prussians to Wellington's aid, the staff work could be described as either careless or deliberately obstructive. Why despatch the Corps farthest from the battlefield first? Or so arrange things that two Corps must cross each other's paths at a road junction? Was Gneisenau so convinced that Wellington would lose that he deliberately delayed the Prussian march? Most likely the arrangements were made in a desperate hurry, and there was good reason to send von Bülow's Corps first, because it had been spared the bloodbath at Ligny, and no one could have foreseen a careless baker setting his house on fire, but if a great allied achievement must be soured by recriminations then it is worth noting that the accusations need not be all one-sided.

And did Wellington belittle the Prussian contribution? There is evidence that he did, but long after the battle was over. In his despatch he acknowledges the Prussian contribution in generous terms:

I should not do justice to my own feelings, or to Marshal Blücher and the Prussian army, if I did not attribute the successful result of this arduous day to the cordial and timely assistance I received from them. The operation of General Bülow upon the enemy's flank was a most decisive one, and, even if I had not found myself in a situation to make the attack which produced the final result, it would have forced the enemy to retire if his attacks should have failed, and would have prevented him from taking advantage of them if they should unfortunately have succeeded.

That seems plain enough: the Prussian intervention was 'most decisive'. The Gneisenau school complains that the Duke still ascribes victory to his own attack, but surely that was justified? The immediate cause of the French army's collapse was the defeat of the Imperial Guard, and the Guard was defeated by Wellington's forces. The Duke does not attempt to deny that the assault by the Guard would have been far worse if the Prussians had not drained Napoleon's reserves into the defence of Plancenoit. This was an allied victory.

Yet as the years passed, the Duke undoubtedly wanted the lion's share of the honour. The battle was his crowning achievement, a victory over Napoleon himself, and from that victory stemmed the Duke's unassailable position as the greatest British hero. He refused to discuss the battle and rejected all requests for information from authors (whom he detested). It was impossible, he said, to tell the story of a battle, but in the 1830s William Siborne, a British army officer, conceived the idea of constructing a massive model of the battle on a scale of nine feet to the mile. The model was built and can be seen today in the National Army Museum in Chelsea. It is a huge and impressive achievement with over 70,000 toy soldiers depicting the three armies at the moment of 'the crisis', which Siborne took to be the defeat of the Imperial Guard. Siborne spent months living at Waterloo to familiarize himself with the battlefield's topography and, with the assistance of the army, wrote to almost every surviving officer with requests for their recollections, and the subsequent replies form a unique archive of eyewitness accounts.

The Duke refused to contribute his own memories, even though it seems he was unhappy with Siborne's work. In March 1837, Lord Fitzroy Somerset wrote to Siborne. Fitzroy Somerset had been the Duke's Military Secretary during the campaign (he later became Lord Raglan of Crimean fame) and was close to Wellington. He wrote amicably enough to Siborne, but noted:

> *I still think that the position you have given to the Prussian troops is not the correct one as regards the moment you wish to represent, and that those who seek the work will deduce from it that the result of the battle was not so much owing to British valour and the great generalship of the chief of the English army, as to the flank movement of the Prussians.*

Siborne offered to make changes, but the government had just purchased the work and it was too late for any more alterations and so the model as we see it today is the one to which Fitzroy Somerset objected. It is probably accurate. And it is probably true that as the Duke grew older he underplayed the Prussian contribution. That was vanity, and he was a vain man with much to be vain about. On hearing of Napoleon's death in 1821 the Duke remarked to Harriet Arbuthnot, probably the closest of his many women friends, 'Now I think I may say I am the most successful General alive!' He was undoubtedly proud of that and jealous of anything that might diminish his reputation.

The battle of Waterloo was an allied victory. That was how it was planned and that was how it turned out. Wellington would never have made his stand if he thought for one moment that the Prussians would let him down. Blücher would never have marched if he thought Wellington would cut and run. It is true that the Prussians arrived later than Wellington hoped, but that probably contributed to the battle's success. If Blücher's forces had arrived two or three hours earlier then Napoleon might have disengaged his army and retreated, but by the time that the Prussians intervened the French army was almost wholly committed to the fight and disengagement was impossible. The Emperor was not just defeated, he was routed.

Frances, Lady Shelley, once asked Wellington if it was true that he had been surprised before Quatre-Bras. She had in mind the evening of the Duchess of Richmond's ball where the Duke declared he had been humbugged. He wrote back to her in March 1820: 'as for the charge of being surprised … supposing I was surprised: I won the battle; and what could you have had more, even if I had not been surprised?'

That surely remains the Duke's answer to all his critics. 'I won the battle; and what could you have had more?'

* * *

An easier question to answer than 'who won the battle?' is 'who lost the battle?', and the answer must be Napoleon. The Duke and Blücher both offered leadership; their men saw them and were encouraged by their presence, but Napoleon left the conduct of the battle to Marshal Ney, who, though braver than most men, did little more than hurl troops against the most skilful defensive general of the age. The French had the time and the men to break Wellington's line, but they failed, partly because the Duke defended so cleverly, and partly because the French never coordinated an all-arms assault on the allied line. They delayed the start of the battle on a day when Wellington was praying for time. They wasted men in the assault on Hougoumont. Ney threw away the French cavalry in a time-consuming attack that lasted much of the afternoon. And why Napoleon entrusted the battle's conduct to Ney is a mystery; Ney was certainly brave, but the Emperor damned him as 'too stupid to be able to succeed', so why rely on him? And, when the French did achieve their one great success, the capture of La Haie Sainte, which enabled them to occupy the forward slope of Wellington's ridge, the Emperor refused to reinforce the centre and so gave the Duke time to bring up his own reinforcements. Finally, when the Imperial Guard did attack it was too few and too late, and by that time the Prussians were on the French flank and threatening their rear.

The Duke, as so often, was right: it is impossible to tell the story of a battle, because there are too many stories woven together and no one can unpick the strands. For some men it was all a blur, a day of terror in which they saw little but smoke. Some battalions only knew where the enemy was by the flash of musket flames in that smoke, and so they fired at those. Afterwards they tried to make sense of the chaos they had endured and so their individual stories were shaped. There was the tale of John Shaw, Corporal of Horse in the 2nd Life Guards, a tall and frighteningly strong man who had been a bare-knuckle boxer. Some said he was blind drunk when he charged with his regiment, but he still killed seven cuirassiers, and when he was last seen his sword was broken and he was using his helmet as a club. He died. Then there was John Dawson, 2nd Earl of Portarlington, who disappeared the night before the battle, probably to keep an assignation with a woman in Brussels. As a result he missed the beginning of the battle, and because he was the commanding officer of the 23rd Dragoons he was in total disgrace. He attached himself to the 18th Hussars instead and charged with them at the battle's end, but his disgrace was such that he was forced to resign his commission. 'He took to dissipation,' the Waterloo Roll Call records, 'and died in an obscure London slum.' Then there was the farmer's wife in Mont St Jean who, knowing the predatory habits of soldiers, took all her poultry into her farmhouse attic and spent the battle guarding her chickens and ducks. A young Prussian wrote home to his parents after the battle and said, 'tell my sister I didn't poop in my pants!' And after the battle Lieutenant Charles Smith of the 95th Rifles had the grim task of burying the dead Greenjackets and, as his work-party sorted through the heaped corpses, they found the body of a French cavalry officer 'of a delicate mould and appearance'. It was a young woman in uniform. We will never know who she was, only that Charles Smith thought her beautiful. Perhaps she could not bear to be parted from her lover?

So many stories, and so few with a happy ending. On the day before Waterloo the Major who was in command of the 40th wrote to his wife. He was a 34-year-old Irishman commanding a Somersetshire battalion, and the letter he wrote is one that many soldiers have written, a last letter in case the writer died. Frenchmen, Dutchmen, Prussians,

Hanoverians, Scotsmen, Irishmen, Welshmen and Englishmen all wrote such letters on the eve of Waterloo. 'My dear Mary,' Major Arthur Heyland wrote:

> *My Mary, let the recollection console you that the happiest days of my life have been from your love and affection, and that I die loving only you, and with a fervent hope that our souls may be reunited hereafter and part no more. What dear children, my Mary, I leave you. My Marianna, gentlest girl, may God bless you. My Anne, my John, may heaven protect you ... My darling Mary, I must tell you again how tranquilly I shall die, should it be my fate to fall; we cannot, my own love, die together; one or other must witness the loss of what we love most. Let my children console you, my love, my Mary.*

Major Arthur Heyland was among the thousands who were killed at the battle of Waterloo.

FROM TOP | *'The Eagle Standards Taken at Waterloo Returned to Wellington', by Mathieu Ignace van Bree.* | *'The Duke of Wellington describing the Field of Waterloo to King George IV', by Benjamin Robert Haydon.*

FROM TOP | *'March of the Allied forces into Paris'*, F. Malek. | *Napoleon on board the 'Northumberland' on its way to St Helena – drawn by a British officer on the ship.*

AFTERWORD

P ARIS SURRENDERED TO THE allies on 4 July 1815. Napoleon
reached Saint Helena in the southern Atlantic on 15 October
1815. He was to live another six years, most of them spent writing a tendentious memoir which fed the Napoleonic cult which still
prevails in France. Basil Jackson, the British staff officer who brought
General Picton the orders to retreat from Quatre-Bras, was one of Saint
Helena's garrison and recorded how the defeated Emperor made a
deliberate policy of constant complaining about 'unnecessary restric-
tions, insults from the governor, scarcity of provisions, miserable
accommodation, insalubrity of climate, and a host of other grievances'.
Few of these whines were justified, but Napoleon succeeded in blacken-
ing the reputation of Sir Hudson Lowe, the island's long-suffering
governor, and in encouraging pity for himself. At his death in 1821
Napoleon was buried in a beautiful high valley overlooking the Atlantic,
but in 1840 his body was moved to France, where he now lies in a lavish
tomb in Les Invalides. Longwood House, built on Saint Helena for
Napoleon's use, was given to the French nation in 1858 and is now a
museum.

Most of the French generals fled into exile after the battle. Almost
all had sworn loyalty to Louis XVIII and feared Royalist vengeance, but
one by one they returned and were restored to favour and high honours.
Marshal Soult, for instance, became Prime Minister. He attended
Queen Victoria's coronation in London's Westminster Abbey, where he

had an amicable encounter with the Duke of Wellington. Grouchy was widely blamed for the Emperor's defeat and he took refuge in the United States, but was forgiven in 1821, the year of Napoleon's death.

Count d'Erlon encountered Marshal Ney during the panicked retreat from Waterloo and advised him to flee into exile. Ney should have taken that advice. Instead he returned to France where, on the restoration of the monarchy, he was arrested and tried for treason. On 7 December 1815, early on a wintry morning, Marshal Ney was executed by a French firing squad. He refused a blindfold, refused to kneel and died in his Marshal's uniform. He deserved better. He was passionate, brave, impetuous and heroic. He was undoubtedly guilty of high treason against Louis XVIII, but so were scores of others, chief among them Marshal Soult who, before the Waterloo campaign, had been Louis's Minister of War, but Soult had powerful political allies in Paris and so escaped punishment. There is a persistent legend that Ney escaped to South Carolina and another man took his place in front of the firing squad, but the basis for the tale seems to be romantic wishfulness.

Louis Canler, the young soldier whose breakfast was flavoured with gunpowder, had a distinguished career as a detective in the Sûreté, the French national police, rising through its ranks to become the organization's chief. Another young man who had a distinguished career was Franz Lieber, the young Prussian who joined the army with such enthusiasm in Berlin. He emigrated to America in 1827, was Professor of Political Economics at South Carolina College, but moved to the north before the Civil War and taught at Columbia University where he compiled the Lieber Code, credited as the first attempt to codify the rules of war. He lived till 1870.

General von Müffling was promoted to Field Marshal. For a time he was commander of the allied garrison that occupied Paris, then he was appointed Chief of the General Staff of the Prussian military. He died in 1851. Carl von Clausewitz is most famous as the author of *Vom Kriege*, known in English as *On War*, the seminal text of war's political implications. Von Clausewitz served as Gneisenau's Chief of Staff, but both men died in the 1831 outbreak of cholera. Field Marshal von Gneisenau is rightly celebrated in Germany as a great patriot and as a man who, with von Scharnhorst, was responsible for reorganizing the Prussian army and readying it for the climactic struggle with Napoleon. His partnership with Blücher was one of the most successful in military history.

Field Marshal von Blücher retired to his estates in Silesia after the wars and died in 1819. Soon after Waterloo he made a visit to London to be celebrated and thanked by the British government for his vital part in the defeat of Napoleon. He had landed at Dover and his route to London took him over Blackheath, where his carriage stopped so he could be shown the great panorama of the British capital stretching westwards. He marvelled at the sight, then said, 'What a city to sack!' He was a splendid man.

Slender Billy proved a better king than a general. His father abdicated in 1840 and the Prince became King William II of the Netherlands, which by then had lost the province of Belgium. He was generally liberal, encouraging electoral reform and accepting constitutional restraints on the monarchy. He ruled till his death in 1849.

Most of the British soldiers who survived the battle remained in the army. Both Ned Costello and John Kincaid became Yeomen Warders of the Tower of London, while others vanished into obscurity and poverty. Others, like Sir John Colborne, had stellar careers in government service. Colborne became Lord Seaton and Lieutenant-Governor of Upper Canada, while Frederick Ponsonby, having been hacked by swordsmen, pierced by a lance and looted by passing infantrymen, survived to become the Governor of Malta. Cavalié Mercer rose to high rank in the Royal Artillery. For all these men, the famous and the obscure, Waterloo was the defining experience of their lives. Nothing that came before had such significance, everything that came after was seen through the prism of that terrible day, and that was most true of the Duke himself. Ever after, despite the high offices he held, he was the victor of Waterloo. He became Prime Minister and it was not a success; his nickname 'the Iron Duke' came not from battle, but from the iron shutters he placed on Apsley House so that the mob stoning the façade would not break his windows. He died, aged eighty-three, in 1852. Despite his political failures he had achieved an eminence and fame that was unrivalled. He was celebrated before Waterloo as the most successful British general since Marlborough, but Waterloo made his reputation unassailable.

The battle marked a turning point. The latter half of the eighteenth century had been a long struggle for supremacy between France and Britain. The Seven Years War drove the French from North America, but France had its revenge in the American Revolution when its army, allied with George Washington's forces, decisively defeated the British and so secured independence for the United States. Ten years later the Revolutionary Wars began, and except for one brief respite in 1802, those wars would last till 1815. Waterloo ended the struggle and ensured that Britain would dominate the nineteenth century, a domination that was sealed by the Duke of Wellington's defence of the ridge at Mont St Jean.

'The Duke of Wellington and officers and soldiers of the Allied army at the end of the Battle of Waterloo', by Jan Willem Pieneman in the Rijksmuseum in Amsterdam. Prince William of Orange lies wounded on a stretcher in the left foreground.

ACKNOWLEDGEMENTS

NO ONE CAN WRITE ABOUT WATERLOO without leaning on the labours of other historians. I am particularly indebted to Mark Adkin, whose book, *The Waterloo Companion*, is indispensable. It is a magnificent compilation of almost everything you might ever wish to know about the battle. The book is lavishly illustrated, the maps are superb, the research exhaustive and the opinions judicious. Whenever I found myself confused, usually by contradictory eyewitness accounts, I discovered that Mark Adkin had already cleared a path through the disagreements. I owe him thanks.

The battlefield today is dominated by the enormous Lion Mound, a memorial erected by Slender Billy's father on the spot where his son was wounded. The Duke of Wellington, on seeing the mound, remarked, 'They have ruined my battlefield,' and so they had because, to make this monstrous lump, tons of soil were removed from the crest of the ridge so that visitors today cannot see the land as it was when the Imperial Guard made their final attack. Nevertheless the battlefield is well worth a visit, and the best guide is David Buttery's *Waterloo Battlefield Guide*, which not only leads the visitor around the locations of the campaign, but tells the story of those four momentous days. The book is an essential companion for anyone visiting the battlefields of the campaign.

Nothing can take us closer to the battle than the words of the men who were there, and no one has done more to preserve those accounts than Gareth Glover. By far the majority of the quotations I used in the book are drawn from Gareth Glover's compilations, either *Letters from the Battle of Waterloo* or his three volumes of *The Waterloo Archive*. I am enormously grateful for his painstaking work.

I was fortunate to meet the late Jac Weller and so had the privilege of listening to his robust opinions on Wellington, Napoleon and the battle of Waterloo. Peter Hofschröer's opinions are just as robust, and the debate he sparked with his writings has broadened our knowledge of the battle. I am grateful to him, and to all the authors whose work has made mine so much easier. Patrick McGrady generously gave me his research on Elizabeth Gale, the five-year-old girl who witnessed the battle.

I have been fortunate, too, in having the same publisher for all my writing career. The support I have received from Susan Watt, Helen Ellis, Liz Dawson, Kate Elton, Jennifer Barth, Jonathan Burnham, Myles Archibald and Julia Koppitz has been extraordinary, thank you! And thank you to my agent, Toby Eady, who has been with me from the first book and without whom there might have been no books.

There would certainly have been no books without my wife's support. Judy has been an inspiration throughout. It can be said of her, as Wellington remarked of the British infantry at Waterloo, that she is 'the best of all instruments'. She is.

Insignia derived from shako plates, buttons and regimental badges appear on the following pages: p. 5 & 8 – Royal Artillery shako plate (1813); p. 15 – Chap. 1, French Imperial eagle; p. 39 – Chap. 2, French Imperial Guard, shako plate; p. 61 – Chap. 3, 95th Rifles 1st Battalion; p. 81 – Chap. 4, bronze totenkopf worn on shakos by Prussian black Hussars; p. 105 – Chap. 5, French Life Guard shako plate; p. 133 – Chap. 6, King's German Legion shako plate; p. 155 – Chap. 7, French 9th Hussars shako plate; p. 181 – Chap. 8, Gordon Highlanders insignia; p. 207 – Chap. 9, Royal Artillery shako plate; p. 229 – Chap. 10, 52nd Foot Infantry insignia; p. 257 – Chap. 11, Saxe Weimar badge; p. 285 – Chap. 12 – French Imperial Guard, shako plate; p. 313 – Aftermath, Royal Scots badge; p. 339 – Afterword – Royal Artillery shako plate.

BIBLIOGRAPHY

Adkin, Mark, *The Waterloo Companion: The Complete Guide to History's Most Famous Land Battle* (London, Aurum Press, 2001)

Alsop, Susan Mary, *The Congress Dances, Vienna 1814–1815* (London, Weidenfeld & Nicolson, 1984)

Asprey, Robert, *The Reign of Napoleon Bonaparte* (New York, Basic Books, 2001)

Bailey, D. W., *British Military Longarms, 1715–1815* (London, Arms and Armour Press, 1971)

Bassford, Christopher, Daniel Moran and Gregory W. Pedlow (eds and translators), *On Waterloo, Clausewitz, Wellington, and the Campaign of 1815* (Clausewitz.com, 2010)

Black, Jeremy, *The Battle of Waterloo* (New York, Random House, 2010)

Brett-James, Antony, *The Hundred Days: Napoleon's Last Campaign from Eye-Witness Accounts* (London, Macmillan, 1964)

Brett-James, Antony (ed.), *Edward Costello: The Peninsular and Waterloo Campaigns* (London, Longman, Green, 1967)

Bryant, Arthur, *Jackets of Green: a study of the history, philosophy and character of the Rifle Brigade* (London, Collins, 1972)

Buttery, David, *Waterloo Battlefield Guide* (Barnsley, Pen and Sword, 2013)

Caldwell, George and Robert Cooper, *Rifle Green at Waterloo* (Leicester, Bugle Horn Publications, 1990)

Chalfont, Lord (ed.), *Waterloo: Battle of Three Armies* (London, Sidgwick and Jackson, 1979)

Chandler, David G. (ed.), *Napoleon's Marshals* (London, Weidenfeld & Nicolson, 1987)

Chandler, David G., *On the Napoleonic Wars* (London, Greenhill Books, 1994)

—— *Waterloo: The Hundred Days* (London, Osprey Publishing, 1980)

Crowdy, T. E., *Incomparable: Napoleon's 9th Light Infantry Regiment* (London, Osprey Publishing, 2013)

Dalton, Charles, *The Waterloo Roll Call*, 2nd edition (London, Eyre and
    Spottiswoode, 1904)

Dobbs, Captain John, *Recollections of an Old 52nd Man* (1863; reprinted
    Staplehurst, Spellmount, 2000)

Elting, John R., *Swords Around a Throne: Napoleon's Grande Armée* (New York,
    The Free Press, 1988)

Fitchett, W. H., *Wellington's Men: Some Soldier Autobiographies* (London, Smith,
    Elder, 1900)

Fremont-Barnes, Gregory and Todd Fisher, *The Napoleonic Wars: The Rise and
    Fall of an Empire* (Oxford, Osprey Publishing, 2004)

Geyl, Pieter, *Napoleon: For and Against* (London, Jonathan Cape, 1949)

Glover, Gareth, *Letters from the Battle of Waterloo* (London, Greenhill Books, 2004)

—— *The Waterloo Archive*, vol. I, *British Sources* (Barnsley, Frontline Books,
    2010)

—— *The Waterloo Archive*, vol. II, *German Sources* (Barnsley, Frontline Books,
    2010)

—— *The Waterloo Archive*, vol. III, *British Sources* (Barnsley, Frontline Books,
    2011)

—— *Wellington as Military Commander* (London, Batsford, 1968)

Griffith, Paddy (ed.), *Wellington Commander: The Iron Duke's Generalship*
    (Chichester, Antony Bird Publications, 1985)

Guedalla, Philip, *Wellington* (New York, Harper and Bros, 1931)

Hathaway, Eileen, *Costello: The True Story of a Peninsular War Rifleman*
    (Swanage, Shinglepicker, 1997)

Haydon, Benjamin Robert, *The Diary of Benjamin Robert Haydon, 1808–1846*
    (Cambridge, MA, Harvard University Press, 1960)

Haythornthwaite, Philip J., *The Napoleonic Source Book* (New York, Facts on File,
    1990)

—— *Redcoats: The British Soldiers of the Napoleonic Wars* (Barnsley, Pen and
    Sword, 2012)

—— *The Waterloo Armies: Men, Organization & Tactics* (Barnsley, Pen and
    Sword, 2007)

—— *Weapons and Equipment of the Napoleonic Wars* (Poole, Blandford Press,
    1979)

—— *Who Was Who in the Napoleonic Wars* (London, Arms and Armour Press,
    1998)

Hibbert, Christopher, *Wellington: A Personal History* (London, HarperCollins,
    1997)

Hofschröer, Peter, *1815, The Waterloo Campaign: Wellington, his German Allies and the Battles of Ligny and Quatre Bras* (London, Greenhill Books, 1998)

Holmes, Richard, *Redcoat: The British Soldier in the Age of Horse and Musket* (London, HarperCollins, 2001)

—— *Wellington: The Iron Duke* (London, HarperCollins, 2002)

Hooper, George, *Waterloo: The Downfall of the First Napoleon: A History of the Campaign of 1815* (London, Smith, Elder, 1862)

Horward, Donald D. *et al.* (eds), *The Consortium on Revolutionary Europe, 1750– 1850: Selected Papers, 2000* (Tallahassee, Florida State University, 2000)

Howarth, David, *A Near Run Thing* (London, Collins, 1968)

Johnson, David, *Napoleon's Cavalry and Its Leaders* (London, Batsford Books, 1978)

Johnson, Paul, *Napoleon* (London, Weidenfeld & Nicolson, 2002)

Johnston, R. M. and Philip Haythornthwaite, *In the Words of Napoleon: The Emperor Day by Day* (London, Greenhill Books, 2002)

Keegan, John, *The Face of Battle* (London, Jonathan Cape, 1976)

—— *The Mask of Command* (New York, Viking, 1987)

Kincaid, John, *Random Shots from a Rifleman* (London, T. and W. Boone, 1847)

Leeke, Rev. William, M.A., *The History of Lord Seaton's Regiment (The 52nd Light Infantry) at the Battle of Waterloo* (2 vols, London, Hatchard, 1866)

Liddell Hart, Captain B. H. (ed.), *The Letters of Private Wheeler 1809–1828* (London, Michael Joseph, 1951)

Lieber, Francis, L.L.D., *Reminiscences, Addresses, and Essays* (vol. I of Lieber's *Miscellaneous Writings*) (Philadelphia, J. B. Lippincott, 1881)

Logie, Jacques, *Waterloo: The 1815 Campaign* (Stroud, Spellmount, 2006)

Longford, Elizabeth, *Wellington: The Years of the Sword* (London, Weidenfeld & Nicolson, 1969)

MacKenzie, Norman, *The Escape from Elba: The Fall and Flight of Napoleon 1814– 1815* (New York, Oxford University Press, 1982)

McLynn, Frank, *Napoleon: A Biography* (London, Jonathan Cape, 1997)

Müffling, Baron Carl von, *The Memoirs of Baron von Müffling: A Prussian Officer in the Napoleonic Wars* (London, Greenhill Books, 1997)

Naylor, John, *Waterloo* (London, Batsford, 1960)

Newark, Tim, *Highlander: The History of the Legendary Highland Soldier* (London, Constable and Robinson, 2009)

Palmer, Alan, *An Encyclopaedia of Napoleon's Europe* (London, Weidenfeld & Nicolson, 1984)

Park, S. J. and G. F. Nafziger, *The British Military, Its System and Organization, 1803–1815* (Cambridge, Ontario, Rafm, 1983)

Parkinson, Roger, *The Hussar General: The Life of Blücher, Man of Waterloo* (London, Peter Davies, 1975)

Richardson, Robert G., *Larrey: Surgeon to Napoleon's Imperial Guard* (London, John Murray, 1974)

Roberts, Andrew, *Napoleon and Wellington* (London, Weidenfeld & Nicolson, 2001)

—— *Waterloo: Napoleon's Last Gamble* (London, HarperCollins, 2005)

Robinaux, Pierre, *Journal de Route du Capitaine Robinaux, 1803–1832* (Paris, Gustave Schlumberger, 1908)

Rogers, Colonel H. C. B., *Napoleon's Army* (Shepperton, Ian Allan, 1974)

Rothenberg, Gunther E., *The Art of Warfare in the Age of Napoleon* (London, Batsford, 1977)

Schom, Alan, *One Hundred Days: Napoleon's Road to Waterloo* (London, Penguin, 1993)

Severn, John Kenneth, *A Wellesley Affair: Richard Marquess Wellesley and the Conduct of Anglo-Spanish Diplomacy, 1809–1812* (Tallahassee, Florida State University, 1981)

Shelley, Lady Frances, *The Diary of Frances Lady Shelley*, vol. I, *1787–1817*, ed. Richard Edgcumbe (New York, Charles Scribner's Sons, 1912); vol. II, *1818–1873*, ed. Richard Edgcumbe (London, John Murray, 1913)

Strawson, John, *The Duke and the Emperor: Wellington and Napoleon* (London, Constable, 1994)

Uffindell, Andrew and Michael Corum, *On the Fields of Glory: The Battlefields of the 1815 Campaign* (London, Greenhill Books, 1996)

Urban, Mark, *Rifles: Six Years with Wellington's Legendary Sharpshooters* (London, Faber and Faber, 2003)

Weller, Jac, *Wellington at Waterloo* (London, Longmans, Green, 1967)

Wise, Terence, *Artillery Equipments of the Napoleonic Wars* (London, Osprey, 1979)

The Waterloo Journal, ed. Ian Fletcher. *The Waterloo Journal* is published three times yearly by The Association of Friends of the Waterloo Committee (www.waterloocommittee.org.uk) and by *A.S.B.L. Pour Les Études Historiques de la Bataille de Waterloo*. I am indebted to the *Journal* for many thought-provoking articles over the years.

INDEX

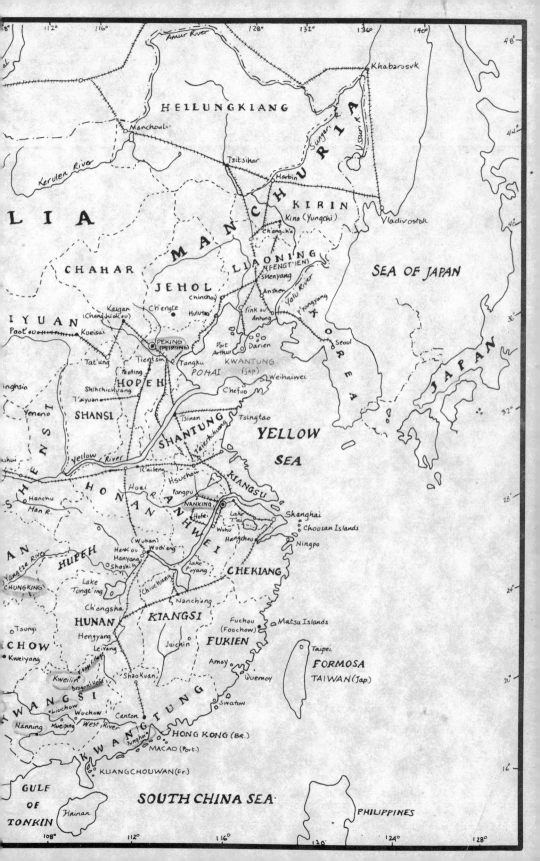